Learning PHP 7

Learn the art of PHP programming through this
example-rich book filled to the brim with tutorials
every PHP developer needs to know

Antonio Lopez

BIRMINGHAM - MUMBAI

Learning PHP 7

First published: March 2016

Production reference: 1210316

Published by Packt Publishing Ltd.
Livery Place
35 Livery Street
Birmingham B3 2PB, UK.

ISBN 978-1-78588-054-4

www.packtpub.com

Credits

Author
Antonio Lopez

Reviewer
Brad Bonkoski

Commissioning Editor
Kunal Parikh

Acquisition Editors
Nikhil Karkal

Divya Poojari

Content Development Editor
Rohit Kumar Singh

Technical Editor
Taabish Khan

Copy Editors
Shruti Iyer

Sonia Mathur

Project Coordinator
Izzat Contractor

Proofreader
Safis Editing

Indexer
Tejal Daruwale Soni

Production Coordinator
Melwyn D'sa

Cover Work
Melwyn D'sa

About the Author

Antonio Lopez is a software engineer with more than 7 years of experience. He has worked with PHP since university, which was 10 years ago, building small personal projects. Later, Antonio started his journey around Europe, working in Barcelona, London, Dublin, and back in Barcelona. He has worked in a number of different areas, from web applications to REST APIs and internal tools. Antonio likes to spend his spare time on personal projects and start-ups and has a strong vocation in education and teaching.

I would like to give thanks to my wife, Neri, for supporting me through the whole process of writing this book without going crazy.

About the Reviewer

Brad Bonkoski has been developing software for over 15 years, specializing in internal operations, systems, tools, and automation. Sometimes, this role is loosely referred to as DevOps. He leans more toward the Dev side of this misunderstood buzzword. After building an incident management system and managing change management for Yahoo, Brad became motivated by metrics and now lives by the mantra that what doesn't get measured doesn't get fixed. Today, he greases the wheels of productivity for Shazam.

www.PacktPub.com

eBooks, discount offers, and more

Did you know that Packt offers eBook versions of every book published, with PDF and ePub files available? You can upgrade to the eBook version at www.PacktPub.com and as a print book customer, you are entitled to a discount on the eBook copy. Get in touch with us at customercare@packtpub.com for more details.

At www.PacktPub.com, you can also read a collection of free technical articles, sign up for a range of free newsletters and receive exclusive discounts and offers on Packt books and eBooks.

https://www2.packtpub.com/books/subscription/packtlib

Do you need instant solutions to your IT questions? PacktLib is Packt's online digital book library. Here, you can search, access, and read Packt's entire library of books.

Why subscribe?

- Fully searchable across every book published by Packt
- Copy and paste, print, and bookmark content
- On demand and accessible via a web browser

Table of Contents

Preface   **ix**

Chapter 1: Setting Up the Environment   **1**

Setting up the environment with Vagrant   **1**
Introducing Vagrant   2
Installing Vagrant   2
Using Vagrant   2
Setting up the environment on OS X   **5**
Installing PHP   5
Installing MySQL   7
Installing Nginx   9
Installing Composer   9
Setting up the environment on Windows   **9**
Installing PHP   10
Installing MySQL   10
Installing Nginx   12
Installing Composer   13
Setting up the environment on Ubuntu   **13**
Installing PHP   14
Installing MySQL   14
Installing Nginx   14
Summary   **16**

Chapter 2: Web Applications with PHP   **17**

The HTTP protocol   **17**
A simple example   18
Parts of the message   18
URL   18
The HTTP method   19
Body   19

Headers	19
The status code	20
A more complex example	20
Web applications	**21**
HTML, CSS, and JavaScript	22
Web servers	**24**
How they work	24
The PHP built-in server	25
Putting things together	26
Summary	**27**
Chapter 3: Understanding PHP Basics	**29**
PHP files	**29**
Variables	**31**
Data types	32
Operators	**33**
Arithmetic operators	34
Assignment operators	34
Comparison operators	35
Logical operators	36
Incrementing and decrementing operators	36
Operator precedence	37
Working with strings	**38**
Arrays	**40**
Initializing arrays	41
Populating arrays	42
Accessing arrays	43
The empty and isset functions	44
Searching for elements in an array	45
Ordering arrays	45
Other array functions	48
PHP in web applications	**49**
Getting information from the user	49
HTML forms	51
Persisting data with cookies	52
Other superglobals	53
Control structures	**54**
Conditionals	54
Switch...case	58
Loops	59
While	59
Do...while	60

For	60
Foreach	61
Functions	**63**
Function declaration	63
Function arguments	64
The return statement	66
Type hinting and return types	66
The filesystem	**68**
Reading files	68
Writing files	70
Other filesystem functions	73
Summary	**73**
Chapter 4: Creating Clean Code with OOP	**75**
Classes and objects	**76**
Class properties	76
Class methods	77
Class constructors	79
Magic methods	80
Properties and methods visibility	**81**
Encapsulation	83
Static properties and methods	**87**
Namespaces	**88**
Autoloading classes	**90**
Using the __autoload function	90
Using the spl_autoload_register function	92
Inheritance	**92**
Introducing inheritance	92
Overriding methods	96
Abstract classes	97
Interfaces	**100**
Polymorphism	105
Traits	**106**
Handling exceptions	**112**
The try…catch block	113
The finally block	115
Catching different types of exceptions	117
Design patterns	**121**
Factory	121
Singleton	124
Anonymous functions	**128**
Summary	**131**

Chapter 5: Using Databases — 133

Introducing databases — 133
MySQL — 134

Schemas and tables — 136
Understanding schemas — 136
Database data types — 138
Numeric data types — 138
String data types — 139
List of values — 139
Date and time data types — 140
Managing tables — 141

Keys and constraints — 143
Primary keys — 143
Foreign keys — 145
Unique keys — 148
Indexes — 149

Inserting data — 149
Querying data — 152
Using PDO — 156
Connecting to the database — 156
Performing queries — 157
Prepared statements — 159

Joining tables — 161
Grouping queries — 164
Updating and deleting data — 165
Updating data — 166
Foreign key behaviors — 168
Deleting data — 169

Working with transactions — 171
Summary — 173

Chapter 6: Adapting to MVC — 175

The MVC pattern — 175
Using Composer — 176
Managing dependencies — 176
Autoloader with PSR-4 — 179
Adding metadata — 180
The index.php file — 181

Working with requests — 181
The request object — 182
Filtering parameters from requests — 183

Mapping routes to controllers   186
The router   189
     URLs matching with regular expressions   190
     Extracting the arguments of the URL   192
     Executing the controller   192
M for model   **194**
The customer model   196
The book model   198
The sales model   203
V for view   **207**
Introduction to Twig   207
The book view   208
Layouts and blocks   210
Paginated book list   211
The sales view   212
The error template   214
The login template   215
C for controller   **215**
The error controller   218
The login controller   219
The book controller   220
Borrowing books   223
The sales controller   225
Dependency injection   **226**
Why is dependency injection necessary?   226
Implementing our own dependency injector   228
Summary   **232**
Chapter 7: Testing Web Applications   **233**
The necessity for tests   **233**
Types of tests   234
Unit tests and code coverage   236
Integrating PHPUnit   **237**
The phpunit.xml file   238
Your first test   239
Running tests   241
Writing unit tests   **242**
The start and end of a test   243
Assertions   244
Expecting exceptions   249
Data providers   250

Testing with doubles	**251**
Injecting models with DI	252
Customizing TestCase	252
Using mocks	254
Database testing	**260**
Test-driven development	**265**
Theory versus practice	270
Summary	**271**
Chapter 8: Using Existing PHP Frameworks	**273**
Reviewing frameworks	**273**
The purpose of frameworks	274
The main parts of a framework	274
Other features of frameworks	**276**
Authentication and roles	276
ORM	276
Cache	277
Internationalization	279
Types of frameworks	**279**
Complete and robust frameworks	279
Lightweight and flexible frameworks	280
An overview of famous frameworks	**280**
Symfony 2	281
Zend Framework 2	281
Other frameworks	281
The Laravel framework	**282**
Installation	282
Project setup	282
Adding the first endpoint	285
Managing users	289
User registration	290
User login	293
Protected routes	295
Setting up relationships in models	295
Creating complex controllers	296
Adding tests	300
The Silex microframework	**303**
Installation	303
Project setup	304
Managing configuration	304
Setting the template engine	305
Adding a logger	306

Adding the first endpoint   306
Accessing the database   307
Silex versus Laravel   **313**
Summary   **313**
Chapter 9: Building REST APIs   **315**
Introducing APIs   **316**
Introducing REST APIs   **316**
The foundations of REST APIs   **317**
HTTP request methods   317
   GET   318
   POST and PUT   318
   DELETE   319
Status codes in responses   320
   2xx – success   320
   3xx – redirection   320
   4xx – client error   321
   5xx – server error   321
REST API security   321
   Basic access authentication   322
   OAuth 2.0   322
Using third-party APIs   **323**
Getting the application's credentials   323
Setting up the application   324
Requesting an access token   325
Fetching tweets   327
The toolkit of the REST API developer   **330**
Testing APIs with browsers   330
Testing APIs using the command line   331
Best practices with REST APIs   **332**
Consistency in your endpoints   332
Document as much as you can   333
Filters and pagination   333
API versioning   333
Using HTTP cache   334
Creating a REST API with Laravel   **334**
Setting OAuth2 authentication   335
   Installing OAuth2Server   335
   Setting up the database   336
   Enabling client-credentials authentication   337
   Requesting an access token   338
Preparing the database   339

Setting up the models	341
Designing endpoints	344
Adding the controllers	346
Testing your REST APIs	**353**
Summary	**358**
Chapter 10: Behavioral Testing	**359**
Behavior-driven development	**359**
Introducing continuous integration	360
Unit tests versus acceptance tests	362
TDD versus BDD	363
Business writing tests	364
BDD with Behat	**365**
Introducing the Gherkin language	366
Defining scenarios	366
Writing Given-When-Then test cases	367
Reusing parts of scenarios	367
Writing step definitions	368
The parameterization of steps	371
Running feature tests	371
Testing with a browser using Mink	**380**
Types of web drivers	381
Installing Mink with Goutte	381
Interaction with the browser	382
Summary	**384**
Index	**385**

Preface

There is no need to state how much weight web applications have in our lives. We use web applications to know what our friends are doing, to get the latest news about politics, to check the results of our favorite football team in a game, or graduate from an online university. And as you are holding this book, you already know that building these applications is not a job that only a selected group of geniuses can perform, and that it's rather the opposite.

There isn't only one way to build web applications; there are actually quite a lot of languages and technologies with the sole purpose of doing this. However, if there is one language that stands out from the rest, either historically or because it is extremely easy to use, it is PHP and all the tools of its ecosystem.

The Internet is full of resources that detail how to use PHP, so why bother reading this book? That's easy. We will not give you the full documentation of PHP as the official website does. Our goal is not that you get a PHP certification, but rather to teach you what you really need in order to build web applications by yourself. From the very beginning, we will use all the information provided in order to build applications, so you can note why each piece of information is useful.

However, we will not stop here. Not only will we show you what the language offers you, but also we will discuss the best approaches to writing code. You will learn all the techniques that any web developer has to master, from OOP and design patterns such as MVC, to testing. You will even work with the existing PHP frameworks that big and small companies use for their own projects.

In short, you will start a journey in which you will learn how to master web development rather than how to master a programming language. We hope you enjoy it.

What this book covers

Chapter 1, Setting Up the Environment, will guide you through the installation of the different software needed.

Chapter 2, Web Applications with PHP, will be an introduction to what web applications are and how they work internally.

Chapter 3, Understanding PHP Basics, will go through the basic elements of the PHP language — from variables to control structures.

Chapter 4, Creating Clean Code with OOP, will describe how to develop web applications following the object-oriented programming paradigm.

Chapter 5, Using Databases, will explain how you can use MySQL databases in your applications.

Chapter 6, Adapting to MVC, will show how to apply the most famous web design pattern, MVC, to your applications.

Chapter 7, Testing Web Applications, will be an extensive introduction to unit testing with PHPUnit.

Chapter 8, Using Existing PHP Frameworks, will introduce you to existing PHP frameworks used by several companies and developers, such as Laravel and Silex.

Chapter 9, Building REST APIs, will explain what REST APIs are, how to use third-party ones, and how to build your own.

Chapter 10, Behavioral Testing, will introduce the concepts of continuous integration and behavioral testing with PHP and Behat.

What you need for this book

In *Chapter 1, Setting Up the Environment,* we will go through the details of how to install PHP and the rest of tools that you need in order to go though the examples of this book. The only thing that you need to start reading is a computer with Windows, OS X, or Linux, and an Internet connection.

Who this book is for

This book is for anyone who wishes to write web applications with PHP. You do not need to be a computer science graduate in order to understand it. In fact, we will assume that you have no knowledge at all of software development, neither with PHP nor with any other language. We will start from the very beginning so that everybody can follow the book.

Experienced readers can still take advantage of the book. You can quickly review the first chapter in order to discover the new features PHP 7 comes with, and then focus on the chapters that might interest you. You do not need to read the book from start to end, but instead keep it as a guide, in order to refresh specific topics whenever they are needed.

Conventions

In this book, you will find a number of text styles that distinguish between different kinds of information. Here are some examples of these styles and an explanation of their meaning.

Code words in text, database table names, folder names, filenames, file extensions, pathnames, dummy URLs, user input, and Twitter handles are shown as follows: "Now, create a `myactions.js` file with the following content."

A block of code is set as follows:

```
#special {
    font-size: 30px;
}
```

When we wish to draw your attention to a particular part of a code block, the relevant lines or items are set in bold:

```
<head>
  <meta charset="UTF-8">
  <title>Your first app</title>
  <link rel="stylesheet" type="text/css" href="mystyle.css">
</head>
```

Any command-line input or output is written as follows:

```
$ sudo apt-get update
```

New terms and **important words** are shown in bold. Words that you see on the screen, for example, in menus or dialog boxes, appear in the text like this: "Click on **Next** until the end of the installation wizard."

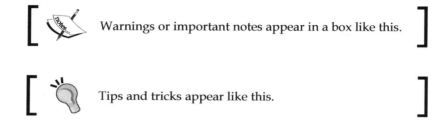

> Warnings or important notes appear in a box like this.

> Tips and tricks appear like this.

Reader feedback

Feedback from our readers is always welcome. Let us know what you think about this book—what you liked or disliked. Reader feedback is important for us as it helps us develop titles that you will really get the most out of.

To send us general feedback, simply e-mail feedback@packtpub.com, and mention the book's title in the subject of your message.

If there is a topic that you have expertise in and you are interested in either writing or contributing to a book, see our author guide at www.packtpub.com/authors.

Customer support

Now that you are the proud owner of a Packt book, we have a number of things to help you to get the most from your purchase.

Downloading the example code

You can download the example code files for this book from your account at http://www.packtpub.com. If you purchased this book elsewhere, you can visit http://www.packtpub.com/support and register to have the files e-mailed directly to you.

You can download the code files by following these steps:

1. Log in or register to our website using your e-mail address and password.
2. Hover the mouse pointer on the **SUPPORT** tab at the top.
3. Click on **Code Downloads & Errata**.

4. Enter the name of the book in the **Search** box.

5. Select the book for which you're looking to download the code files.

6. Choose from the drop-down menu where you purchased this book from.

7. Click on **Code Download**.

Once the file is downloaded, please make sure that you unzip or extract the folder using the latest version of:

- WinRAR / 7-Zip for Windows
- Zipeg / iZip / UnRarX for Mac
- 7-Zip / PeaZip for Linux

Errata

Although we have taken every care to ensure the accuracy of our content, mistakes do happen. If you find a mistake in one of our books—maybe a mistake in the text or the code—we would be grateful if you could report this to us. By doing so, you can save other readers from frustration and help us improve subsequent versions of this book. If you find any errata, please report them by visiting http://www.packtpub. com/submit-errata, selecting your book, clicking on the **Errata Submission Form** link, and entering the details of your errata. Once your errata are verified, your submission will be accepted and the errata will be uploaded to our website or added to any list of existing errata under the Errata section of that title.

To view the previously submitted errata, go to https://www.packtpub.com/books/ content/support and enter the name of the book in the search field. The required information will appear under the **Errata** section.

Piracy

Piracy of copyrighted material on the Internet is an ongoing problem across all media. At Packt, we take the protection of our copyright and licenses very seriously. If you come across any illegal copies of our works in any form on the Internet, please provide us with the location address or website name immediately so that we can pursue a remedy.

Please contact us at copyright@packtpub.com with a link to the suspected pirated material.

We appreciate your help in protecting our authors and our ability to bring you valuable content.

Questions

If you have a problem with any aspect of this book, you can contact us at questions@packtpub.com, and we will do our best to address the problem.

1
Setting Up the Environment

You are about to start a journey—a long one, in which you will learn how to write web applications with PHP. However, first, you need to set up your environment, something that has proven to be tricky at times. This task includes installing PHP 7, the language of choice for this book; MySQL, the database that we will use in some chapters; Nginx, the web server that will allow us to visualize our applications with a browser; and Composer, the favorite PHP dependencies management tool. We will do all of this with Vagrant and also on three different platforms: Windows, OS X, and Ubuntu.

In this chapter, you will learn about:

- Using Vagrant to set up a development environment
- Setting up your environment manually on the main platforms

Setting up the environment with Vagrant

Not so long ago, every time you started working for a new company, you would spend an important part of your first few days setting up your new environment—that is, installing all the necessary tools on your new computer in order to be able to code. This was incredibly frustrating because even though the software to install was the same, there was always something that failed or was missing, and you would spend less time being productive.

Introducing Vagrant

Luckily for us, people tried to fix this big problem. First, we have virtual machines, which are emulations of computers inside your own computer. With this, we can have Linux inside our MacBook, which allows developers to share environments. It was a good step, but it still had some problems; for example, VMs were quite big to move between different environments, and if developers wanted to make a change, they had to apply the same change to all the existing virtual machines in the organization.

After some deliberation, a group of engineers came up with a solution to these issues and we got **Vagrant**. This amazing software allows you to manage virtual machines with simple configuration files. The idea is simple: a configuration file specifies which base virtual machine we need to use from a set of available ones online and how you would like to customize it—that is, which commands you will want to run the first time you start the machine—this is called "provisioning". You will probably get the Vagrant configuration from a public repository, and if this configuration ever changes, you can get the changes and reprovision your machine. It's easy, right?

Installing Vagrant

If you still do not have Vagrant, installing it is quite easy. You will need to visit the Vagrant download page at `https://www.vagrantup.com/downloads.html` and select the operating system that you are working with. Execute the installer, which does not require any extra configuration, and you are good to go.

Using Vagrant

Using Vagrant is quite easy. The most important piece is the `Vagrantfile` file. This file contains the name of the base image we want to use and the rest of the configuration that we want to apply. The following content is the configuration needed in order to get an Ubuntu VM with PHP 7, MySQL, Nginx, and Composer. Save it as `Vagrantfile` at the root of the directory for the examples of this book.

```
VAGRANTFILE_API_VERSION = "2"

Vagrant.configure(VAGRANTFILE_API_VERSION) do |config|
  config.vm.box = "ubuntu/trusty32"
  config.vm.network "forwarded_port", guest: 80, host: 8080
  config.vm.provision "shell", path: "provisioner.sh"
end
```

As you can see, the file is quite small. The base image's name is `ubuntu/trusty32`, messages to our port `8080` will be redirected to the port `80` of the virtual machine, and the provision will be based on the `provisioner.sh` script. You will need to create this file, which will be the one that contains all the setup of the different components that we need. This is what you need to add to this file:

```bash
#!/bin/bash

sudo apt-get install python-software-properties -y
sudo LC_ALL=en_US.UTF-8 add-apt-repository ppa:ondrej/php -y
sudo apt-get update
sudo apt-get install php7.0 php7.0-fpm php7.0-mysql -y
sudo apt-get --purge autoremove -y
sudo service php7.0-fpm restart

sudo debconf-set-selections <<< 'mysql-server mysql-server/root_
password password root'
sudo debconf-set-selections <<< 'mysql-server mysql-server/root_
password_again password root'
sudo apt-get -y install mysql-server mysql-client
sudo service mysql start

sudo apt-get install nginx -y
sudo cat > /etc/nginx/sites-available/default <<- EOM
server {
    listen 80 default_server;
    listen [::]:80 default_server ipv6only=on;

    root /vagrant;
    index index.php index.html index.htm;

    server_name server_domain_or_IP;

    location / {
        try_files \$uri \$uri/ /index.php?\$query_string;
    }

    location ~ \.php\$ {
        try_files \$uri /index.php =404;
        fastcgi_split_path_info ^(.+\.php)(/.+)\$;
        fastcgi_pass unix:/var/run/php/php7.0-fpm.sock;
        fastcgi_index index.php;
        fastcgi_param SCRIPT_FILENAME \$document_root\$fastcgi_script_
name;
        include fastcgi_params;
    }
}
EOM
sudo service nginx restart
```

The file looks quite long, but we will do quite a lot of stuff with it. With the first part of the file, we will add the necessary repositories to be able to fetch PHP 7, as it does not come with the official ones, and then install it. Then, we will try to install MySQL, server and client. We will set the root password on this provisioning because we cannot introduce it manually with Vagrant. As this is a development machine, it is not really a problem, but you can always change the password once you are done. Finally, we will install and configure Nginx to listen to the port 8080.

To start the virtual machine, you need to execute the following command in the same directory where Vagrantfile is:

```
$ vagrant up
```

The first time you execute it, it will take some time as it will have to download the image from the repository, and then it will execute the provisioner.sh file. The output should be something similar to this one followed by some more output messages:

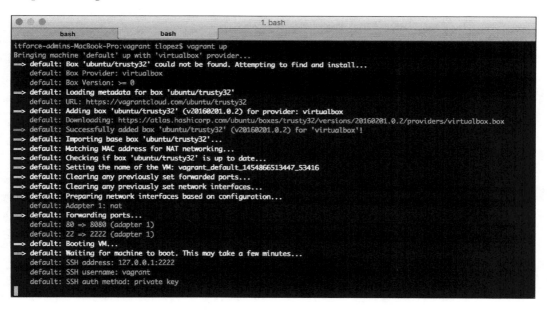

In order to access your new VM, run the following command on the same directory where you have your Vagrantfile file:

```
$ vagrant ssh
```

Vagrant will start an SSH session to the VM, which means that you are inside the VM. You can do anything you would do with the command line of an Ubuntu system. To exit, just press *Ctrl* + *D*.

Sharing files from your laptop to the VM is easy; just move or copy them to the same directory where your `Vagrantfile` file is, and they will "magically" appear on the `/vagrant` directory of your VM. They will be synchronized, so any changes that you make while in your VM will be reflected on the files of your laptop.

Once you have a web application and you want to test it through a web browser, remember that we will forward the ports. This means that in order to access the port `80` of your VM, the common one for web applications, you will have to point to the port `8080` on your browsers; here's an example: `http://localhost:8080`.

Setting up the environment on OS X

If you are not convinced with Vagrant and prefer to use a Mac to develop PHP applications, this is your section. Installing all the necessary tools on a Mac might be a bit tricky, depending on the version of your OS X. At the time of writing this book, Oracle has not released a MySQL client that you can use via the command line that works with El Capitan, so we will describe how to install another tool that can do a similar job.

Installing PHP

If it is the first time you are using a Mac to develop applications of any kind, you will have to start by installing Xcode. You can find this application for free on the App Store:

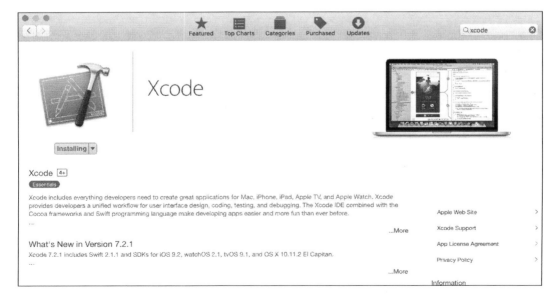

Another indispensable tool for Mac users is Brew. This is the package manager for OS X and will help us install PHP with almost no pain. To install it, run the following command on your command line:

```
$ ruby -e "$(curl -fsSL https://raw.githubusercontent.com/Homebrew/
install/master/install)"
```

If you already have Brew installed, you can make sure that everything works fine by running these two commands:

```
$ brew doctor
```

```
$ brew update
```

It is time to install PHP 7 using Brew. To do so, you will just need to run one command, as follows:

```
$ brew install homebrew/php/php70
```

The result should be as shown in the following screenshot:

Make sure to add the binary to your `PATH` environment variable by executing this command:

```
$ export PATH="$(brew --prefix homebrew/php/php70)/bin:$PATH"
```

You can check whether your installation was successful by asking which version of PHP your system is using with the `$ php -v` command.

Installing MySQL

As pointed out at the beginning of this section, MySQL is a tricky one for Mac users. You need to download the MySQL server installer and MySQL Workbench as the client. The MySQL server installer can be found at `https://dev.mysql.com/downloads/mysql/`. You should find a list of different options, as shown here:

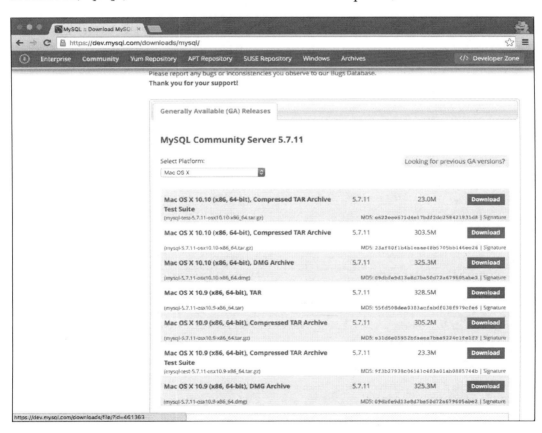

The easiest way to go is to download **DMG Archive**. You will be asked to log in with your Oracle account; you can create one if you do not have any. After this, the download will start. As with any DMG package, just double-click on it and go through the options—in this case, just click on **Next** all the time. Be careful because at the end of the process, you will be prompted with a message similar to this:

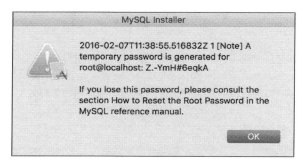

Make a note of it; otherwise, you will have to reset the root password. The next one is MySQL Workbench, which you can find at `http://www.mysql.com/products/workbench/`. The process is the same; you will be asked to log in, and then you will get a DMG file. Click on **Next** until the end of the installation wizard. Once done, you can launch the application; it should look similar to this:

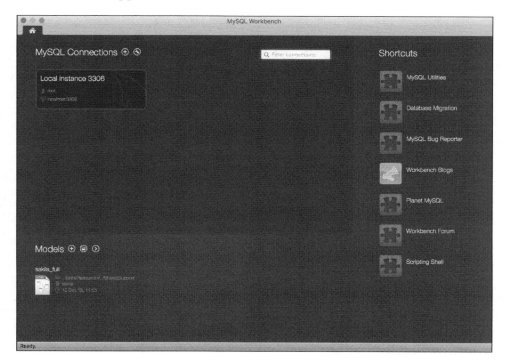

Installing Nginx

In order to install Nginx, we will use Brew, as we did with PHP. The command is the following:

```
$ brew install nginx
```

If you want to make Nginx start every time you start your laptop, run the following command:

```
$ ln -sfv /usr/local/opt/nginx/*.plist ~/Library/LaunchAgents
```

If you have to change the configuration of Nginx, you will find the file in /usr/local/etc/nginx/nginx.conf. You can change things, such as the port that Nginx is listening to or the root directory where your code is (the default directory is /usr/local/Cellar/nginx/1.8.1/html/). Remember to restart Nginx to apply the changes with the sudo nginx command.

Installing Composer

Installing Composer is as easy as downloading it with the curl command; move the binary to /usr/local/bin/ with the following two commands:

```
$ curl -sS https://getcomposer.org/installer | php
$ mv composer.phar /usr/local/bin/composer
```

Setting up the environment on Windows

Even though it is not very professional to pick sides based on personal opinions, it is well known among developers how hard it can be to use Windows as a developer machine. They prove to be extremely tricky when it comes to installing all the software since the installation mode is always very different from OS X and Linux systems, and quite often, there are dependency or configuration problems. In addition, the command line has different interpreters than Unix systems, which makes things a bit more confusing. This is why most developers would recommend you use a virtual machine with Linux if you only have a Windows machine at your disposal.

However, to be fair, PHP 7 is the exception to the rule. It is surprisingly simple to install it, so if you are really comfortable with your Windows and would prefer not to use Vagrant, here you have a short explanation on how to set up your environment.

Installing PHP

In order to install PHP 7, you will first download the installer from the official website. For this, go to `http://windows.php.net/download`. The options should be similar to the following screenshot:

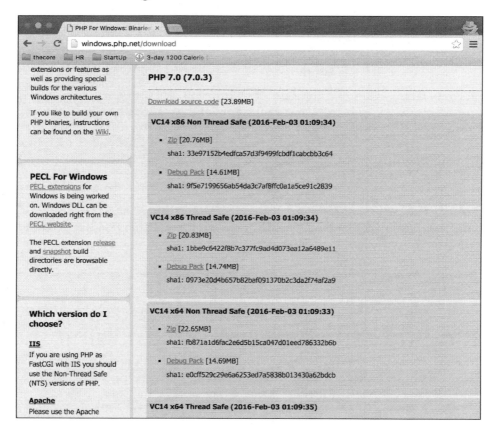

Choose **x86 Thread Safe** for Windows 32-bit or **x64 Thread Safe** for the 64-bit one. Once downloaded, uncompress it in `C:\php7`. Yes, that is it!

Installing MySQL

Installing MySQL is a little more complex. Download the installer from `http://dev.mysql.com/downloads/installer/` and execute it. After accepting the license agreement, you will get a window similar to the following one:

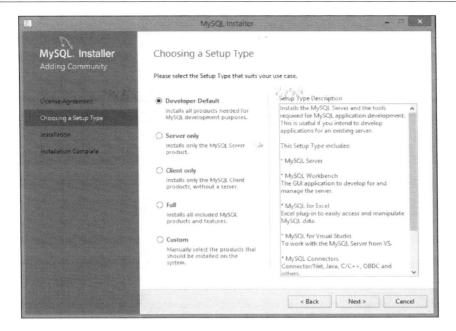

For the purposes of the book—and actually for any development environment—you should go for the first option: **Developer Default**. Keep going forward, leaving all the default options, until you get a window similar to this:

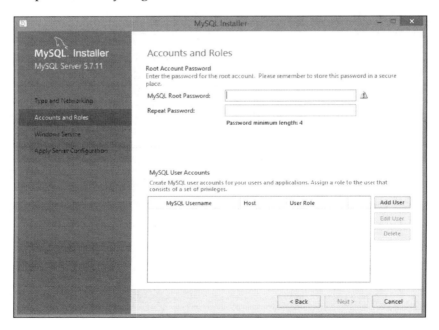

Depending on your preferences, you can either just set a password for the root user, which is enough as it is only a development machine, or you can add an extra user by clicking on **Add User**. Make sure to set the correct name, password, and permissions. A user named test with administration permissions should look similar to the following screenshot:

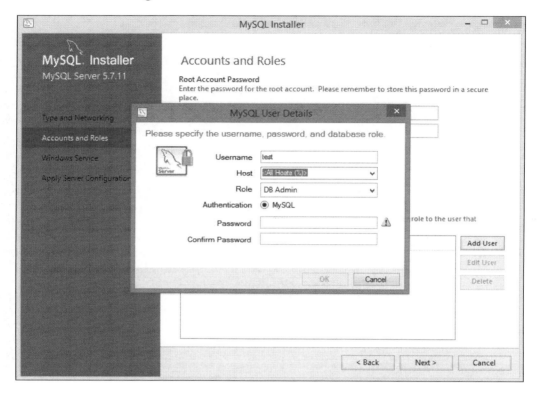

For the rest of the installation process, you can select all the default options.

Installing Nginx

The installation for Nginx is almost identical to the PHP 7 one. First, download the ZIP file from http://nginx.org/en/download.html. At the time of writing, the versions available are as follows:

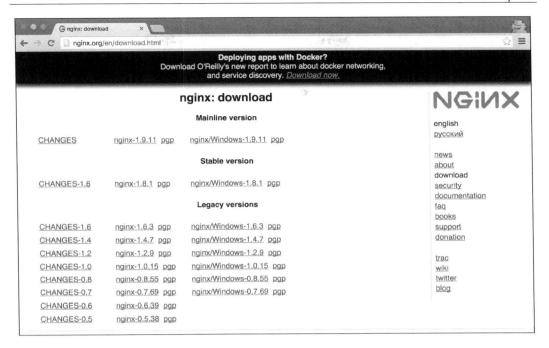

You can safely download the mainline version 1.9.10 or a later one if it is stable. Once the file is downloaded, uncompress it in `C:\nginx` and run the following commands to start the web server:

```
$ cd nginx
$ start nginx
```

Installing Composer

To finish with the setup, we need to install Composer. To go for the automatic installation, just download the installer from `https://getcomposer.org/Composer-Setup.exe`. Once downloaded, execute it in order to install Composer on your system and to update your PATH environment variable.

Setting up the environment on Ubuntu

Setting up your environment on Ubuntu is the easiest of the three platforms. In fact, you could take the `provisioner.sh` script from the *Setting up the environment with Vagrant* section and execute it on your laptop. That should do the trick. However, just in case you already have some of the tools installed or you want to have a sense of control on what is going on, we will detail each step.

Installing PHP

The only thing to consider in this section is to remove any previous PHP versions on your system. To do so, you can run the following command:

```
$ sudo apt-get -y purge php.*
```

The next step is to add the necessary repositories in order to fetch the correct PHP version. The commands to add and update them are:

```
$ sudo apt-get install python-software-properties
$ sudo LC_ALL=en_US.UTF-8 add-apt-repository ppa:ondrej/php -y
$ sudo apt-get update
```

Finally, we need to install PHP 7 together with the driver for MySQL. For this, just execute the following three commands:

```
$ sudo apt-get install php7.0 php7.0-fpm php7.0-mysql -y
$ sudo apt-get --purge autoremove -y
$ sudo service php7.0-fpm start
```

Installing MySQL

Installing MySQL manually can be slightly different than with the Vagrant script. As we can interact with the console, we do not have to specify the root password previously; instead, we can force MySQL to prompt for it. Run the following command and keep in mind that the installer will ask you for the password:

```
$ sudo apt-get -y install mysql-server mysql-client
```

Once done, if you need to start the MySQL server, you can do it with the following command:

```
$ sudo service mysql start
```

Installing Nginx

The first thing that you need to know is that you can only have one web server listening on the same port. As port 80 is the default one for web applications, if you are running Apache on your Ubuntu machine, you will not be able to start an Nginx web server listening on the same port 80. To fix this, you can either change the ports for Nginx or Apache, stop Apache, or uninstall it. Either way, the installation command for Nginx is as follows:

```
$ sudo apt-get install nginx -y
```

Now, you will need to enable a site with Nginx. The sites are files under `/etc/nginx/sites-available`. There is already one file there, `default`, which you can safely replace with the following content:

```
server {
    listen 80 default_server;
    listen [::]:80 default_server ipv6only=on;

    root /var/www/html;
    index index.php index.html index.htm;

    server_name server_domain_or_IP;

    location / {
        try_files $uri $uri/ /index.php?$query_string;
    }

    location ~ \.php$ {
        try_files $uri /index.php =404;
        fastcgi_split_path_info ^(.+\.php)(/.+)$;
        fastcgi_pass unix:/var/run/php/php7.0-fpm.sock;
        fastcgi_index index.php;
        fastcgi_param SCRIPT_FILENAME $document_root$fastcgi_script_name;
        include fastcgi_params;
    }
}
```

This configuration basically points the root directory of your web application to the `/var/www/html` directory. You can choose the one that you prefer, but make sure that it has the right permissions. It also listens on the port 80, which you can change with the one you prefer; just keep this in mind that when you try to access your application via a browser. Finally, to apply all the changes, run the following command:

```
$ sudo service nginx restart
```

Downloading the example code

You can download the example code files for this book from your account at http://www.packtpub.com. If you purchased this book elsewhere, you can visit http://www.packtpub.com/support and register to have the files e-mailed directly to you.

You can download the code files by following these steps:

- Log in or register to our website using your e-mail address and password.
- Hover the mouse pointer on the **SUPPORT** tab at the top.
- Click on **Code Downloads & Errata**.
- Enter the name of the book in the **Search** box.
- Select the book for which you're looking to download the code files.
- Choose from the drop-down menu where you purchased this book from.
- Click on **Code Download**.

Once the file is downloaded, please make sure that you unzip or extract the folder using the latest version of:

- WinRAR / 7-Zip for Windows
- Zipeg / iZip / UnRarX for Mac
- 7-Zip / PeaZip for Linux

Summary

In this chapter, you learned how easy it is to set up a development environment using Vagrant. If this did not convince you, you still got the chance to set up all the tools manually. Either way, now you are able to work on the next chapters.

In the next chapter, we will take a look at the idea of web applications with PHP, going from the protocols used to how the web server serves requests, thus setting the foundation for the following chapters.

2
Web Applications with PHP

Web applications are a common thing in our lives, and they are usually very user friendly; users do not need to understand how they work behind the scenes. As a developer, though, you need to understand how your application works internally.

In this chapter, you will learn about:

- HTTP and how web applications make use of it
- Web applications and how to build a simple one
- Web servers and how to launch your PHP built-in web server

The HTTP protocol

If you check the RFC2068 standard at `https://tools.ietf.org/html/rfc2068`, you will see that its description is almost endless. Luckily, what you need to know about this protocol, at least for starters, is way shorter.

HTTP stands for **HyperText Transfer Protocol**. As any other protocol, the goal is to allow two entities or nodes to communicate with each other. In order to achieve this, the messages need to be formatted in a way that they both understand, and the entities must follow some pre-established rules.

A simple example

The following diagram shows a very basic interchange of messages:

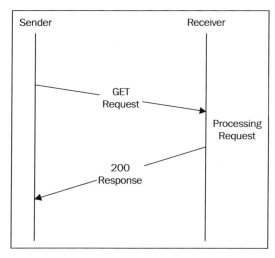

A simple GET request

Do not worry if you do not understand all the elements in this diagram; we will describe them shortly. In this representation, there are two entities: **sender** and **receiver**. The sender sends a message to the receiver. This message, which starts the communication, is called the request. In this case, the message is a GET request. The receiver receives the message, processes it, and generates a second message: the response. In this case, the response shows a 200 status code, meaning that the request was processed successfully.

HTTP is stateless; that is, it treats each request independently, unrelated to any previous one. This means that with this request and response sequence, the communication is finished. Any new requests will not be aware of this specific interchange of messages.

Parts of the message

An HTTP message contains several parts. We will define only the most important of them.

URL

The URL of the message is the destination of the message. The request will contain the receiver's URL, and the response will contain the sender's.

As you might know, the URL can contain extra parameters, known as a query string. This is used when the sender wants to add extra data. For example, consider this URL: `http://myserver.com/greeting?name=Alex`. This URL contains one parameter: `name` with the value `Alex`. It could not be represented as part of the URL `http://myserver.com/greeting`, so the sender chose to add it at the end of it. You will see later that this is not the only way that we can add extra information into a message.

The HTTP method

The HTTP method is the verb of the message. It identifies what kind of action the sender wants to perform with this message. The most common ones are GET and POST.

- **GET**: This asks the receiver about something, and the receiver usually sends this information back. The most common example is asking for a web page, where the receiver will respond with the HTML code of the requested page.

- **POST**: This means that the sender wants to perform an action that will update the data that the receiver is holding. For example, the sender can ask the receiver to update his profile name.

There are other methods, such as **PUT**, **DELETE**, or **OPTION**, but they are less used in web development, although they play a crucial role in REST APIs, which will be explained in *Chapter 9*, *Building REST APIs*.

Body

The body part is usually present in response messages even though a request message can contain it too. The body of the message contains the content of the message itself; for example, if the user requested a web page, the body of the response would consist of the HTML code that represents this page.

Soon, we will discuss how the request can also contain a body, which is used to send extra information as part of the request, such as form parameters.

The body can contain text in any format; it can be an HTML text that represents a web page, plain text, the content of an image, JSON, and so on.

Headers

The headers on an HTTP message are the metadata that the receiver needs in order to understand the content of the message. There are a lot of headers, and you will see some of them in this book.

Headers consist of a map of key-value pairs. The following could be the headers of a request:

```
Accept: text/html
Cookie: name=Richard
```

This request tells the receiver, which is a server, that it will accept text as HTML, which is the common way of representing a web page; and that it has a cookie named Richard.

The status code

The status code is present in responses. It identifies the status of the request with a numeric code so that browsers and other tools know how to react. For example, if we try to access a URL that does not exist, the server should reply with a status code 404. In this way, the browser knows what happened without even looking at the content of the response.

Common status codes are:

- **200**: The request was successful
- **401**: Unauthorized; the user does not have permission to see this resource
- **404**: Page not found
- **500**: Internal server error; something wrong happened on the server side and it could not be recovered

A more complex example

The following diagram shows a POST request and its response:

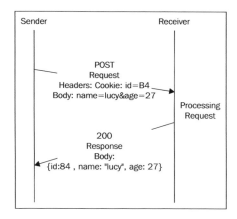

A more complex POST request

In this exchange of messages, we can see the other important method, POST, in action. In this case, the sender tries to send a request in order to update some entity's data. The message contains a cookie ID with the value **84**, which may identify the entity to update. It also contains two parameters in the body: name and age. This is the data that the receiver has to update.

> **Submitting web forms**
>
> Representing the parameters as part of the body is a common way to send information when submitting a form, but not the only one. You can add a query string to the URL, add JSON to the body of the message, and so on.

The response has a status code of 200, meaning that the request was processed successfully. In addition, the response also contains a body, this time formatted as JSON, which represents the new status of the updated entity.

Web applications

Maybe you have noticed that in the previous sections, I used the not very intuitive terms of sender and receiver as they do not represent any specific scenario that you might know but rather all of them in a generic way. The main reason for this choice of terminology is to try to separate HTTP from web applications. You will see at the end of the book that HTTP is used for more than just websites.

If you are reading this book, you already know what a web application is. Alternatively, maybe you know it by other terms, such as website or web page. Let's try to give some definitions.

A **web page** is a single document with content. It contains links that open other web pages with different content.

A **website** is the set of web pages that usually live in the same server and are related to each other.

A **web application** is just a piece of software that runs on a client, which is usually a browser, and communicates with a *server*. A server is a remote machine that receives requests from a client, processes them, and generates a response. This response will go back to the client, generally rendered by the browser in order to display it to the user.

Even though this is out of the scope of this book, you may be interested to know that not only browsers can act as clients, generating requests and sending them to the servers; even servers can be the ones taking the initiative of sending messages to the browsers.

So, what is the difference between a website and a web application? Well, the web application can be a small part of a bigger website with a specific functionality. Also, not all websites are web applications as a web application always does something but a website can just display information.

HTML, CSS, and JavaScript

Web applications are rendered by the browser so that the user can see its content. To do this, the server needs to send the content of the page or document. The document uses HTML to describe its elements and how they are organized. Elements can be links, buttons, input fields, and so on. A simple example of a web page looks like this:

```html
<!DOCTYPE html>
<html lang="en">
<head>
  <meta charset="UTF-8">
  <title>Your first app</title>
</head>
<body>
  <a id="special" class="link" href="http://yourpage.com">Your page</a>
  <a class="link" href="http://theirpage.com">Their page</a>
</body>
</html>
```

Let's focus on the highlighted code. As you can see, we are describing two `<a>` links with some properties. Both links have a class, a destination, and a text. The first one also contains an ID. Save this code into a file named `index.html` and execute it. You will see how your default browser opens a very simple page with two links.

If we want to add some styles, or change the color, size, and position of the links, we need to add CSS. CSS describes how elements from the HTML are displayed. There are several ways to include CSS, but the best approach is to have it in a separated file and then reference it from the HTML. Let's update our `<head>` section as shown in the following code:

```html
<head>
  <meta charset="UTF-8">
  <title>Your first app</title>
  <link rel="stylesheet" type="text/css" href="mystyle.css">
</head>
```

Now, let's create a new `mystyle.css` file in the same folder with the following content:

```
.link {
    color: green;
    font-weight: bold;
}

#special {
    font-size: 30px;
}
```

This CSS file contains two style definitions: one for the `link` class and one for the `special` ID. The class style will be applied to both the links as they both define this class, and it sets them as green and bold. The ID style that increases the font of the link is only applied to the first link.

Finally, in order to add behavior to our web page, we need to add JS or JavaScript. JS is a programming language that would need an entire book for itself, and in fact, there are quite a lot of them. If you want to give it a chance, we recommend the free online book *Eloquent JavaScript, Marijn Haverbeke*, which you can find at http://eloquentjavascript.net/. As with CSS, the best approach would be to add a separate file and then reference it from our HTML. Update the `<body>` section with the following highlighted code:

```
<body>
  <a id="special" class="link" href="http://yourpage.com">Your page</a>
  <a class="link" href="http://theirpage.com">Their page</a>
  <script src="myactions.js"></script>
</body>
```

Now, create a `myactions.js` file with the following content:

```
document.getElementById("special").onclick = function() {
    alert("You clicked me?");
}
```

The JS file adds a function that will be called when the `special` link is clicked on. This function just pops up an alert. You can save all your changes and refresh the browser to see how it looks now and how the links behave.

Different ways of including JS

You might notice that we included the CSS file reference at the end of the <head> section and JS at the end of <body>. You can actually include JS in both the <head> and the <body>; just bear in mind that the script will be executed as soon as it is included. If your script references fields that are not yet defined or other JS files that will be included later, JS will fail.

Congratulations! You just wrote your very first web page. Not impressed? Well, then you are reading the correct book! You will have the chance to work with more HTML, CSS, and JS during the book, even though the book focuses especially on PHP.

Web servers

So, it is about time that you learn what those famous web servers are. A web server is no more than a piece of software running on a machine and listening to requests from a specific port. Usually, this port is 80, but it can be any other that is available.

How they work

The following diagram represents the flow of request-response on the server side:

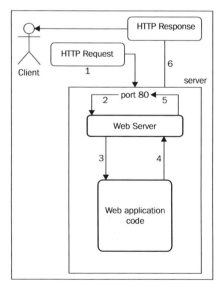

Request-response flow on the server side

The job of a web server is to route external requests to the correct application so that they can be processed. Once the application returns a response, the web server will send this response to the client. Let's take a close look at all the steps:

1. The client, which is a browser, sends a request. This can be of any type—GET or POST—and contain anything as long as it is valid.

2. The server receives the request, which points to a port. If there is a web server listening on this port, the web server will then take control of the situation.

3. The web server decides which web application—usually a file in the filesystem—needs to process the request. In order to decide, the web server usually considers the path of the URL; for example, `http://myserver.com/app1/hi` would try to pass the request to the `app1` application, wherever it is in the filesystem. However, another scenario would be `http://app1.myserver.com/hi`, which would also go to the same application. The rules are very flexible, and it is up to both the web server and the user as to how to set them.

4. The web application, after receiving a request from the web server, generates a response and sends it to the web server.

5. The web server sends the response to the indicated port.

6. The response finally arrives to the client.

The PHP built-in server

There are powerful web servers that support high loads of traffic, such as Apache or Nginx, which are fairly simple to install and manage. For the purpose of this book, though, we will use something even simpler: a PHP built-in server. The reason to use this is that you will not need extra package installations, configurations, and headaches as it comes with PHP. With just one command, you will have a web server running on your machine.

Production web servers

Note that the PHP built-in web server is good for testing purposes, but it is highly recommended not to use it in production environments. If you have to set up a server that needs to be public and your application is written in PHP, I highly recommend you to choose either of the classics: Apache (http://httpd.apache.org) or Nginx (https://www.nginx.com). Both can run almost on any server, are free and easy to install and configure, and, more importantly, have a huge community that will support you on virtually any problem you might encounter.

Finally, hands on! Let's try to create our very first web page using the built-in server. For this, create an index.php file inside your workspace directory — for example, Documents/workspace/index.php. The content of this file should be:

```
<?php
echo 'hello world';
```

Now, open your command line, go to your workspace directory, probably by running the cd Documents/workspace command, and run the following command:

```
$ php -S localhost:8000
```

The command line will prompt you with some information, the most important one being what is listening, which should be localhost:8000 as specified, and how to stop it, usually by pressing *Ctrl + C*. Do not close the command line as it will stop the web server too.

Now, let's open a browser and go to http://localhost:8000. You should see a **hello world** message on a white page. Yay, success! If you are interested, you can check your command line, and you will see log entries of each request you are sending via your browser.

So, how does it really work? Well, if you check again in the previous diagram, the php -S command started a web server — in our case, listening to port 8000 instead of 80. Also, PHP knows that the web application code will be on the same directory that you started the web server: your workspace. There are more specific options, but by default, PHP will try to execute the index.php file in your workspace.

Putting things together

Let's try to include our first project (index.html with its CSS and JS files) as part of the built-in server. To do this, you just need to open the command line and go to the directory in which these files are and start the web server with php -S localhost:8000. If you check localhost:8000 in your browser, you will see our two-link page, as is expected.

Let's now move our new `index.php` file to the same directory. You do not need to restart your web server; PHP will know about the changes automatically. Go to your browser and refresh the page. You should now see the **hello world** message instead of the links. What happened here?

If you do not change the default options, PHP will always try to find an `index.php` file in the directory in which you started the web server. If this is not found, PHP will try to find an `index.html` file. Previously, we only had the `index.html` file, so PHP failed to find `index.php`. Now that it can find its first option, `index.php`, it will load it.

If we want to see our `index.html` file from the browser, we can always specify it in the URL like `http://localhost:8000/index.html`. If the web server notices that you are trying to access a specific file, it will try to load it instead of the default options.

Finally, if we try to access a file that is not on our filesystem, the web server will return a response with status code 404 — that is, not found. We can see this code if we open the **Developer tools** section of our browser and go to the **Network** section.

Developer tools are your friends

As a web developer, you will find very few tools more useful than the developer tools of your browser. It changes from browser to browser, but all of the big names, such as Chrome or Firefox, have it. It is very important that you get familiar with how to use it as it allows you to debug your applications from the client side.

I will introduce you to some of these tools during the course of this book.

Summary

In this chapter, you learned what HTTP is and how web applications use it in order to interact with the server. You also now know how web servers work and how to launch a light built-in server with PHP. Finally, you took the first steps toward building your first web application. Congratulations!

In the next chapter, we will take a look at the basics of PHP so that you can start building simple applications.

3
Understanding PHP Basics

Learning a new language is not easy. You need to understand not only the syntax of the language, but also its grammatical rules, that is, when and why to use each element of the language. Luckily for you, some languages come from the same root. For example, Spanish and French are Romance languages, as they both evolved from spoken Latin; that means that these two languages share a lot of rules, and if you already know French, learning Spanish becomes much easier.

Programming languages are quite the same. If you already know another programming language, it will be very easy for you to go through this chapter. If this is your first time though, you will need to understand all those grammatical rules from scratch, and so, it might take some more time. But fear not! We are here to help you in this endeavor.

In this chapter, you will learn about the following:

- PHP files
- Variables, strings, arrays, and operators in PHP
- PHP in web applications
- Control structures in PHP
- Functions in PHP
- The PHP filesystem

PHP files

From now on, we will work on your `index.php` file, so you can just start the web server, and go to `http://localhost:8080` to see the results.

You might have already noticed that in order to write PHP code, you have to start the file with `<?php`. There are other options, and you can also finish the file with `?>`, but none of them are needed. What is important to know is that you can mix PHP code with other content, like HTML, CSS, or JavaScript, in your PHP file as soon as you enclose the PHP bits with the `<?php ?>` tags.

```php
<?php
  echo 'hello world';
?>
bye world
```

If you check the result of the preceding code snippet in your browser, you will see that it prints both messages, **hello world** and **bye world**. The reason why this happens is simple: you already know that the PHP code there prints the **hello world** message. What happens next is that anything outside the PHP tags will be interpreted as is. If there is an HTML code for instance, it would not be printed as is, but will be interpreted by the browser.

You will learn in *Chapter 6*, *Adapting to MVC*, why it is usually a bad idea to mix PHP and HTML. For now, assuming that it is bad, let's try to avoid it. For that, you can include one file from another PHP file using any one of these four functions:

- `include`: This will try to find and include the specified file each time it is invoked. If the file is not found, PHP will throw a warning, but will continue with the execution.

- `require`: This will do the same as `include`, but PHP will throw an error instead of a warning if the file is not found.

- `include_once`: This function will do what `include` does, but it will include the file only the first time that it is invoked. Subsequent calls will be ignored.

- `require_once`: This works the same as `require`, but it will include the file only the first time that it is invoked. Subsequent calls will be ignored.

Each function has its own usage, so it is not right to say that one is better than the other. Just think carefully what your scenario is, and then decide. For example, let's try to include our `index.html` file from our `index.php` file such that we do not mix PHP with HTML, but have the best of both worlds:

```php
<?php
echo 'hello world';
require 'index.html';
```

We chose `require` as we know the file is there—and if it is not, we are not interested in continuing the execution. Moreover, as it is some HTML code, we might want to include it multiple times, so we did not choose the `require_once` option. You can try to require a file that does not exist, and see what the browser says.

PHP does not consider empty lines; you can add as many as you want to make your code easier to read, and it will not have any repercussion on your application. Another element that helps in writing understandable code, and which is ignored by PHP, is comments. Let's see both in action:

```php
<?php

/*
 * This is the first file loaded by the web server.
 * It prints some messages and html from other files.
 */

// let's print a message from php
echo 'hello world';

// and then include the rest of html
require 'index.html';
```

The code does the same job as the previous one, but now everyone will easily understand what we are trying to do. We can see two types of comments: single-line comments and multiple-line comments. The first type consists of a single line starting with //, and the second type encloses multiple lines within /* and */. We start each commented line with an asterisk, but that is completely optional.

Variables

Variables keep a value for future reference. This value can change if we want it to; that is why they are called variables. Let's take a look at them in an example. Save this code in your index.php file:

```php
<?php
$a = 1;
$b = 2;
$c = $a + $b;
echo $c; // 3
```

In this preceding piece of code, we have three variables: $a has value 1, $b has 2, and $c contains the sum of $a and $b, hence, $c equals 3. Your browser should print the value of the variable $c, which is 3.

Assigning a value to a variable means to give it a value, and it is done with the equals sign as shown in the previous example. If you did not assign a value to a variable, we will get a notice from PHP when it checks its contents. A notice is just a message telling us that something is not exactly right, but it is a minor problem and you can continue with the execution. The value of an unassigned variable will be null, that is, nothing.

PHP variables start with the $ sign followed by the variable name. A valid variable name starts with a letter or an underscore followed by any combination of letters, numbers, and/or underscores. It is case sensitive. Let's see some examples:

```php
<?php
$_some_value = 'abc'; // valid
$1number = 12.3; // not valid!
$some$signs% = '&^%'; // not valid!
$go_2_home = "ok"; // valid
$go_2_Home = 'no'; // this is a different variable
$isThisCamelCase = true; // camel case
```

Remember that everything after // is a comment, and is thus ignored by PHP.

In this piece of code, we can see that variable names like $_some_value and $go_2_ home are valid. $1number and $some$signs% are not valid as they start with a number, or they contain invalid symbols. As names are case sensitive, $go_2_home and $go_2_Home are two different variables. Finally, we show the CamelCase convention, which is the preferred option among most developers.

Data types

We can assign more than just numbers to variables. PHP has eight primitive types, but for now, we will focus on its four scalar types:

- **Booleans**: These take just true or false values
- **Integers**: These are numeric values without a decimal point, for example, 2 or 5
- **Floating point numbers or floats**: These are numbers with a decimal point, for example, 2.3
- **Strings**: These are concatenations of characters which are surrounded by either single or double quotes, like 'this' or "that"

Even though PHP defines these types, it allows the user to assign different types of data to the same variable. Check the following code to see how it works:

```php
<?php
$number = 123;
var_dump($number);
$number = 'abc';
var_dump($number);
```

If you check the result on your browser, you will see the following:

```
int(123) string(3) "abc"
```

The code first assigns the value 123 to the variable $number. As 123 is an integer, the type of the variable will be integer int. That is what we see when printing the content of the variable with var_dump. After that, we assign another value to the same variable, this time a string. When printing the new content, we see that the type of the variable changed from integer to string, yet PHP did not complain at any time. This is called **type juggling**.

Let's check another piece of code:

```php
<?php
$a = "1";
$b = 2;
var_dump($a + $b); // 3
var_dump($a . $b); // 12
```

You already know that the + operator returns the sum of two numeric values. You will see later that the . operator concatenates two strings. Thus, the preceding code assigns a string and an integer to two variables, and then tries to add and concatenate them.

When trying to add them, PHP knows that it needs two numeric values, and so it tries to adapt the string to an integer. In this case, it is easy as the string represents a valid number. That is the reason why we see the first result as an integer 3 (*1 + 2*).

In the last line, we are performing a string concatenation. We have an integer in $b, so PHP will first try to convert it to a string—which is "2"—and then concatenate it with the other string, "1". The result is the string "12".

Type juggling

PHP tries to convert the data type of a variable only when there is a context where the type of variable needed is different. But PHP does not change the value and type of the variable itself. Instead, it will take the value and try to transform it, leaving the variable intact.

Operators

Using variables is nice, but if we cannot make them interact with each other, there is nothing much we can do. **Operators** are elements that take some expressions— operands—and perform actions on them to get a result. The most common examples of operators are arithmetic operators, which you already saw previously.

An **expression** is almost anything that has a value. Variables, numbers, or text are examples of expressions, but you will see that they can get way more complicated. Operators expect expressions of a specific type, for example, arithmetic operators expect either integers or floats. But as you already know, PHP takes care of transforming the types of the expressions given whenever possible.

Let's take a look at the most important groups of operators.

Arithmetic operators

Arithmetic operators are very intuitive, as you already know. Addition, subtraction, multiplication, and division (+, -, *, and /) do as their names say. Modulus (%) gives the remainder of the division of two operands. Exponentiation (**) raises the first operand to the power of the second. Finally, negation (-) negates the operand. This last one is the only arithmetic operator that takes just one operand.

Let's see some examples:

```php
<?php
$a = 10;
$b = 3;
var_dump($a + $b); // 13
var_dump($a - $b); // 7
var_dump($a * $b); // 30
var_dump($a / $b); // 3.333333...
var_dump($a % $b); // 1
var_dump($a ** $b); // 1000
var_dump(-$a); // -10
```

As you can see, they are quite easy to understand!

Assignment operators

You already know this one too, as we have been using it in our examples. The assignment operator assigns the result of an expression to a variable. Now you know that an expression can be as simple as a number, or, for example, the result of a series of arithmetic operations. The following example assigns the result of an expression to a variable:

```php
<?php
$a = 3 + 4 + 5 - 2;
var_dump($a); // 10
```

There are a series of assignment operators that work as shortcuts. You can build them combining an arithmetic operator and the assignment operator. Let's see some examples:

```
$a = 13;
$a += 14; // same as $a = $a + 14;
var_dump($a);
$a -= 2; // same as $a = $a - 2;
var_dump($a);
$a *= 4; // same as $a = $a * 4;
var_dump($a);
```

Comparison operators

Comparison operators are one of the most used groups of operators. They take two operands and compare them, returning the result of the comparison usually as a Boolean, that is, `true` or `false`.

There are four comparisons that are very intuitive: < (less than), <= (less or equal to), > (greater than), and >= (greater than or equal to). There is also the special operator <=> (spaceship) that compares both the operands and returns an integer instead of a Boolean. When comparing *a* with *b*, the result will be less than 0 if *a* is less than *b*, 0 if *a* equals *b*, and greater than 0 if *a* is greater than *b*. Let's see some examples:

```
<?php
var_dump(2 < 3); // true
var_dump(3 < 3); // false
var_dump(3 <= 3); // true
var_dump(4 <= 3); // false
var_dump(2 > 3); // false
var_dump(3 >= 3); // true
var_dump(3 > 3); // false
var_dump(1 <=> 2); // int less than 0
var_dump(1 <=> 1); // 0
var_dump(3 <=> 2); // int greater than 0
```

There are comparison operators to evaluate if two expressions are equal or not, but you need to be careful with type juggling. The == (equals) operator evaluates two expressions *after* type juggling, that is, it will try to transform both expressions to the same type, and then compare them. Instead, the === (identical) operator evaluates two expressions *without* type juggling, so even if they look the same, if they are not of the same type, the comparison will return `false`. The same applies to != or <> (not equal to) and !== (not identical):

```
<?php
$a = 3;
$b = '3';
```

```
$c = 5;
var_dump($a == $b); // true
var_dump($a === $b); // false
var_dump($a != $b); // false
var_dump($a !== $b); // true
var_dump($a == $c); // false
var_dump($a <> $c); // true
```

You can see that when asking if a string and an integer that represent the same number are equal, it replies affirmatively; PHP first transforms both to the same type. On the other hand, when asked if they are identical, it replies they are not as they are of different types.

Logical operators

Logical operators apply a logic operation—also known as a binary operation—to its operands, returning a Boolean response. The most used ones are ! (not), && (and), and || (or). && will return true only if both operands evaluate to true. || will return true if any or both of the operands are true. ! will return the negated value of the operand, that is, true if the operand is false or false if the operand is true. Let's see some examples:

```
<?php
var_dump(true && true); // true
var_dump(true && false); // false
var_dump(true || false); // true
var_dump(false || false); // false
var_dump(!false); // true
```

Incrementing and decrementing operators

Incrementing/decrementing operators are also shortcuts like += or -=, and they only work on variables. There are four of them, and they need special attention. We've already seen the first two:

- ++: This operator on the left of the variable will increase the variable by 1, and then return the result. On the right, it will return the content of the variable, and after that increase it by 1.

- --: This operator works the same as ++ but decreases the value by 1 instead of increasing by 1.

Let's see an example:

```php
<?php
$a = 3;
$b = $a++; // $b is 3, $a is 4
var_dump($a, $b);
$b = ++$a; // $a and $b are 5
var_dump($a, $b);
```

In the preceding code, on the first assignment to $b, we use $a++. The operator on the right will return first the value of $a, which is 3, assign it to $b, and only then increase $a by 1. In the second assignment, the operator on the left first increases $a by 1, changes the value of $a to 5, and then assigns that value to $b.

Operator precedence

You can add multiple operators to an expression to make it as long as it needs to be, but you need to be careful as some operators have higher precedence than others, and thus, the order of execution might not be the one you expect. The following table shows the order of precedence of the operators that we've studied until now:

Operator	Type
**	Arithmetic
++, --	Increasing/decreasing
!	Logical
*, /, %	Arithmetic
+, -	Arithmetic
<, <=, >, >=	Comparison
==, !=, ===, !==	Comparison
&&	Logical
||	Logical
=, +=, -=, *=, /=, %=, **=	Assignment

The preceding table shows us that the expression 3+2*3 will first evaluate the product 2*3 and then the sum, so the result is 9 rather than 15. If you want to perform operations in a specific order, different from the natural order of precedence, you can force it by enclosing the operation within parentheses. Hence, (3+2)*3 will first perform the sum and then the product, giving the result 15 this time.

Let's see some examples to clarify this quite tricky subject:

```php
<?php
$a = 1;
$b = 3;
$c = true;
$d = false;
$e = $a + $b > 5 || $c; // true
var_dump($e);
$f = $e == true && !$d; // true
var_dump($f);
$g = ($a + $b) * 2 + 3 * 4; // 20
var_dump($g);
```

This preceding example could be endless, and still not be able to cover all the scenarios you can imagine, so let's keep it simple. In the first highlighted line, we have a combination of arithmetic, comparison, and logical operators, plus the assignment operator. As there are no parentheses, the order is the one detailed in the previous table. The operator with the highest preference is the sum, so we perform it first: $a + $b equals 4. The next one is the comparison operator, so 4 > 5, which is false. Finally, the logical operator, false || $c ($c is true) results in true.

The second example might need a bit more explanation. The first operator we see in the table is the negation, so we resolve it. !$d is !false, so it is true. The expression is now, $e == true && true. First we need to solve the comparison $e == true. Knowing that $e is true, the comparison results in true. The final operation then is the logical end, and it results in true.

Try to work out the last example by yourself to get some practice. Do not be afraid if you think we are not covering operators enough. During the next few sections, we will see a lot of examples.

Working with strings

Working with strings in real life is really easy. Actions like *Check if this string contains this* or *Tell me how many times this character appears* are very easy to perform. But when programming, strings are concatenations of characters that you cannot see at once when searching for something. Instead, you have to look one by one and keep track of what the content is. In this scenario, those really easy actions are not that easy any more.

Luckily for you, PHP brings a whole set of predefined functions that help you in interacting with strings. You can find the entire list of functions at http://php.net/manual/en/ref.strings.php, but we will only cover the ones that are used the most. Let's look at some examples:

```php
<?php

$text = '   How can a clam cram in a clean cream can? ';

echo strlen($text); // 45
$text = trim($text);
echo $text; // How can a clam cram in a clean cream can?
echo strtoupper($text); // HOW CAN A CLAM CRAM IN A CLEAN CREAM CAN?
echo strtolower($text); // how can a clam cram in a clean cream can?
$text = str_replace('can', 'could', $text);
echo $text; // How could a clam cram in a clean cream could?
echo substr($text, 2, 6); // w coul
var_dump(strpos($text, 'can')); // false
var_dump(strpos($text, 'could')); // 4
```

In the preceding long piece of code, we are playing with a string with different functions:

- strlen: This function returns the number of characters that the string contains.

- trim: This function returns the string, removing all the blank spaces to the left and to the right.

- strtoupper and strtolower: These functions return the string with all the characters in upper or lower case respectively.

- str_replace: This function replaces all occurrences of a given string by the replacement string.

- substr: This function extracts the string contained between the positions specified by parameters, with the first character being at position 0.

- strpos: This function shows the position of the first occurrence of the given string. It returns false if the string cannot be found.

Additionally, there is an operator for strings (.) which concatenates two strings (or two variables transformed to a string when possible). Using it is really simple: in the following example, the last statement will concatenate all the strings and variables forming the sentence, *I am Hiro Nakamura!*.

```php
<?php
$firstname = 'Hiro';
$surname = 'Nakamura';
echo 'I am ' . $firstname . ' ' . $surname . '!';
```

Another thing to note about strings is the way they are represented. So far, we have been enclosing the strings within single quotes, but you can also enclose them within double quotes. The difference is that within single quotes, a string is exactly as it is represented, but within double quotes, some rules are applied before showing the final result. There are two elements that double quotes treat differently than single quotes: escape characters and variable expansions.

- **Escape characters**: These are special characters than cannot be represented easily. Examples of escape characters are new lines or tabs. To represent them, we use escape sequences, which are the concatenation of a backslash (\) followed by some other character. For example, \n represents a new line, and \t represents a tabulation.

- **Variable expanding**: This allows you to include variable references inside the string, and PHP replaces them by their current value. You have to include the $ sign too.

Have a look at the following example:

```php
<?php
$firstname = 'Hiro';
$surname = 'Nakamura';
echo "My name is $firstname $surname.\nI am a master of time and
space. \"Yatta!\"";
```

The preceding piece of code will print the following in the browser:

```
My name is Hiro Nakamura.
I am a master of time and space. "Yatta!"
```

Here, \n inserted a new line. \" added the double quotes (you need to escape them too, as PHP would understand that you want to end your string), and the variables $firstname and $surname were replaced by their values.

Arrays

If you have some experience with other programming languages or data structures in general, you might be aware of two data structures that are very common and useful: **lists** and **maps**. A list is an ordered set of elements, whereas a map is a set of elements identified by keys. Let's see an example:

```
List: ["Harry", "Ron", "Hermione"]

Map: {
  "name": "James Potter",
  "status": "dead"
}
```

The first element is a list of names that contains three values: Harry, Ron, and Hermione. The second one is a map, and it defines two values: James Potter and dead. Each of these two values is identified with a key: name and status respectively.

In PHP, we do not have lists and maps; we have arrays. An array is a data structure that implements both, a list and a map.

Initializing arrays

You have different options for initializing an array. You can initialize an empty array, or you can initialize an array with data. There are different ways of writing the same data with arrays too. Let's see some examples:

```php
<?php
$empty1 = [];
$empty2 = array();
$names1 = ['Harry', 'Ron', 'Hermione'];
$names2 = array('Harry', 'Ron', 'Hermione');
$status1 = [
    'name' => 'James Potter',
    'status' => 'dead'
];
$status2 = array(
    'name' => 'James Potter',
    'status' => 'dead'
);
```

In the preceding example, we define the list and map from the previous section. $names1 and $names2 are exactly the same array, just using a different notation. The same happens with $status1 and $status2. Finally, $empty1 and $empty2 are two ways of creating an empty array.

Later you will see that lists are handled like maps. Internally, the array $names1 is a map, and its keys are ordered numbers. In this case, another initialization for $names1 that leads to the same array could be as follows:

```php
$names1 = [
    0 => 'Harry',
    1 => 'Ron',
    2 => 'Hermione'
];
```

Keys of an array can be any alphanumeric value, like strings or numbers. Values of an array can be anything: strings, numbers, Booleans, other arrays, and so on. You could have something like the following:

```php
<?php
$books = [
    '1984' => [
        'author' => 'George Orwell',
        'finished' => true,
        'rate' => 9.5
    ],
    'Romeo and Juliet' => [
        'author' => 'William Shakespeare',
        'finished' => false
    ]
];
```

This array is a list that contains two arrays—maps. Each map contains different values like strings, doubles, and Booleans.

Populating arrays

Arrays are not immutable, that is, they can change after being initialized. You can change the content of an array either by treating it as a map or as a list. Treating it as a map means that you specify the key that you want to override, whereas treating it as a list means appending another element to the end of the array:

```php
<?php
$names = ['Harry', 'Ron', 'Hermione'];
$status = [
    'name' => 'James Potter',
    'status' => 'dead'
];
$names[] = 'Neville';
$status['age'] = 32;
print_r($names, $status);
```

In the preceding example, the first highlighted line appends the name Neville to the list of names, hence the list will look like *['Harry', 'Ron', 'Hermione', 'Neville']*. The second change actually adds a new key-value to the array. You can check the result from your browser by using the function print_r. It does something similar to var_dump, just without the type and size of each value.

print_r and var_dump in a browser

When printing the content of an array, it is useful to see one key-value per line, but if you check your browser, you will see that it displays the whole array in one line. That happens because what the browser tries to display is HTML, and it ignores new lines or whitespaces. To check the content of the array as PHP wants you to see it, check the source code of the page—you will see the option by right-clicking on the page.

If you need to remove an element from the array, instead of adding or updating one, you can use the `unset` function:

```php
<?php
$status = [
    'name' => 'James Potter',
    'status' => 'dead'
];
unset($status['status']);
print_r ($status);
```

The new `$status` array contains the key name only.

Accessing arrays

Accessing an array is as easy as specifying the key as when you were updating it. For that, you need to understand how lists work. You already know that lists are treated internally as a map with numeric keys in order. The first key is always 0; so, an array with *n* elements will have keys from 0 to *n-1*.

You can add any key to a given array, even if it previously consisted of numeric entries. The problem arises when adding numeric keys, and later, you try to append an element to the array. What do you think will happen?

```php
<?php
$names = ['Harry', 'Ron', 'Hermione'];
$names['badguy'] = 'Voldemort';
$names[8] = 'Snape';
$names[] = 'McGonagall';
print_r($names);
```

The result of that last piece of code is as follows:

```
Array
(
    [0] => Harry
```

```
[1] => Ron
[2] => Hermione
[badguy] => Voldemort
[8] => Snape
[9] => McGonagall
)
```

When trying to append a value, PHP inserts it after the last numeric key, in this case 8.

You might've already figured it out by yourself, but you can always print any part of the array by specifying its key:

```php
<?php
$names = ['Harry', 'Ron', 'Hermione'];
print_r($names[1]); // prints 'Ron'
```

Finally, trying to access a key that does not exist in an array will return you a null and throw a notice, as PHP identifies that you are doing something wrong in your code.

```php
<?php
$names = ['Harry', 'Ron', 'Hermione'];
var_dump($names[4]); // null and a PHP notice
```

The empty and isset functions

There are two useful functions for enquiring about the content of an array. If you want to know if an array contains any element at all, you can ask if it is empty with the empty function. That function actually works with strings too, an empty string being a string with no characters (' '). The isset function takes an array position, and returns true or false depending on whether that position exists or not:

```php
<?php
$string = '';
$array = [];
$names = ['Harry', 'Ron', 'Hermione'];
var_dump(empty($string)); // true
var_dump(empty($array)); // true
var_dump(empty($names)); // false
var_dump(isset($names[2])); // true
var_dump(isset($names[3])); // false
```

In the preceding example, we can see that an array with no elements or a string with no characters will return `true` when asked if it is empty, and `false` otherwise. When we use `isset($names[2])` to check if the position 2 of the array exists, we get `true`, as there is a value for that key: `Hermione`. Finally, `isset($names[3])` evaluates to `false` as the key 3 does not exist in that array.

Searching for elements in an array

Probably, one of the most used functions with arrays is `in_array`. This function takes two values, the value that you want to search for and the array. The function returns `true` if the value is in the array and `false` otherwise. This is very useful, because a lot of times what you want to know from a list or a map is if it contains an element, rather than knowing that it does or its location.

Even more useful sometimes is `array_search`. This function works in the same way except that instead of returning a Boolean, it returns the key where the value is found, or `false` otherwise. Let's see both functions:

```php
<?php
$names = ['Harry', 'Ron', 'Hermione'];
$containsHermione = in_array('Hermione', $names);
var_dump($containsHermione); // true
$containsSnape = in_array('Snape', $names);
var_dump($containsSnape); // false
$wheresRon = array_search('Ron', $names);
var_dump($wheresRon); // 1
$wheresVoldemort = array_search('Voldemort', $names);
var_dump($wheresVoldemort); // false
```

Ordering arrays

An array can be sorted in different ways, so there are a lot of chances that the order that you need is different from the current one. By default, the array is sorted by the order in which the elements were added to it, but you can sort an array by its key or by its value, both ascending and descending. Furthermore, when sorting an array by its values, you can choose to preserve their keys or to generate new ones as a list.

There is a complete list of these functions on the official documentation website at `http://php.net/manual/en/array.sorting.php`, but here we will display the most important ones:

Name	Sorts by	Maintains key association	Order of sort
sort	Value	No	Low to high
rsort	Value	No	High to low
asort	Value	Yes	Low to high
arsort	Value	Yes	High to low
ksort	Key	Yes	Low to high
krsort	Key	Yes	High to low

These functions always take one argument, the array, and they do not return anything. Instead, they directly sort the array we pass to them. Let's see some of them:

```php
<?php
$properties = [
    'firstname' => 'Tom',
    'surname' => 'Riddle',
    'house' => 'Slytherin'
];
$properties1 = $properties2 = $properties3 = $properties;
sort($properties1);
var_dump($properties1);
asort($properties3);
var_dump($properties3);
ksort($properties2);
var_dump($properties2);
```

Okay, there is a lot going on in the last example. First of all, we initialize an array with some key values and assign it to `$properties`. Then we create three variables that are copies of the original array—the syntax should be intuitive. Why do we do that? Because if we sort the original array, we will not have the original content any more. This is not what we want in this specific example, as we want to see how the different sort functions affect the same array. Finally, we perform three different sorts, and print each of the results. The browser should show you something like the following:

```
array(3) {
  [0]=>
  string(6) "Riddle"
  [1]=>
```

```
        string(9) "Slytherin"
    [2]=>
    string(3) "Tom"
}
array(3) {
    ["surname"]=>
    string(6) "Riddle"
    ["house"]=>
    string(9) "Slytherin"
    ["firstname"]=>
    string(3) "Tom"
}
array(3) {
    ["firstname"]=>
    string(3) "Tom"
    ["house"]=>
    string(9) "Slytherin"
    ["surname"]=>
    string(6) "Riddle"
}
```

The first function, sort, orders the values alphabetically. Also, if you check the keys, now they are numeric as in a list, instead of the original keys. Instead, asort orders the values in the same way, but keeps the association of key-values. Finally, ksort orders the elements by their keys, alphabetically.

How to remember so many function names

PHP has a lot of function helpers that will save you from writing customized functions by yourself, for example, it provides you with up to 13 different sorting functions. And you can always rely on the official documentation. But, of course, you would like to write code without going back and forth from the docs. So, here are some tips to remember what each sorting function does:

- An a in the name means **associative**, and thus, will preserve the key-value association.

- An r in the name means **reverse**, so the order will be from high to low.

- A k means **key**, so the sorting will be based on the keys instead of the values.

Other array functions

There are around 80 different functions related to arrays. As you can imagine, you will never even hear about some of them, as they have very specific purposes. The complete list can be found at http://php.net/manual/en/book.array.php.

We can get a list of the keys of the array with array_keys, and a list of its values with array_values:

```php
<?php
$properties = [
    'firstname' => 'Tom',
    'surname' => 'Riddle',
    'house' => 'Slytherin'
];
$keys = array_keys($properties);
var_dump($keys);
$values = array_values($properties);
var_dump($values);
```

We can get the number of elements in an array with the count function:

```php
<?php
$names = ['Harry', 'Ron', 'Hermione'];
$size = count($names);
var_dump($size); // 3
```

And we can merge two or more arrays into one with array_merge:

```php
<?php
$good = ['Harry', 'Ron', 'Hermione'];
$bad = ['Dudley', 'Vernon', 'Petunia'];
$all = array_merge($good, $bad);
var_dump($all);
```

The last example will print the following array:

```
array(6) {
  [0]=>
  string(5) "Harry"
  [1]=>
  string(3) "Ron"
  [2]=>
  string(8) "Hermione"
  [3]=>
  string(6) "Dudley"
  [4]=>
```

```
    string(6) "Vernon"
    [5]=>
    string(7) "Petunia"
}
```

As you can see, the keys of the second array are now different, as originally, both the arrays had the same numeric keys, and an array cannot have two values for the same key.

PHP in web applications

Even though the main purpose of this chapter is to show you the basics of PHP, doing it in a reference-manual kind of a way is not interesting enough, and if we were to copy-paste what the official documentation says, you might as well go there and read it by yourself. Keeping in mind the main purpose of this book and your main goal is to write web applications with PHP, let us show you how to apply everything you are learning as soon as possible, before you get too bored.

In order to do that, we will now start on a journey towards building an online bookstore. At the very beginning, you might not see the usefulness of it, but that is just because we've still not shown all that PHP can do.

Getting information from the user

Let's start by building a home page. In this page, we are going to figure out if the user is looking for a book or just walking by. How do we find that out? The easiest way right now is to inspect the URL that the user used to access our application, and extract some information from there.

Save this content as your index.php:

```php
<?php
$looking = isset($_GET['title']) || isset($_GET['author']);
?>
<!DOCTYPE html>
<html lang="en">
<head>
    <meta charset="UTF-8">
    <title>Bookstore</title>
</head>
<body>
    <p>You lookin'? <?php echo (int) $looking; ?></p>
    <p>The book you are looking for is</p>
    <ul>
```

```
            <li><b>Title</b>: <?php echo $_GET['title']; ?></li>
            <li><b>Author</b>: <?php echo $_GET['author']; ?></li>
        </ul>
    </body>
    </html>
```

Now access the link, `http://localhost:8000/?author=HarperLee&title=To Kill a Mockingbird`. You will see that the page prints some of the information that you passed on to the URL.

For each request, PHP stores all the parameters that come from the query string in an array called `$_GET`. Each key of the array is the name of the parameter, and its associated value is the value of the parameter. So `$_GET` contains two entries: `$_GET['author']` contains `Harper Lee` and `$_GET['title']` has the value `To Kill a Mockingbird`.

In the first highlighted line, we assign a Boolean value to the variable `$looking`. If either `$_GET['title']` or `$_GET['author']` exists, that variable will be `true`, otherwise `false`. Just after that, we close the PHP tag and then we print some HTML, but as you can see, we are actually mixing the HTML with some PHP code.

Another interesting line here is the second highlighted one. Before printing the content of `$looking`, we cast the value. **Casting** means forcing PHP to transform a type of value to another one. Casting a Boolean to an integer means that the resultant value will be `1` if the Boolean is `true` or `0` if the Boolean is `false`. As `$looking` is `true` since `$_GET` contains valid keys, the page shows a "1".

If we try to access the same page without sending any information, as in `http://localhost:8000`, the browser will say **Are you looking for a book? 0**. Depending on the settings of your PHP configuration, you will see two notice messages complaining that you are trying to access keys of the array that do not exist.

Casting versus type juggling

We already know that when PHP needs a specific type of variable, it will try to transform it, which is called type juggling. But PHP is quite flexible, so sometimes, you have to be the one specifying the type that you need. When printing something with `echo`, PHP tries to transform everything it gets into strings. Since the string version of the Boolean `false` is an empty string, that would not be useful for our application. Casting the Boolean to an integer first assures that we will see a value, even if it is just a 0.

HTML forms

HTML forms are one of the most popular ways of collecting information from the user. They consist of a series of fields—called input in the HTML world—and a final submit button. In HTML, the form tag contains two attributes: action points where the form will be submitted, and method, which specifies the HTTP method that the form will use (GET or POST). Let's see how it works. Save the following content as login.html and go to http://localhost:8000/login.html.

```
<!DOCTYPE html>
<html lang="en">
<head>
    <meta charset="UTF-8">
    <title>Bookstore - Login</title>
</head>
<body>
    <p>Enter your details to login:</p>
    <form action="authenticate.php" method="post">
        <label>Username</label>
        <input type="text" name="username" />
        <label>Password</label>
        <input type="password" name="password" />
        <input type="submit" value="Login"/>
    </form>
</body>
</html>
```

The form defined in the preceding code contains two fields, one for the username and one for the password. You can see that they are identified by the attribute name. If you try to submit this form, the browser will show you a **Page Not Found** message, as it is trying to access http://localhost:8000/authenticate.php and the web server cannot find it. Let's create it then:

```
<?php
$submitted = !empty($_POST);
?>
<!DOCTYPE html>
<html lang="en">
<head>
    <meta charset="UTF-8">
    <title>Bookstore</title>
</head>
<body>
    <p>Form submitted? <?php echo (int) $submitted; ?></p>
    <p>Your login info is</p>
```

```
    <ul>
        <li><b>username</b>: <?php echo $_POST['username']; ?></li>
        <li><b>password</b>: <?php echo $_POST['password']; ?></li>
    </ul>
</body>
</html>
```

As with $_GET, $_POST is an array that contains the parameters received by POST. In this preceding piece of code, we first ask if that array is not empty—note the ! operator. Afterwards, we just display the information received, just as in index.php. Notice that the keys of the $_POST array are the values for the argument name of each input field.

Persisting data with cookies

When we want the browser to remember some data like whether you are logged in or not on your web application, your basic info, and so on, we use **cookies**. Cookies are stored on the client side and are sent to the server when making a request as headers. As PHP is oriented towards web applications, it allows you to manage cookies in a very easy way.

There are few things you need to know about cookies and PHP. You can write cookies with the setcookie function that accepts several arguments:

- A valid name for the cookie as a string.

- The value of the cookie—only strings or values that can be casted to a string. This parameter is optional, and if not set, PHP will actually remove the cookie.

- Expiration time as a timestamp. If not set, the cookie will be removed once the browser is closed.

Timestamps

Computers use different ways for describing dates and times, and a very common one, especially on Unix systems, is the use of timestamps. They represent the number of seconds passed since January 1, 1970. For example, the timestamp that represents October 4, 2015 at 6:30 p.m. would be 1,443,954,637, which is the number of seconds since that date.

You can get the current timestamp with PHP using the time function.

There are other arguments related to security, but they are out of the scope of this section. Also note that you can only set cookies if there is no previous output from your application, that is, before HTML, echo calls, and any other similar functions that send some output.

To read the cookies that the client sends to us, we just need to access the array, $_COOKIE. It works as the other two arrays, so the keys of the array will be the name of the cookies and the value of the array will be their values.

A very common usage for cookies is authenticating the user. There are several different ways of doing so, depending on the level of security you need for your application. Let's try to implement one very simple—albeit insecure one (do not use it for live web applications). Leaving the HTML intact, update the PHP part of your authenticate.php file with the following content:

```php
<?php
setcookie('username', $_POST['username']);
$submitted = !empty($_POST);
?>
```

Do the same with the body tag in your index.php:

```html
<body>
    <p>You are <?php echo $_COOKIE['username']; ?></p>
    <p>Are you looking for a book? <?php echo (int) $lookingForBook; ?></p>
    <p>The book you are looking for is</p>
    <ul>
        <li><b>Title</b>: <?php echo $_GET['title']; ?></li>
        <li><b>Author</b>: <?php echo $_GET['author']; ?></li>
    </ul>
</body>
```

If you access http://localhost:8000/login.html again, try to log in, open a new tab (in the same browser), and go to the home page at http://localhost:8000, you will see how the browser still remembers your username.

Other superglobals

$_GET, $_POST, and $_COOKIE are special variables called **superglobals**. There are other superglobals too, like $_SERVER or $_ENV, which will give you extra information. The first one shows you information about headers, paths accessed, and other information related to the request. The second one contains the environment variables of the machine where your application is running. You can see the full list of these arrays and their elements at http://php.net/manual/es/language.variables.superglobals.php.

In general, using superglobals is useful, since it allows you to get information from the user, the browser, the request, and so on. This is of immeasurable value when writing web applications that need to interact with the user. But with great power comes great responsibility, and you should be very careful when using these arrays. Most of those values come from the users themselves, which could lead to security issues.

Control structures

So far, our files have been executed line by line. Due to that, we have been getting notices on some scenarios, such as when the array does not contain what we are looking for. Would it not be nice if we could choose which lines to execute? Control structures to the rescue!

A **control structure** is like a traffic diversion sign. It directs the execution flow depending on some predefined conditions. There are different control structures, but we can categorize them in **conditionals** and **loops**. A conditional allows us to choose whether to execute a statement or not. A loop executes a statement as many times as you need. Let's take a look at each one of them.

Conditionals

A conditional evaluates a Boolean expression, that is, something that returns a value. If the expression is `true`, it will execute everything inside its block of code. A block of code is a group of statements enclosed by {}. Let's see how it works:

```php
<?php
echo "Before the conditional.";
if (4 > 3) {
    echo "Inside the conditional.";
}
if (3 > 4) {
    echo "This will not be printed.";
}
echo "After the conditional.";
```

In the preceding piece of code, we use two conditionals. A conditional is defined by the keyword `if` followed by a Boolean expression in parentheses and by a block of code. If the expression is `true`, it will execute the block, otherwise it will skip it.

You can increase the power of conditionals by adding the keyword `else`. This tells PHP to execute some block of code if the previous conditions were not satisfied. Let's see an example:

```php
if (2 > 3) {
    echo "Inside the conditional.";
} else {
    echo "Inside the else.";
}
```

The preceding example will execute the code inside the `else` as the condition of the `if` was not satisfied.

Finally, you can also add an `elseif` keyword followed by another condition and a block of code to continue asking PHP for more conditions. You can add as many `elseif` as you need after an `if`. If you add an `else`, it has to be the last one of the chain of conditions. Also keep in mind that as soon as PHP finds a condition that resolves to `true`, it will stop evaluating the rest of conditions.

```php
<?php
if (4 > 5) {
    echo "Not printed";
} elseif (4 > 4) {
    echo "Not printed";
} elseif (4 == 4) {
    echo "Printed.";
} elseif (4 > 2) {
    echo "Not evaluated.";
} else {
    echo "Not evaluated.";
}
if (4 == 4) {
    echo "Printed";
}
```

In the last example, the first condition that evaluates to `true` is the highlighted one. After that, PHP does not evaluate any more conditions until a new `if` starts.

With this knowledge, let's try to clean up our application a bit, executing statements only when needed. Copy this code to your `index.php` file:

```html
<!DOCTYPE html>
<html lang="en">
<head>
    <meta charset="UTF-8">
    <title>Bookstore</title>
```

```php
</head>
<body>
    <p>
<?php
if (isset($_COOKIE[username'])) {
    echo "You are " . $_COOKIE['username'];
} else {
    echo "You are not authenticated.";
}
?>
    </p>
<?php
if (isset($_GET['title']) && isset($_GET['author'])) {
?>
    <p>The book you are looking for is</p>
    <ul>
        <li><b>Title</b>: <?php echo $_GET['title']; ?></li>
        <li><b>Author</b>: <?php echo $_GET['author']; ?></li>
    </ul>
<?php
} else {
?>
    <p>You are not looking for a book?</p>
<?php
}
?>
</body>
</html>
```

In this new code, we have mixed conditionals and HTML code in two different ways. The first one opens a PHP tag, and adds an if...else clause that will print whether we are authenticated or not with an echo. No HTML is merged within the conditionals, which makes it clear.

The second option—the second highlighted block—shows an uglier solution, but sometimes necessary. When you have to print a lot of HTML code, echo is not that handy, and it is better to close the PHP tag, print all HTML you need, and then open the tag again. You can do that even inside the code block of an if clause as you can see in the code.

Mixing PHP and HTML

If you feel that the last file we edited looks rather ugly, you are right. Mixing PHP and HTML is confusing, and you should avoid it. In *Chapter 6, Adapting to MVC,* we will see how to do things properly.

Let's edit our `authenticate.php` file too, as it is trying to access the `$_POST` entries that might not be there. The new content of the file would be as follows:

```php
<?php
$submitted = isset($_POST['username']) && isset($_POST['password']);
if ($submitted) {
    setcookie('username', $_POST['username']);
}
?>
<!DOCTYPE html>
<html lang="en">
<head>
    <meta charset="UTF-8">
    <title>Bookstore</title>
</head>
<body>
<?php if ($submitted): ?>
    <p>Your login info is</p>
    <ul>
        <li><b>username</b>: <?php echo $_POST['username']; ?></li>
        <li><b>password</b>: <?php echo $_POST['password']; ?></li>
    </ul>
<?php else: ?>
    <p>You did not submit anything.</p>
<?php endif; ?>
</body>
</html>
```

This code also contains conditionals, which we already know. We are setting a variable to know if we submitted a login or not, and set the cookies if so. But the highlighted lines show you a new way of including conditionals with HTML. This makes the code more readable when working with HTML code, avoiding the use of {}, and instead using `:` and `endif`. Both syntaxes are correct, and you should use the one that you consider more readable in each case.

Switch...case

Another control structure similar to `if...else` is `switch...case`. This structure evaluates only one expression, and executes the block depending on its value. Let's see an example:

```php
<?php
switch ($title) {
    case 'Harry Potter':
        echo "Nice story, a bit too long.";
        break;
    case 'Lord of the Rings':
        echo "A classic!";
        break;
    default:
        echo "Dunno that one.";
        break;
}
```

The `switch` clause takes an expression, in this case a variable, and then defines a series of cases. When the case matches the current value of the expression, PHP executes the code inside it. As soon as PHP finds a `break` statement, it exits the `switch...case`. In case none of the cases are suitable for the expression, PHP executes the default, if there is one, but that is optional.

You also need to know that breaks are mandatory if you want to exit the `switch...case`. If you do not specify any, PHP will keep on executing statements, even if it encounters a new case. Let's see a similar example, but without the breaks:

```php
<?php
$title = 'Twilight';
switch ($title) {
    case 'Harry Potter':
        echo "Nice story, a bit too long.";
    case 'Twilight':
        echo 'Uh...';
    case 'Lord of the Rings':
        echo "A classic!";
    default:
        echo "Dunno that one.";
}
```

If you test this code in your browser, you will see that it prints **Uh...A classic! Dunno that one**. PHP found that the second case is valid, so it executes its content. But as there are no breaks, it keeps on executing until the end. This might be the desired behavior sometimes but not usually, so be careful when using it!

Loops

Loops are control structures that allow you to execute certain statements several times, as many times as you need. You might use them in several different scenarios, but the most common one is when interacting with arrays. For example, imagine you have an array with elements, but you do not know what is in it. You want to print all its elements, so you loop through all of them.

There are four types of loops. Each of them has its own use cases, but in general, you can transform one type of loop into another. Let's look at them closely.

While

The `while` loop is the simplest of the loops. It executes a block of code until the expression to evaluate returns `false`. Let's see one example:

```php
<?php
$i = 1;
while ($i < 4) {
    echo $i . " ";
    $i++;
}
```

In the preceding example, we define a variable with value 1. Then we have a `while` clause in which the expression to evaluate is `$i < 4`. This loop executes the content of the block of code until that expression is `false`. As you can see, inside the loop we are incrementing the value of `$i` by 1 each time, so the loop ends after 4 iterations. Check the output of that script and you will see "0 1 2 3". The last value printed is 3, so at that time the value of `$i` was 3. After that, we increased its value to 4, so when the `while` clause evaluates if `$i < 4`, the result is `false`.

Whiles and infinite loops

One of the most common problems with the `while` loops is creating an infinite loop. If you do not add any code inside the `while` loop that updates any of the variables considered in the `while` expression such that it can be `false` at some point, PHP will never exit the loop!

Do...while

The do...while loop is very similar to while in the sense that it evaluates an expression each time, and will execute the block of code until that expression is false. The only difference is that when this expression is evaluated, the while clause evaluates the expression before executing the code, so sometimes, we might not even enter the loop if the expression evaluates to false the very first time. On the other hand, do...while evaluates the expression after it executes its block of code, so even if the expression is false from the very beginning, the loop will be executed at least once.

```php
<?php
echo "with while: ";
$i = 1;
while ($i < 0) {
    echo $i . " ";
    $i++;
}
echo "with do-while: ";
$i = 1;
do {
    echo $i . " ";
    $i++;
} while ($i < 0);
```

The preceding piece of code defines two loops with the same expression and block of code, but if you execute them, you will see that only the code inside the do...while is executed. In both cases, the expression is false since the beginning, so while does not even enter the loop, whereas the do...while enters the loop once.

For

The for loop is the most complex of the four loops. It defines an initialization expression, an exit condition, and the end of an iteration expression. When PHP first encounters the loop, it executes what is defined as the initialization expression. Then, it evaluates the exit condition and if it resolves to true, it enters the loop. After executing everything inside the loop, it executes the end of the iteration expression. Once done, it evaluates the end condition again, going through the loop code and the end of the iteration expression, until it evaluates to false. As always, an example will clarify it:

```php
<?php
for ($i = 1; $i < 10; $i++) {
    echo $i . " ";
}
```

The initialization expression is $i = 1$, and is executed only the first time. The exit condition is $i < 10$, and it is evaluated at the beginning of each iteration. The end of the iteration expression is $i++$, which is executed at the end of each iteration. This example prints the numbers from 1 to 9. Another more common usage of the `for` loop is with arrays:

```php
<?php
$names = ['Harry', 'Ron', 'Hermione'];
for ($i = 0; $i < count($names); $i++) {
    echo $names[$i] . " ";
}
```

In this example, we have an array of names. Since it is defined as a list, its keys will be 0, 1, and 2. The loop initializes the variable $i to 0, and it iterates until the value of $i is not less than the number of elements in the array, that is, 3. In the first iteration, $i is 0, in the second, it is 1, and in the third one it is equal to 2. When $i is 3, it will not enter the loop, as the exit condition evaluates to `false`.

On each iteration, we print the content of the position $i of the array, hence the result of this code will be all three names in the array.

Be careful with exit conditions

It is very common to set an exit condition that is not exactly what we need, especially with arrays. Remember that arrays start with 0 if they are a list, so an array of three elements will have entries of 0, 1, and 2. Defining the exit condition as $i <= count($array) will cause an error in your code, as when $i is 3, it also satisfies the exit condition and will try to access the key 3, which does not exist.

Foreach

The last, but not least, type of loop is `foreach`. This loop is exclusive for arrays, and it allows you to iterate an array entirely, even if you do not know its keys. There are two options for the syntax, as you can see in the following examples:

```php
<?php
$names = ['Harry', 'Ron', 'Hermione'];
foreach ($names as $name) {
    echo $name . " ";
}
foreach ($names as $key => $name) {
    echo $key . " -> " . $name . " ";
}
```

The `foreach` loop accepts an array—in this case `$names`—and it specifies a variable which will contain the value of the entry of the array. You can see that we do not need to specify any end condition, as PHP will know when the array has been iterated. Optionally, you can specify a variable that contains the key of each iteration, as in the second loop.

The `foreach` loops are also useful with maps, where the keys are not necessarily numeric. The order in which PHP iterates the array will be the same order that you used to insert the contents in the array.

Let's use some loops in our application. We want to show the available books in our home page. We have the list of books in an array, so we will have to iterate all of them with a `foreach` loop, printing some information from each one. Append the following code to the `body` tag in `index.php`:

```php
<?php endif;
    $books = [
        [
            'title' => 'To Kill A Mockingbird',
            'author' => 'Harper Lee',
            'available' => true,
            'pages' => 336,
            'isbn' => 9780061120084
        ],
        [
            'title' => '1984',
            'author' => 'George Orwell',
            'available' => true,
            'pages' => 267,
            'isbn' => 9780547249643
        ],
        [
            'title' => 'One Hundred Years Of Solitude',
            'author' => 'Gabriel Garcia Marquez',
            'available' => false,
            'pages' => 457,
            'isbn' => 9785267006323
        ],
    ];
?>
<ul>
<?php foreach ($books as $book): ?>
        <li>
            <i><?php echo $book['title']; ?></i>
            - <?php echo $book['author']; ?>
```

```php
<?php if (!$book['available']): ?>
        <b>Not available</b>
<?php endif; ?>
        </li>
<?php endforeach; ?>
    </ul>
```

The highlighted code shows a `foreach` loop using the : notation as well, which is better when mixing it with HTML. It iterates all of the `$books` array, and for each book, it prints some information as an HTML list. Notice also that we have a conditional inside a loop, which is perfectly fine. Of course, this conditional will be executed for each entry in the array, so you should keep the block of code of your loops as simple as possible.

Functions

A function is a reusable block of code that, given an input, performs some actions and, optionally, returns some result. You already know several predefined functions like `empty`, `in_array`, or `var_dump`. Those functions come with PHP so you do not have to reinvent the wheel, but you can create your own very easily. You can define functions when you identify portions of your application that have to be executed several times, or just to encapsulate some functionality.

Function declaration

Declaring a function means writing it down so it can be used later. A function has a name, takes some arguments, and has a block of code. Optionally, it can define what kind of value is to be returned. The name of the function has to follow the same rules as variable names, that is, it has to start with a letter or an underscore, and can contain any letters, numbers, or underscore. It cannot be a reserved word.

Let's see a simple example:

```php
function addNumbers($a, $b) {
    $sum = $a + $b;
    return $sum;
}
$result = addNumbers(2, 3);
```

The preceding function's name is `addNumbers`, and it takes two arguments: `$a` and `$b`. The block of code defines a new variable `$sum`, which is the sum of both arguments, and then returns its content with `return`. In order to use this function, you just need to call it by its name while sending all the required arguments, as shown in the highlighted line.

PHP does not support **overloaded functions**. Overloading refers to the ability of declaring two or more functions with the same name but different arguments. As you can see, you can declare the arguments without knowing what their types are, so PHP would not be able to decide which function to use.

Another important thing to note is the **variable scope**. We are declaring a variable $sum inside the block of code, so once the function ends, the variable will not be accessible any more. That means that the scope of variables declared inside the function is just the function itself. Furthermore, if you had a variable $sum declared outside the function, it would not be affected at all since the function cannot access that variable unless we send it as an argument.

Function arguments

A function gets information from outside via arguments. You can define any number of arguments—including 0 (none). These arguments need at least a name so they can be used inside the function; there cannot be two arguments with the same name. When invoking the function, you need to send the arguments in the same order as declared.

A function may contain **optional arguments**, that is, you are not forced to provide a value for those arguments. When declaring the function, you need to provide a default value for those arguments. So, in case the user does not provide a value, the function will use the default one.

```
function addNumbers($a, $b, $printResult = false) {
    $sum = $a + $b;
    if ($printResult) {
        echo 'The result is ' . $sum;
    }
    return $sum;
}

$sum1 = addNumbers(1, 2);
$sum1 = addNumbers(3, 4, false);
$sum1 = addNumbers(5, 6, true); // it will print the result
```

This new function in the last example takes two mandatory arguments and an optional one. The default value of the optional argument is false, and it is then used normally inside the function. The function will print the result of the sum if the user provides true as the third argument, which happens only the third time that the function is invoked. For the first two, $printResult is set to false.

The arguments that the function receives are just copies of the values that the user provided. That means that if you modify these arguments inside the function, it will not affect the original values. This feature is known as sending arguments by value. Let's see an example:

```
function modify($a) {
    $a = 3;
}

$a = 2;
modify($a);
var_dump($a); // prints 2
```

We are declaring a variable $a with value 2, and then calling the modify method sending that $a. The modify method modifies the argument $a, setting its value to 3, but this does not affect the original value of $a, which remains 2 as you can see from var_dump.

If what you want is to actually change the value of the original variable used in the invocation, you need to pass the argument by reference. To do that, you add an ampersand (&) before the argument when declaring the function:

```
function modify(&$a) {
    $a = 3;
}
```

Now, on invoking the function modify, $a will always be 3.

Arguments by value versus by reference

PHP allows you to do it, and in fact, some native functions of PHP use arguments by reference. Remember the array sorting functions? They did not return the sorted array, but sorted the array provided instead. But using arguments by reference is a way of confusing developers. Usually, when someone uses a function, they expect a result, and they do not want the arguments provided by them to be modified. So try to avoid it; people will be grateful!

The return statement

You can have as many `return` statements as you want inside your function, but PHP will exit the function as soon as it finds one. That means that if you have two consecutive `return` statements, the second one will never be executed. Still, having multiple `return` statements can be useful if they are inside conditionals. Add this function inside your `functions.php` file:

```php
function loginMessage() {
    if (isset($_COOKIE['username'])) {
        return "You are " . $_COOKIE['username'];
    } else {
        return "You are not authenticated.";
    }
}
```

And let's use the last example in your `index.php` file by replacing the highlighted content (note that to save some trees, I replaced most of the code that was not changed at all with //...):

```php
//...
<body>
    <p><?php echo loginMessage(); ?></p>
<?php if (isset($_GET['title']) && isset($_GET['author'])): ?>
//...
```

Additionally, you can omit the `return` statement if you do not want the function to return anything. In this case, the function will end once it reaches the end of the block of code.

Type hinting and return types

With the release of PHP 7, the language allows the developer to be more specific about what functions are getting and returning. You can—always optionally—specify the type of argument that the function needs (**type hinting**), and the type of result the function will return (**return type**). Let's first see an example:

```php
<?php

declare(strict_types=1);

function addNumbers(int $a, int $b, bool $printSum): int {
    $sum = $a + $b;
    if ($printSum) {
        echo 'The sum is ' . $sum;
```

```
    }
    return $sum;
}

addNumbers(1, 2, true);
addNumbers(1, '2', true); // it fails when strict_types is 1
addNumbers(1, 'something', true); // it always fails
```

This preceding function states that the arguments need to be integer, integer, and Boolean, and that the result will be an integer. Now, you know that PHP has type juggling, so it can usually transform a value of one type to its equivalent value of another type, for example, the string "2" can be used as integer 2. To stop PHP from using type juggling with the arguments and results of functions, you can declare the directive `strict_types` as shown in the first highlighted line. This directive has to be declared at the top of each file where you want to enforce this behavior.

The three invocations work as follows:

- The first invocation sends two integers and a Boolean, which is what the function expects, so regardless of the value of `strict_types`, it will always work.

- The second invocation sends an integer, a string, and a Boolean. The string has a valid integer value, so if PHP was allowed to use type juggling, the invocation would resolve just normally. But in this example, it will fail because of the declaration at the top of the file.

- The third invocation will always fail as the string "something" cannot be transformed into a valid integer.

Let's try to use a function within our project. In our `index.php`, we have a `foreach` loop that iterates the books and prints them. The code inside the loop is kind of hard to understand as it is a mix of HTML with PHP, and there is a conditional too. Let's try to abstract the logic inside the loop into a function. First, create the new `functions.php` file with the following content:

```php
<?php
function printableTitle(array $book): string {
    $result = '<i>' . $book['title'] . '</i> - ' . $book['author'];
    if (!$book['available']) {
        $result .= ' <b>Not available</b>';
    }
    return $result;
}
```

This file will contain our functions. The first one, `printableTitle`, takes an array representing a book, and builds a string with a nice representation of the book in HTML. The code is the same as before, just encapsulated in a function.

Now `index.php` will have to include the `functions.php` file, and then use the function inside the loop. Let's see how:

```php
<?php require_once 'functions.php' ?>
<!DOCTYPE html>
<html lang="en">

//...

?>
    <ul>
<?php foreach ($books as $book): ?>
    <li><?php echo printableTitle($book); ?> </li>
<?php endforeach; ?>
    </ul>

//...
```

Well, now our loop looks way cleaner, right? Also, if we need to print the title of the book somewhere else, we can reuse the function instead of duplicating code!

The filesystem

As you might have already noticed, PHP comes with a lot of native functions that help you to manage arrays and strings in an easier way as compared to other languages. The filesystem is another of those areas where PHP tried to make it as easy as possible. The list of functions extends to over 80 different ones, so we will cover here just the ones that you are more likely to use.

Reading files

In our code, we define a list of books. So far, we have only three books, but you can guess that if we want to make this application useful, the list will grow way more. Storing the information inside your code is not practical at all, so we have to start thinking about externalizing it.

If we think in terms of separating the code from the data, there is no need to keep using PHP arrays to define the books. Using a less language-restrictive system will allow people who do not know PHP to edit the content of the file. There are many solutions for this, like CSV or XML files, but nowadays, one of the most used systems to represent data in web applications is JSON. PHP allows you to convert arrays to JSON and vice versa using just a couple of functions: `json_encode` and `json_decode`. Easy, right?

Save the following into `books.json`:

```json
[
    {
        "title": "To Kill A Mockingbird",
        "author": "Harper Lee",
        "available": true,
        "pages": 336,
        "isbn": 9780061120084
    },
    {
        "title": "1984",
        "author": "George Orwell",
        "available": true,
        "pages": 267,
        "isbn": 9780547249643
    },
    {
        "title": "One Hundred Years Of Solitude",
        "author": "Gabriel Garcia Marquez",
        "available": false,
        "pages": 457,
        "isbn": 9785267006323
    }
]
```

The preceding code snippet is a JSON representation of our array in PHP. Now, let's read this information with the function `file_get_contents`, and transform it to a PHP array with `json_decode`. Replace the array with these two lines:

```php
$booksJson = file_get_contents('books.json');
$books = json_decode($booksJson, true);
```

With just one function, we are able to store all the content from the JSON file in a variable as a string. With the function, we transform this JSON string into an array. The second argument in `json_decode` tells PHP to transform it to an array, otherwise it would use objects, which we have not covered as yet.

When referencing files within PHP functions, you need to know whether to use absolute or relative paths. When using relative paths, PHP will try to find the file inside the same directory where the PHP script is. If not found, PHP will try to find it in other directories defined in the `include_path` directive, but that is something you would like to avoid. Instead, you could use absolute paths, which is a way to make sure the reference will not be misunderstood. Let's see two examples:

```php
$booksJson = file_get_contents('/home/user/bookstore/books.json');
$booksJson = file_get_contents(__DIR__, '/books.json');
```

The constant `__DIR__` contains the directory name of the current PHP file, and if we prefix it to the name of our file, we will have an absolute path. In fact, even though you might think that writing down the whole path by yourself is better, using `__DIR__` allows you to move your application anywhere else without needing to change anything in the code, as its content will always match the directory of the script, whereas the hardcoded path from the first example will not be valid anymore.

Writing files

Let's add some functionality to our application. Imagine that we want to allow the user to take the book that he or she is looking for, but only if it is available. If you remember, we identify the book by the query string. That is not very practical, so let's help the user by adding links to the list of books, so when you click on a link, the query string will contain that book's information.

```php
<?php require_once 'functions.php' ?>
<!DOCTYPE html>
<html lang="en">
<head>
    <meta charset="UTF-8">
    <title>Bookstore</title>
</head>
<body>
    <p><?php echo loginMessage(); ?></p>
<?php
$booksJson = file_get_contents('books.json');
$books = json_decode($booksJson, true);
if (isset($_GET['title'])) {
    echo '<p>Looking for <b>' . $_GET['title'] . '</b></p>';
} else {
    echo '<p>You are not looking for a book?</p>';
}
?>
    <ul>
```

```php
<?php foreach ($books as $book): ?>
    <li>
        <a href="?title=<?php echo $book['title']; ?>">
            <?php echo printableTitle($book); ?>
        </a>
    </li>
<?php endforeach; ?>
    </ul>
</body>
</html>
```

If you try the preceding code in your browser, you will see that the list contains links, and by clicking on them, the page refreshes with the new title as part of the query string. Let's now check if the book is available or not, and if it is, let's update its available field to `false`. Add the following function in your `functions.php`:

```php
function bookingBook(array &$books, string $title): bool {
    foreach ($books as $key => $book) {
        if ($book['title'] == $title) {
            if ($book['available']) {
                $books[$key]['available'] = false;
                return true;
            } else {
                return false;
            }
        }
    }
    return false;
}
```

We have to pay attention as the code starts getting complex. This function takes an array of books and a title, and returns a Boolean, being `true` if it could book it or `false` if not. Moreover, the array of books is passed by reference, which means that all changes to that array will affect the original array too. Even though we discouraged this previously, in this case, it is a reasonable approach.

We iterate the whole array of books, asking each time if the title of the current book matches the one we are looking for. Only if that is `true`, we will check if the book is available or not. If it is, we will update the availability to `false` and return `true`, meaning that we booked the book. If the book is not available, we will just return `false`.

Finally, note that `foreach` defines `$key` and `$book`. We do so because the `$book` variable is a copy of the `$books` array, and if we edit it, the original one will not be affected. Instead, we ask for the key of that book too, so when editing the array, we use `$books[$key]` instead of `$book`.

We can use this function from the `index.php` file:

```
//...
    echo '<p>Looking for <b>' . $_GET['title'] . '</b></p>';
    if (bookingBook($books, $_GET['title'])) {
        echo 'Booked!';
    } else {
        echo 'The book is not available...';
    }
} else {
//...
```

Try it out in your browser. By clicking on an available book, you will get the **Booked!** message. We are almost done! We are just missing the last part: persist this information back to the filesystem. In order to do that, we have to construct the new JSON content and then to write it back to the `books.json` file. Of course, let's do that only if the book was available.

```
function updateBooks(array $books) {
    $booksJson = json_encode($books);
    file_put_contents(__DIR__ . '/books.json', $booksJson);
}
```

The `json_encode` function does the opposite of `json_decode`: it takes an array—or any other variable—and transforms it to JSON. The `file_put_contents` function is used to write to the file referenced as the first argument, the content sent as the second argument. Would you know how to use this function?

```
//...
if (bookingBook($books, $_GET['title'])) {
    echo 'Booked!';
    updateBooks($books);
} else {
    echo 'The book is not available...';
}
//...
```

Files versus databases

Storing information in JSON files is better than having it in your code, but it is still not the best option. In *Chapter 5, Using Databases,* you will learn how to store data of the application in a database, which is a way better solution.

Other filesystem functions

If you want to make your application more robust, you could check that the `books.json` file exists, that you have read and write permission, and/or that the previous content was a valid JSON. You can use some PHP functions for that:

- `file_exists`: This function takes the path of the file, and returns a Boolean: `true` when the file exists and `false` otherwise.

- `is_writable`: This function works the same as `file_exists`, but checks whether the file is writable or not.

You can find the full list of functions at `http://uk1.php.net/manual/en/book.filesystem.php`. You can find functions to move, copy, or remove files, create directories, give permissions and ownership, and so on.

Summary

In this chapter, we went through all the basics of procedural PHP while writing simple examples in order to practice them. You now know how to use variables and arrays with control structures and functions, how to get information from HTTP requests, and how to interact with the filesystem among other things.

In the next chapter, we will study the other and most used paradigm: OOP. That is one step closer to writing clean and well-structured applications.

4
Creating Clean Code with OOP

When applications start growing, representing more complex data structures becomes necessary. Primitive types like integers, strings, or arrays are not enough when you want to associate specific behavior to data. More than half a century ago, computer scientists started using the concept of objects to refer to the encapsulation of properties and functionality that represented an object in real life.

Nowadays, OOP is one of the most used programming paradigms, and you will be glad to know that PHP supports it. Knowing OOP is not just a matter of knowing the syntax of the language, but knowing when and how to use it. But do not worry, after this chapter and a bit of practice, you will become a confident OOP developer.

In this chapter, you will learn about the following:

- Classes and objects
- Visibility, static properties, and methods
- Namespaces
- Autoloading classes
- Inheritance, interfaces, and traits
- Handling exceptions
- Design patterns
- Anonymous functions

Classes and objects

Objects are representations of real-life elements. Each object has a set of attributes that differentiates it from the rest of the objects of the same class, and is capable of a set of actions. A **class** is the definition of what an object looks like and what it can do, like a pattern for objects.

Let's take our bookstore example, and think of the kind of real-life objects it contains. We store books, and let people take them if they are available. We could think of two types of objects: books and customers. We can define these two classes as follows:

```php
<?php

class Book {
}

class Customer {
}
```

A class is defined by the keyword `class` followed by a valid class name—that follows the same rules as any other PHP label, like variable names—and a block of code. But if we want to have a specific book, that is, an object `Book`—or instance of the class `Book`—we have to instantiate it. To instantiate an object, we use the keyword `new` followed by the name of the class. We assign the instance to a variable, as if it was a primitive type:

```php
$book = new Book();
$customer = new Customer();
```

You can create as many instances as you need, as long as you assign them to different variables:

```php
$book1 = new Book();
$book2 = new Book();
```

Class properties

Let's think about the properties of books first: they have a title, an author, and an ISBN. They can also be available or unavailable. Write the following code inside `Book.php`:

```php
<?php

class Book {
    public $isbn;
    public $title;
```

```
    public $author;
    public $available;
}
```

This preceding snippet defines a class that represents the properties that a book has. Do not bother about the word `public`; we will explain what it means when talking about visibility in the next section. For now, just think of properties as variables inside the class. We can use these variables in objects. Try adding this code at the end of the `Book.php` file:

```
$book = new Book();
$book->title = "1984";
$book->author = "George Orwell";
$book->available = true;
var_dump($book);
```

Printing the object shows the value of each of its properties, in a way similar to the way arrays do with their keys. You can see that properties have a type at the moment of printing, but we did not define this type explicitly; instead, the variable took the type of the value assigned. This works exactly the same way that normal variables do.

When creating multiple instances of an object and assigning values to their properties, each object will have their own values, so you will not override them. The next bit of code shows you how this works:

```
$book1 = new Book();
$book1->title = "1984";
$book2 = new Book();
$book2->title = "To Kill a Mockingbird";
var_dump($book1, $book2);
```

Class methods

Methods are functions defined inside a class. Like functions, methods get some arguments and perform some actions, optionally returning a value. The advantage of methods is that they can use the properties of the object that invoked them. Thus, calling the same method in two different objects might have two different results.

Even though it is usually a bad idea to mix HTML with PHP, for the sake of learning, let's add a method in our class `Book` that returns the book as in our already existing function `printableTitle`:

```
<?php

class Book {
    public $isbn;
```

```php
    public $title;
    public $author;
    public $available;

    public function getPrintableTitle(): string {
        $result = '<i>' . $this->title
            . '</i> - ' . $this->author;
        if (!$this->available) {
            $result .= ' <b>Not available</b>';
        }
        return $result;
    }
}
```

As with properties, we add the keyword `public` at the beginning of the function, but other than that, the rest looks just as a normal function. The other special bit is the use of `$this`: it represents the object itself, and allows you to access the properties and methods of that same object. Note how we refer to the title, author, and available properties.

You can also update the values of the current object from one of its functions. Let's use the available property as an integer that shows the number of units available instead of just a Boolean. With that, we can allow multiple customers to borrow different copies of the same book. Let's add a method to give one copy of a book to a customer, updating the number of units available:

```php
public function getCopy(): bool {
    if ($this->available < 1) {
        return false;
    } else {
        $this->available--;
        return true;
    }
}
```

In this preceding method, we first check if we have at least one available unit. If we do not, we return `false` to let them know that the operation was not successful. If we do have a unit for the customer, we decrease the number of available units, and then return `true`, letting them know that the operation was successful. Let's see how you can use this class:

```php
<?php
$book = new Book();
$book->title = "1984";
$book->author = "George Orwell";
```

```
$book->isbn = 9785267006323;
$book->available = 12;

if ($book->getCopy()) {
    echo 'Here, your copy.';
} else {
    echo 'I am afraid that book is not available.';
}
```

What would this last piece of code print? Exactly, **Here, your copy.** But what would be the value of the property available? It would be 11, which is the result of the invocation of getCopy.

Class constructors

You might have noticed that it looks like a pain to instantiate the Book class, and set all its values each time. What if our class has 30 properties instead of four? Well, hopefully, you will never do that, as it is very bad practice. Still, there is a way to mitigate that pain: **constructors**.

Constructors are functions that are invoked when someone creates a new instance of the class. They look like normal methods, with the exception that their name is always __construct, and that they do not have a return statement, as they always have to return the new instance. Let's see an example:

```
public function __construct(int $isbn, string $title, string $author,
int $available) {
    $this->isbn = $isbn;
    $this->title = $title;
    $this->author = $author;
    $this->available = $available;
}
```

The constructor takes four arguments, and then assigns the value of one of the arguments to each of the properties of the instance. To instantiate the Book class, we use the following:

```
$book = new Book("1984", "George Orwell", 9785267006323, 12);
```

This object is exactly the same as the object when we set the value to each of its properties manually. But this one looks cleaner, right? This does not mean you cannot set new values to this object manually, it just helps you in constructing new objects.

As a constructor is still a function, it can use default arguments. Imagine that the number of units will usually be 0 when creating the object, and later, the librarian will add units when available. We could set a default value to the `$available` argument of the constructor, so if we do not send the number of units when creating the object, the object will be instantiated with its default value:

```
public function __construct(
    int $isbn,
    string $title,
    string $author,
    int $available = 0
) {
    $this->isbn = $isbn;
    $this->title = $title;
    $this->author = $author;
    $this->available = $available;
}
```

We could use the preceding constructor in two different ways:

```
$book1 = new Book("1984", "George Orwell", 9785267006323, 12);
$book2 = new Book("1984", "George Orwell", 9785267006323);
```

`$book1` will set the number of units available to `12`, whereas `$book2` will set it to the default value of 0. But do not trust me; try it by yourself!

Magic methods

There is a special group of methods that have a different behavior than the normal ones. Those methods are called **magic methods**, and they usually are triggered by the interaction of the class or object, and not by invocations. You have already seen one of them, the constructor of the class, `__construct`. This method is not invoked directly, but rather used when creating a new instance with `new`. You can easily identify magic methods, because they start with `__`. The following are some of the most used magic methods:

- `__toString`: This method is invoked when we try to cast an object to a string. It takes no parameters, and it is expected to return a string.

- `__call`: This is the method that PHP calls when you try to invoke a method on a class that does not exist. It gets the name of the method as a string and the list of parameters used in the invocation as an array, through the argument.

- `__get`: This is a version of `__call` for properties. It gets the name of the property that the user was trying to access through parameters, and it can return anything.

You could use the __toString method to replace the current getPrintableTitle method in our Book class. To do that, just change the name of the method as follows:

```php
public function __toString() {
    $result = '<i>' . $this->title . '</i> - ' . $this->author;
    if (!$this->available) {
        $result .= ' <b>Not available</b>';
    }
    return $result;
}
```

To try the preceding code, you can just add the following snippet that creates an object book and then casts it to a string, invoking the __toString method:

```php
$book = new Book(1234, 'title', 'author');
$string = (string) $book; // title - author Not available
```

As the name suggests, those are magic methods, so most of the time their features will look like magic. For obvious reasons, we personally encourage developers to use constructors and maybe __toString, but be careful about when to use the rest, as you might make your code quite unpredictable for people not familiar with it.

Properties and methods visibility

So far, all the properties and methods defined in our Book class were tagged as public. That means that they are accessible to anyone, or more precisely, from anywhere. This is called the **visibility** of the property or method, and there are three types of visibility. In the order of being more restrictive to less, they are as follows:

- private: This type allows access only to members of the same class. If A and B are instances of the class C, A can access the properties and methods of B.

- protected: This type allows access to members of the same class and instances from classes that inherit from that one only. You will see inheritance in the next section.

- public: This type refers to a property or method that is accessible from anywhere. Any classes or code in general from outside the class can access it.

In order to show some examples, let's first create a second class in our application. Save this into a Customer.php file:

```php
<?php

class Customer {
    private $id;
```

```
        private $firstname;
        private $surname;
        private $email;

        public function __construct(
            int $id,
            string $firstname,
            string $surname,
            string $email
        ) {
            $this->id = $id;
            $this->firstname = $firstname;
            $this->surname = $surname;
            $this->email = $email;
        }
    }
```

This class represents a customer, and its properties consist of the general information that the bookstores usually know about their customers. But for security reasons, we cannot let everybody know about the personal data of our customers, so we set every property as `private`.

So far, we have been adding the code to create objects in the same `Book.php` file, but since now we have two classes, it seems natural to leave the classes in their respective files, and create and play with objects in a separate file. Let's name this third file `init.php`. In order to instantiate objects of a given class, PHP needs to know where the class is. For that, just include the file with `require_once`.

```php
<?php

require_once __DIR__ . '/Book.php';
require_once __DIR__ . '/Customer.php';

$book1 = new Book("1984", "George Orwell", 9785267006323, 12);
$book2 = new Book("To Kill a Mockingbird", "Harper Lee",
9780061120084, 2);

$customer1 = new Customer(1, 'John', 'Doe', 'johndoe@mail.com');
$customer2 = new Customer(2, 'Mary', 'Poppins', 'mp@mail.com');
```

You do not need to include the files every single time. Once you include them, PHP will know where to find the classes, even though your code is in a different file.

Conventions for classes

When working with classes, you should know that there are some conventions that everyone tries to follow in order to ensure clean code which is easy to maintain. The most important ones are as follows:

- Each class should be in a file named the same as the class along with the .php extension
- Class names should be in CamelCase, that is, each word should start with an uppercase letter, followed by the rest of the word in lowercase
- A file should contain only the code of one class
- Inside a class, you should first place the properties, then the constructor, and finally, the rest of the methods

To show how visibility works, let's try the following code:

```
$book1->available = 2; // OK
$customer1->id = 3; // Error!
```

We already know that the properties of the Book class' objects are public, and therefore, editable from outside. But when trying to change a value from Customer, PHP complains, as its properties are private.

Encapsulation

When working with objects, one of the most important concepts you have to know and apply is **encapsulation**. Encapsulation tries to group the data of the object with its methods in an attempt to hide the internal structure of the object from the rest of the world. In simple words, you could say that you use encapsulation if the properties of an object are private, and the only way to update them is through public methods.

The reason for using encapsulation is to make it easier for a developer to make changes to the internal structure of the class without directly affecting the external code that uses that class. For example, imagine that our Customer class, that now has two properties to define its name—firstname and surname—has to change. From now on, we only have one property name that contains both. If we were accessing its properties straightaway, we should change all of those accesses!

Instead, if we set the properties as private and enable two public methods, getFirstname and getSurname, even if we have to change the internal structure of the class, we could just change the implementation of those two methods—which is at one place only—and the rest of the code that uses our class will not be affected at all. This concept is also known as **information hiding**.

The easiest way to implement this idea is by setting all the properties of the class as private and enabling two methods for each of the properties: one will get the current value (also known as **getter**), and the other will allow you to set a new value (known as **setter**). That's at least the most common and easy way to encapsulate data.

But let's go one step further: when defining a class, think of the data that you want the user to be able to change and to retrieve, and only add setters and getters for them. For example, customers might change their e-mail address, but their name, surname, and ID remains the same once we create them. The new definition of the class would look like the following:

```php
<?php

class Customer {
    private $id;
    private $name;
    private $surname;
    private $email;

    public function __construct(
        int $id,
        string $firstname,
        string $surname,
        string $email
    ) {
        $this->id = $id;
        $this->firstname = $firstname;
        $this->surname = $surname;
        $this->email = $email;
    }

    public function getId(): id {
        return $this->id;
    }
    public function getFirstname(): string {
        return $this->firstname;
    }
    public function getSurname(): string {
        return $this->surname;
    }
    public function getEmail(): string {
        return $this->email;
    }
    public function setEmail(string $email) {
```

```php
        $this->email = $email;
    }
}
```

On the other hand, our books also remain almost the same. The only change possible is the number of available units. But we usually take or add one book at a time instead of setting the specific number of units available, so a setter here is not really useful. We already have the getCopy method that takes one copy when possible; let's add an addCopy method, plus the rest of the getters:

```php
<?php

class Book {
    private $isbn;
    private $title;
    private $author;
    private $available;

    public function __construct(
        int $isbn,
        string $title,
        string $author,
        int $available = 0
    ) {
        $this->isbn = $isbn;
        $this->title = $title;
        $this->author = $author;
        $this->available = $available;
    }
    public function getIsbn(): int {
        return $this->isbn;
    }
    public function getTitle(): string {
        return $this->title;
    }
    public function getAuthor(): string {
        return $this->author;
    }
    public function isAvailable(): bool {
        return $this->available;
    }

    public function getPrintableTitle(): string {
        $result = '<i>' . $this->title . '</i> - ' . $this->author;
        if (!$this->available) {
```

```
                        $result .= ' <b>Not available</b>';
            }
            return $result;
        }

        public function getCopy(): bool {
            if ($this->available < 1) {
                return false;
            } else {
                $this->available--;
                return true;
            }
        }

        public function addCopy() {
            $this->available++;
        }
    }
```

When the number of classes in your application, and with it, the number of relationships between classes increases, it is helpful to represent these classes in a diagram. Let's call this diagram a UML diagram of classes, or just an hierarchic tree. The hierarchic tree for our two classes would look as follows:

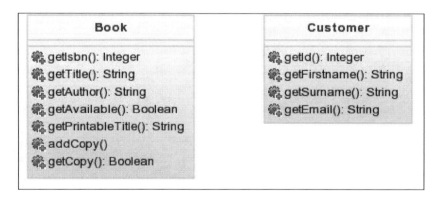

We only show public methods, as the protected or private ones cannot be called from outside the class, and thus, they are not useful for a developer who just wants to use these classes externally.

Static properties and methods

So far, all the properties and methods were linked to a specific instance; so two different instances could have two different values for the same property. PHP allows you to have properties and methods linked to the class itself rather than to the object. These properties and methods are defined with the keyword `static`.

```
private static $lastId = 0;
```

Add the preceding property to the `Customer` class. This property shows the last ID assigned to a user, and is useful in order to know the ID that should be assigned to a new user. Let's change the constructor of our class as follows:

```
public function __construct(
    int $id,
    string $name,
    string $surname,
    string $email
) {
    if ($id == null) {
        $this->id = ++self::$lastId;
    } else {
        $this->id = $id;
        if ($id > self::$lastId) {
            self::$lastId = $id;
        }
    }
    $this->name = $name;
    $this->surname = $surname;
    $this->email = $email;
}
```

Note that when referring to a static property, we do not use the variable `$this`. Instead, we use `self::`, which is not tied to any instance but to the class itself. In this last constructor, we have two options. We are either provided with an ID value that is not null, or we send a null in its place. When the received ID is null, we use the static property `$lastId` to know the last ID used, increase it by one, and assign it to the property `$id`. If the last ID we inserted was 5, this will update the static property to 6, and then assign it to the instance property. Next time we create a new customer, the `$lastId` static property will be 6. Instead, if we get a valid ID as part of the arguments, we assign it, and check if the assigned `$id` is greater than the static `$lastId`. If it is, we update it. Let's see how we would use this:

```
$customer1 = new Customer(3, 'John', 'Doe', 'johndoe@mail.com');
$customer2 = new Customer(null, 'Mary', 'Poppins', 'mp@mail.com');
$customer3 = new Customer(7, 'James', 'Bond', '007@mail.com');
```

In the preceding example, $customer1 specifies that his ID is 3, probably because he is an existing customer and wants to keep the same ID. That sets both his ID and the last static ID to 3. When creating the second customer, we do not specify the ID, so the constructor will take the last ID, increase it by 1, and assign it to the customer. So $customer2 will have the ID 4, and the latest ID will be 4 too. Finally, our secret agent knows what he wants, so he forces the system to have the ID as 7. The latest ID will be updated to 7 too.

Another benefit of static properties and methods is that we do not need an object to use them. You can refer to a static property or method by specifying the name of the class, followed by : :, and the name of the property/method. That is, of course, if the visibility rules allow you to do that, which, in this case, it does not, as the property is private. Let's add a public static method to retrieve the last ID:

```
public static function getLastId(): int {
    return self::$lastId;
}
```

You can reference it either using the class name or an existing instance, from anywhere in the code:

```
Customer::getLastId();
$customer1::getLastId();
```

Namespaces

You know that you cannot have two classes with the same name, since PHP would not know which one is being referred to when creating a new object. To solve this issue, PHP allows the use of **namespaces**, which act as paths in a filesystem. In this way, you can have as many classes with the same name as you need, as long as they are all defined in different namespaces. It is worth noting that, even though namespaces and the file path will usually be the same, this is enforced by the developer rather than by the language; you could actually use any namespace that has nothing to do with the filesystem.

Specifying a namespace has to be the first thing that you do in a file. In order to do that, use the namespace keyword followed by the namespace. Each section of the namespace is separated by \, as if it was a different directory. If you do not specify the namespace, the class will belong to the base namespace, or root. At the beginning of both files—Book.php and Customer.php—add the following:

```
<?php

namespace Bookstore\Domain;
```

The preceding line of code sets the namespace of our classes as `Bookstore\Domain`. The full name of our classes then is `Bookstore\Domain\Book` and `Bookstore\Domain\Customer`. If you try to access the `init.php` file from your browser, you will see an error saying that either the class `Book` or the class `Customer` were not found. But we included the files, right? That happens because PHP thinks that you are trying to access `\Book` and `\Customer` from the root. Do not worry, there are several ways to amend this.

One way would be to specify the full name of the classes when referencing them, that is, using `$customer = new Bookstore\Domain\Book();` instead of `$book = new Book();`. But that does not sound practical, does it?

Another way would be to say that the `init.php` file belongs to the `BookStore\Domain` namespace. That means that all the references to classes inside `init.php` will have the `BookStore\Domain` prefixed to them, and you will be able to use `Book` and `Customer`. The downside of this solution is that you cannot easily reference other classes from other namespaces, as any reference to a class will be prefixed with that namespace.

The best solution is to use the keyword `use`. This keyword allows you to specify a full class name at the beginning of the file, and then use the simple name of the class in the rest of that file. Let's see an example:

```php
<?php

use Bookstore\Domain\Book;
use Bookstore\Domain\Customer;

require_once __DIR__ . '/Book.php';
require_once __DIR__ . '/Customer.php';
//...
```

In the preceding file, each time that we reference `Book` or `Customer`, PHP will know that we actually want to use the full class name, that is, with `Bookstore\Domain\` prefixed to it. This solution allows you to have a clean code when referencing those classes, and at the same time, to be able to reference classes from other namespaces if needed.

But what if you want to include two different classes with the same name in the same file? If you set two `use` statements, PHP will not know which one to choose, so we still have the same problem as before! To fix that, either you use the full class name—with namespace—each time you want to reference any of the classes, or you use aliases.

Imagine that we have two `Book` classes, the first one in the namespace `Bookstore\Domain` and the second one in `Library\Domain`. To solve the conflict, you could do as follows:

```
use Bookstore\Domain\Book;
use Library\Domain\Book as LibraryBook;
```

The keyword `as` sets an alias to that class. In that file, whenever you reference the class `LibraryBook`, you will actually be referencing the class `Library\Domain\Book`. And when referencing `Book`, PHP will just use the one from `Bookstore`. Problem solved!

Autoloading classes

As you already know, in order to use a class, you need to include the file that defines it. So far, we have been including the files manually, as we only had a couple of classes and used them in one file. But what happens when we use several classes in several files? There must be a smarter way, right? Indeed there is. **Autoloading** to the rescue!

Autoloading is a PHP feature that allows your program to search and load files automatically given some set of predefined rules. Each time you reference a class that PHP does not know about, it will ask the **autoloader**. If the autoloader can figure out which file that class is in, it will load it, and the execution of the program will continue as normal. If it does not, PHP will stop the execution.

So, what is the autoloader? It is no more than a PHP function that gets a class name as a parameter, and it is expected to load a file. There are two ways of implementing an autoloader: either by using the `__autoload` function or the `spl_autoload_register` one.

Using the __autoload function

Defining a function named `__autoload` tells PHP that the function is the autoloader that it must use. You could implement an easy solution:

```php
function __autoload($classname) {
    $lastSlash = strpos($classname, '\\') + 1;
    $classname = substr($classname, $lastSlash);
    $directory = str_replace('\\', '/', $classname);
    $filename = __DIR__ . '/' . $directory . '.php';
    require_once($filename);
}
```

Our intention is to keep all PHP files in src, that is, the source. Inside this directory, the directory tree will emulate the namespace tree of the classes excluding the first section BookStore, which is useful as a namespace but not necessary as a directory. That means that our Book class, with full class name BookStore\Domain\Book, will be in src/Domain/Book.php.

In order to achieve that, our __autoload function tries to find the first occurrence of the backslash \ with strpos, and then extracts from that position until the end with substr. This, in practice, just removes the first section of the namespace, BookStore. After that, we replace all \ by / so that the filesystem can understand the path. Finally, we concatenate the current directory, the class name as a directory, and the .php extension.

Before trying that, remember to create the src/Domain directory and move the two classes inside it. Also, to make sure that we are testing the autoloader, save the following as your init.php, and go to http://localhost:8000/init.php:

```php
<?php

use Bookstore\Domain\Book;
use Bookstore\Domain\Customer;

function __autoload($classname) {
    $lastSlash = strpos($classname, '\\') + 1;
    $classname = substr($classname, $lastSlash);
    $directory = str_replace('\\', '/', $classname);
    $filename = __DIR__ . '/src/' . $directory . '.php'
    require_once($filename);
}

$book1 = new Book("1984", "George Orwell", 9785267006323, 12);
$customer1 = new Customer(5, 'John', 'Doe', 'johndoe@mail.com');
```

The browser does not complain now, and there is no explicit require_once. Also remember that the __autoload function has to be defined only once, not in each file. So from now on, when you want to use your classes, as soon as the class is in a namespace and file that follows the convention, you only need to define the use statement. Way cleaner than before, right?

Using the spl_autoload_register function

The `__autoload` solution looks pretty good, but it has a small problem: what if our code is so complex that we do not have only one convention, and we need more than one implementation of the `__autoload` function? As we cannot define two functions with the same name, we need a way to tell PHP to keep a list of possible implementations of the autoloader, so it can try all of them until one works.

That is the job of `spl_autoload_register`. You define your autoloader function with a valid name, and then invoke the function `spl_autoload_register`, sending the name of your autoloader as an argument. You can call this function as many times as the different autoloaders you have in your code. In fact, even if you have only one autoloader, using this system is still a better option than the `__autoload` one, as you make it easier for someone else who has to add a new autoloader later:

```php
function autoloader($classname) {
    $lastSlash = strpos($classname, '\\') + 1;
    $classname = substr($classname, $lastSlash);
    $directory = str_replace('\\', '/', $classname);
    $filename = __DIR__ . '/' . $directory . '.php';
    require_once($filename);
}
spl_autoload_register('autoloader');
```

Inheritance

We have presented the object-oriented paradigm as the panacea for complex data structures, and even though we have shown that we can define objects with properties and methods, and it looks pretty and fancy, it is not something that we could not solve with arrays. Encapsulation was one feature that made objects more useful than arrays, but their true power lies in inheritance.

Introducing inheritance

Inheritance in OOP is the ability to pass the implementation of the class from parents to children. Yes, classes can have parents, and the technical way of referring to this feature is that a class *extends* from another class. When extending a class, we get all the properties and methods that are not defined as private, and the child class can use them as if they were its own. The limitation is that a class can only extend from one parent.

To show an example, let's consider our `Customer` class. It contains the properties `firstname`, `surname`, `email`, and `id`. A customer is actually a specific type of person, one that is registered in our system, so he/she can get books. But there can be other types of persons in our system, like librarian or guest. And all of them would have some common properties to all people, that is, `firstname` and `surname`. So it would make sense if we create a `Person` class, and make the `Customer` class extend from it. The hierarchic tree would look as follows:

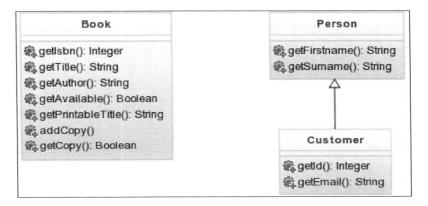

Note how `Customer` is connected to `Person`. The methods in `Person` are not defined in `Customer`, as they are implicit from the extension. Now save the new class in `src/Domain/Person.php`, following our convention:

```php
<?php

namespace Bookstore\Domain;

class Person {
    protected $firstname;
    protected $surname;

    public function __construct(string $firstname, string $surname) {
        $this->firstname = $firstname;
        $this->surname = $surname;
    }

    public function getFirstname(): string {
        return $this->firstname;
    }

    public function getSurname(): string {
        return $this->surname;
    }
}
```

The class defined in the preceding code snippet does not look special; we have just defined two properties, a constructor and two getters. Note though that we defined the properties as protected, because if we defined them as private, the children would not be able to access them. Now we can update our Customer class by removing the duplicate properties and its getters:

```php
<?php

namespace Bookstore\Domain;

class Customer extends Person {
    private static $lastId = 0;
    private $id;
    private $email;

    public function __construct(
        int $id,
        string $name,
        string $surname,
        string $email
    ) {
        if (empty($id)) {
            $this->id = ++self::$lastId;
        } else {
            $this->id = $id;
            if ($id > self::$lastId) {
                self::$lastId = $id;
            }
        }
        $this->name = $name;
        $this->surname = $surname;
        $this->email = $email;
    }

    public static function getLastId(): int {
        return self::$lastId;
    }

    public function getId(): int {
        return $this->id;
    }

    public function getEmail(): string {
        return $this->email;
```

```
    }

    public function setEmail($email): string {
        $this->email = $email;
    }
}
```

Note the new keyword `extends`; it tells PHP that this class is a child of the `Person` class. As both `Person` and `Customer` are in the same namespace, you do not have to add any `use` statement, but if they were not, you should let it know how to find the parent. This code works fine, but we can see that there is a bit of duplication of code. The constructor of the `Customer` class is doing the same job as the constructor of the `Person` class! We will try to fix it really soon.

In order to reference a method or property of the parent class from the child, you can use `$this` as if the property or method was in the same class. In fact, you could say it actually is. But PHP allows you to redefine a method in the child class that was already present in the parent. If you want to reference the parent's implementation, you cannot use `$this`, as PHP will invoke the one in the child. To force PHP to use the parent's method, use the keyword `parent::` instead of `$this`. Update the constructor of the `Customer` class as follows:

```
public function __construct(
    int $id,
    string $firstname,
    string $surname,
    string $email
) {
    parent::__construct($firstname, $surname);
    if (empty($id)) {
        $this->id = ++self::$lastId;
    } else {
        $this->id = $id;
        if ($id > self::$lastId) {
            self::$lastId = $id;
        }
    }
    $this->email = $email;
}
```

This new constructor does not duplicate code. Instead, it calls the constructor of the parent class `Person`, sending `$firstname` and `$surname`, and letting the parent do what it already knows how to do. We avoid code duplication and, on top of that, we make it easier for any future changes to be made in the constructor of `Person`. If we need to change the implementation of the constructor of `Person`, we will change it in one place only, instead of in all the children.

Overriding methods

As said before, when extending from a class, we get all the methods of the parent class. That is implicit, so they are not actually written down inside the child's class. What would happen if you implement another method with the same signature and/or name? You will be *overriding the method*.

As we do not need this feature in our classes, let's just add some code in our init.php file to show this behavior, and then you can just remove it. Let's define a class Pops, a class Child that extends from the parent, and a sayHi method in both of them:

```php
class Pops {
    public function sayHi() {
        echo "Hi, I am pops.";
    }
}

class Child extends Pops{
    public function sayHi() {
        echo "Hi, I am a child.";
    }
}

$pops = new Pops();
$child = new Child();
echo $pops->sayHi(); // Hi, I am pops.
echo $child->sayHi(); // Hi, I am Child.
```

The highlighted code shows you that the method has been overridden, so when invoking it from a child's point of view, we will be using it rather than the one inherited from its father. But what happens if we want to reference the inherited one too? You can always reference it with the keyword parent. Let's see how it works:

```php
class Child extends Pops{
    public function sayHi() {
        echo "Hi, I am a child.";
        parent::sayHi();
    }
}

$child = new Child();
echo $child->sayHi(); // Hi, I am Child. Hi I am pops.
```

Now the child is saying hi for both himself and his father. It seems very easy and handy, right? Well, there is a restriction. Imagine that, as in real life, the child was very shy, and he would not say hi to everybody. We could try to set the visibility of the method as protected, but see what happens:

```
class Child extends Pops{
    protected function sayHi() {
        echo "Hi, I am a child.";
    }
}
```

When trying this code, even without trying to instantiate it, you will get a fatal error complaining about the access level of that method. The reason is that when overriding, the method has to have at least as much visibility as the one inherited. That means that if we inherit a protected one, we can override it with another protected or a public one, but never with a private one.

Abstract classes

Remember that you can extend only from one parent class each time. That means that Customer can only extend from Person. But if we want to make this hierarchic tree more complex, we can create children classes that extend from Customer, and those classes will extend implicitly from Person too. Let's create two types of customer: basic and premium. These two customers will have the same properties and methods from Customer and from Person, plus the new ones that we implement in each one of them.

Save the following code as src/Domain/Customer/Basic.php:

```php
<?php

namespace Bookstore\Domain\Customer;

use Bookstore\Domain\Customer;

class Basic extends Customer {
    public function getMonthlyFee(): float {
        return 5.0;
    }

    public function getAmountToBorrow(): int {
        return 3;
    }

    public function getType(): string {
        return 'Basic';
    }
}
```

And the following code as `src/Domain/Customer/Premium.php`:

```php
<?php

namespace Bookstore\Domain\Customer;

use Bookstore\Domain\Customer;

class Premium extends Customer {
    public function getMonthlyFee(): float {
        return 10.0;
    }

    public function getAmountToBorrow(): int {
        return 10;
    }

    public function getType(): string {
        return 'Premium';
    }
}
```

Things to note in the preceding two codes are that we extend from `Customer` in two different classes, and it is perfectly legal— we can extend from classes in different namespaces. With this addition, the hierarchic tree for `Person` would look as follows:

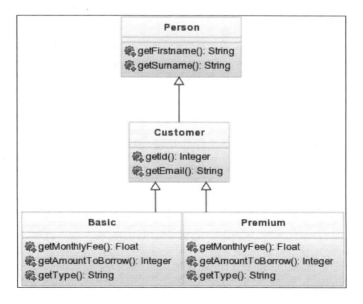

We define the same methods in these two classes, but their implementations are different. The aim of this approach is to use both types of customers indistinctively, without knowing which one it is each time. For example, we could temporally have the following code in our init.php. Remember to add the use statement to import the class Customer if you do not have it.

```
function checkIfValid(Customer $customer, array $books): bool {
    return $customer->getAmountToBorrow() >= count($books);
}
```

The preceding function would tell us if a given customer could borrow all the books in the array. Notice that the type hinting of the method says Customer, without specifying which one. This will accept objects that are instances of Customer or any class that extends from Customer, that is, Basic or Premium. Looks legit, right? Let's try to use it then:

```
$customer1 = new Basic(5, 'John', 'Doe', 'johndoe@mail.com');
var_dump(checkIfValid($customer1, [$book1])); // ok
$customer2 = new Customer(7, 'James', 'Bond', 'james@bond.com');
var_dump(checkIfValid($customer2, [$book1])); // fails
```

The first invocation works as expected, but the second one fails, even though we are sending a Customer object. The problem arises because the parent does not know about any getAmountToBorrow method! It also looks dangerous that we rely on the children to always implement that method. The solution lies in using abstract classes.

An **abstract class** is a class that cannot be instantiated. Its sole purpose is to make sure that its children are correctly implemented. Declaring a class as abstract is done with the keyword abstract, followed by the definition of a normal class. We can also specify the methods that the children are forced to implement, without implementing them in the parent class. Those methods are called abstract methods, and are defined with the keyword abstract at the beginning. Of course, the rest of the normal methods can stay there too, and will be inherited by its children:

```php
<?php
abstract class Customer extends Person {
//...
    abstract public function getMonthlyFee();
    abstract public function getAmountToBorrow();
    abstract public function getType();
//...
}
```

The preceding abstraction solves both problems. First, we will not be able to send any instance of the class Customer, because we cannot instantiate it. That means that all the objects that the checkIfValid method is going to accept are only the children from Customer. On the other hand, declaring abstract methods forces all the children that extend the class to implement them. With that, we make sure that all objects will implement getAmountToBorrow, and our code is safe.

The new hierarchic tree will define the three abstract methods in Customer, and will omit them for its children. It is true that we are implementing them in the children, but as they are enforced by Customer, and thanks to abstraction, we are sure that all classes extending from it will have to implement them, and that it is safe to do so. Let's see how this is done:

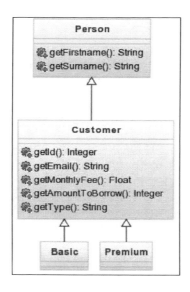

With the last new addition, your init.php file should fail. The reason is that it is trying to instantiate the class Customer, but now it is abstract, so you cannot. Instantiate a concrete class, that is, one that is not abstract, to solve the problem.

Interfaces

An **interface** is an OOP element that groups a set of function declarations without implementing them, that is, it specifies the name, return type, and arguments, but not the block of code. Interfaces are different from abstract classes, since they cannot contain any implementation at all, whereas abstract classes could mix both method definitions and implemented ones. The purpose of interfaces is to state what a class can do, but not how it is done.

From our code, we can identify a potential usage of interfaces. Customers have an expected behavior, but its implementation changes depending on the type of customer. So, Customer could be an interface instead of an abstract class. But as an interface cannot implement any function, nor can it contain properties, we will have to move the concrete code from the Customer class to somewhere else. For now, let's move it up to the Person class. Edit the Person class as shown:

```php
<?php

namespace Bookstore\Domain;

class Person {

    private static $lastId = 0;
    protected $id;
    protected $firstname;
    protected $surname;
    protected $email;

    public function __construct(
        int $id,
        string $firstname,
        string $surname,
        string $email
    ) {
        $this->firstname = $firstname;
        $this->surname = $surname;
        $this->email = $email;

        if (empty($id)) {
            $this->id = ++self::$lastId;
        } else {
            $this->id = $id;
            if ($id > self::$lastId) {
                self::$lastId = $id;
            }
        }
    }

    public function getFirstname(): string {
        return $this->firstname;
    }
    public function getSurname(): string {
        return $this->surname;
```

```
    }
    public static function getLastId(): int {
        return self::$lastId;
    }
    public function getId(): int {
        return $this->id;
    }
    public function getEmail(): string {
        return $this->email;
    }
}
```

Complicating things more than necessary

Interfaces are very useful, but there is always a place and a time for everything. As our application is very simple due to its didactic nature, there is no real place for them. The abstract class already defined in the previous section is the best approach for our scenario. But just for the sake of showing how interfaces work, we will be adapting our code to them.

Do not worry though, as most of the code that we are going to introduce now will be replaced by better practices once we introduce databases and the MVC pattern in *Chapter 5, Using Databases*, and *Chapter 6, Adapting to MVC*.

When writing your own applications, do not try to complicate things more than necessary. It is a common pattern to see very complex code from developers that try to show up all the skills they have in a very simple scenario. Use only the necessary tools to leave clean code that is easy to maintain, and of course, that works as expected.

Change the content of Customer.php with the following:

```php
<?php

namespace Bookstore\Domain;

interface Customer {
    public function getMonthlyFee(): float;
    public function getAmountToBorrow(): int;
    public function getType(): string;
}
```

Note that an interface is very similar to an abstract class. The differences are that it is defined with the keyword interface, and that its methods do not have the word abstract. Interfaces cannot be instantiated, since their methods are not implemented as with abstract classes. The only thing you can do with them is make a class to implement them.

Implementing an interface means implementing all the methods defined in it, like
when we extended an abstract class. It has all the benefits of the extension of
abstract classes, such as belonging to that type—useful when type hinting. From the
developer's point of view, using a class that implements an interface is like writing
a contract: you ensure that your class will always have the methods declared in
the interface, regardless of the implementation. Because of that, interfaces only
care about public methods, which are the ones that other developers can use. The
only change you need to make in your code is to replace the keywords `extends` by
`implements`:

```
class Basic implements Customer {
```

So, why would someone use an interface if we could always use an abstract class that
not only enforces the implementation of methods, but also allows inheriting code as
well? The reason is that you can only extend from one class, but you can implement
multiple instances at the same time. Imagine that you had another interface that
defined payers. This could identify someone that has the ability to pay something,
regardless of what it is. Save the following code in `src/Domain/Payer.php`:

```php
<?php

namespace Bookstore\Domain;

interface Payer {
    public function pay(float $amount);
    public function isExtentOfTaxes(): bool;
}
```

Now our basic and premium customers can implement both the interfaces. The basic
customer will look like the following:

```php
//...
use Bookstore\Domain\Customer;
use Bookstore\Domain\Person;

class Basic extends Person implements Customer {
    public function getMonthlyFee(): float {
//...
```

And the premium customer will change in the same way:

```php
//...
use Bookstore\Domain\Customer;
use Bookstore\Domain\Person;

class Premium extends Person implements Customer {
    public function getMonthlyFee(): float {
//...
```

You should see that this code would no longer work. The reason is that although we implement a second interface, the methods are not implemented. Add these two methods to the basic customer class:

```
public function pay(float $amount) {
    echo "Paying $amount.";
}

public function isExtentOfTaxes(): bool {
    return false;
}
```

Add these two methods to the premium customer class:

```
public function pay(float $amount) {
    echo "Paying $amount.";
}

public function isExtentOfTaxes(): bool {
    return true;
}
```

If you know that *all* customers will have to be payers, you could even make the `Customer` interface to inherit from the `Payer` interface:

```
interface Customer extends Payer {
```

This change does not affect the usage of our classes at all. Other developers will see that our basic and premium customers inherit from `Payer` and `Customer`, and so they contain all the necessary methods. That these interfaces are independent, or they extend from each other is something that will not affect too much.

Interfaces can only extend from other interfaces, and classes can only extend from other classes. The only way to mix them is when a class implements an interface, but neither does a class extend from an interface, nor does an interface extend from a class. But from the point of view of type hinting, they can be used interchangeably.

To summarize this section and make things clear, let's show what the hierarchic tree looks like after all the new additions. As in abstract classes, the methods declared in an interface are shown in the interface rather than in each of the classes that implement it.

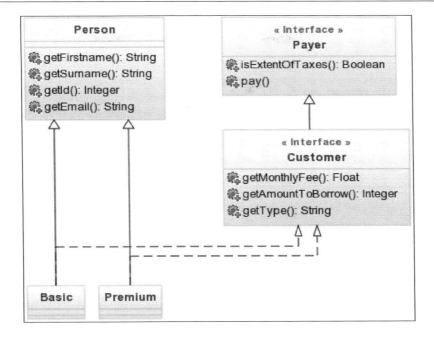

Polymorphism

Polymorphism is an OOP feature that allows us to work with different classes that implement the same interface. It is one of the beauties of object-oriented programming. It allows the developer to create a complex system of classes and hierarchic trees, but offers a simple way of working with them.

Imagine that we have a function that, given a payer, checks whether it is exempt of taxes or not, and makes it pay some amount of money. This piece of code does not really mind if the payer is a customer, a librarian, or someone who has nothing to do with the bookstore. The only thing that it cares about is that the payer has the ability to pay. The function could be as follows:

```
function processPayment(Payer $payer, float $amount) {
    if ($payer->isExtentOfTaxes()) {
        echo "What a lucky one...";
    } else {
        $amount *= 1.16;
    }
    $payer->pay($amount);
}
```

You could send basic or premium customers to this function, and the behavior will be different. But, as both implement the `Payer` interface, both objects provided are valid types, and both are capable of performing the actions needed.

The `checkIfValid` function takes a customer and a list of books. We already saw that sending any kind of customer makes the function work as expected. But what happens if we send an object of the class `Librarian`, which extends from `Payer`? As `Payer` does not know about `Customer` (it is rather the other way around), the function will complain as the type hinting is not accomplished.

One useful feature that comes with PHP is the ability to check whether an object is an instance of a specific class or interface. The way to use it is to specify the variable followed by the keyword `instanceof` and the name of the class or interface. It returns a Boolean, which is `true` if the object is from a class that extends or implements the specified one, or `false` otherwise. Let's see some examples:

```
$basic = new Basic(1, "name", "surname", "email");
$premium = new Premium(2, "name", "surname", "email");
var_dump($basic instanceof Basic); // true
var_dump($basic instanceof Premium); // false
var_dump($premium instanceof Basic); // false
var_dump($premium instanceof Premium); // true
var_dump($basic instanceof Customer); // true
var_dump($basic instanceof Person); // true
var_dump($basic instanceof Payer); // true
```

Remember to add all the `use` statements for each of the class or interface, otherwise PHP will understand that the specified class name is inside the namespace of the file.

Traits

So far, you have learned that extending from classes allows you to inherit code (properties and method implementations), but it has the limitation of extending only from one class each time. On the other hand, you can use interfaces to implement multiple behaviors from the same class, but you cannot inherit code in this way. To fill this gap, that is, to be able to inherit code from multiple places, you have traits.

Traits are mechanisms that allow you to reuse code, "inheriting", or rather copy-pasting code, from multiple sources at the same time. Traits, as abstract classes or interfaces, cannot be instantiated; they are just containers of functionality that can be used from other classes.

If you remember, we have some code in the Person class that manages the assignment of IDs. This code is not really part of a person, but rather part of an ID system that could be used by some other entity that has to be identified with IDs too. One way to extract this functionality from Person—and we are not saying that it is the best way to do so, but for the sake of seeing traits in action, we choose this one—is to move it to a trait.

To define a trait, do as if you were defining a class, just use the keyword trait instead of class. Define its namespace, add the use statements needed, declare its properties and implement its methods, and place everything in a file that follows the same conventions. Add the following code to the src/Utils/Unique.php file:

```php
<?php

namespace Bookstore\Utils;

trait Unique {
    private static $lastId = 0;
    protected $id;

    public function setId(int $id) {
        if (empty($id)) {
            $this->id = ++self::$lastId;
        } else {
            $this->id = $id;
            if ($id > self::$lastId) {
                self::$lastId = $id;
            }
        }
    }

    public static function getLastId(): int {
        return self::$lastId;
    }
    public function getId(): int {
        return $this->id;
    }
}
```

Observe that the namespace is not the same as usual, since we are storing this code in a different file. This is a matter of conventions, but you are entirely free to use the file structure that you consider better for each case. In this case, we do not think that this trait represents "business logic" like customers and books do; instead, it represents a utility for managing the assignment of IDs.

We include all the code related to IDs from `Person`. That includes the properties, the getters, and the code inside the constructor. As the trait cannot be instantiated, we cannot add a constructor. Instead, we added a `setId` method that contains the code. When constructing a new instance that uses this trait, we can invoke this `setId` method to set the ID based on what the user sends as an argument.

The class `Person` will have to change too. We have to remove all references to IDs and we will have to define somehow that the class is using the trait. To do that, we use the keyword `use`, like in namespaces, but inside the class. Let's see what it would look like:

```php
<?php

namespace Bookstore\Domain;

use Bookstore\Utils\Unique;

class Person {
    use Unique;

    protected $firstname;
    protected $surname;
    protected $email;

    public function __construct(
        int $id,
        string $firstname,
        string $surname,
        string $email
    ) {
        $this->firstname = $firstname;
        $this->surname = $surname;
        $this->email = $email;
        $this->setId($id);
    }

    public function getFirstname(): string {
        return $this->firstname;
    }
    public function getSurname(): string {
        return $this->surname;
    }
    public function getEmail(): string {
        return $this->email;
```

```
    }
    public function setEmail(string $email) {
        $this->email = $email;
    }
}
```

We add the `use Unique;` statement to let the class know that it is using the trait. We remove everything related to IDs, even inside the constructor. We still get an ID as the first argument of the constructor, but we ask the method `setId` from the trait to do everything for us. Note that we refer to that method with `$this`, as if the method was inside the class. The updated hierarchic tree would look like the following (note that we are not adding all the methods for all the classes or interfaces that are not involved in the recent changes in order to keep the diagram as small and readable as possible):

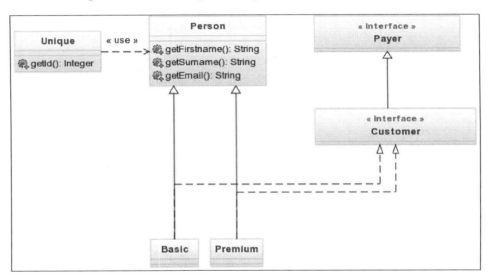

Let's see how it works, even though it does so in the way that you probably expect. Add this code into your `init.php` file, include the necessary `use` statements, and execute it in your browser:

```
$basic1 = new Basic(1, "name", "surname", "email");
$basic2 = new Basic(null, "name", "surname", "email");
var_dump($basic1->getId()); // 1
var_dump($basic2->getId()); // 2
```

The preceding code instantiates two customers. The first of them has a specific ID, whereas the second one lets the system choose an ID for it. The result is that the second basic customer has the ID 2. That is to be expected, as both customers are basic. But what would happen if the customers are of different types?

```
$basic = new Basic(1, "name", "surname", "email");
$premium = new Premium(null, "name", "surname", "email");
var_dump($basic->getId()); // 1
var_dump($premium->getId()); // 2
```

The IDs are still the same. That is to be expected, as the trait is included in the Person class, so the static property $lastId will be shared across all the instances of the class Person, including Basic and Premium customers. If you used the trait from Basic and Premium customer instead of Person (but you should not), you would have the following result:

```
var_dump($basic->getId()); // 1
var_dump($premium->getId()); // 1
```

Each class will have its own static property. All Basic instances will share the same $lastId, different from the $lastId of Premium instances. This should make clear that the static members in traits are linked to whichever class uses them, rather than the trait itself. That could also be reflected on testing the following code which uses our original scenario where the trait is used from Person:

```
$basic = new Basic(1, "name", "surname", "email");
$premium = new Premium(null, "name", "surname", "email");
var_dump(Person::getLastId()); // 2
var_dump(Unique::getLastId()); // 0
var_dump(Basic::getLastId()); // 2
var_dump(Premium::getLastId()); // 2
```

If you have a good eye for problems, you might start thinking about some potential issues around the usage of traits. What happens if we use two traits that contain the same method? Or what happens if you use a trait that contains a method that is already implemented in that class?

Ideally, you should avoid running into these kinds of situations; they are warning lights for possible bad design. But as there will always be extraordinary cases, let's see some isolated examples on how they would behave.

The scenario where the trait and the class implement the same method is easy. The method implemented explicitly in the class is the one with more precedence, followed by the method implemented in the trait, and finally, the method inherited from the parent class. Let's see how it works. Take for example the following trait and class definitions:

```php
<?php

trait Contract {
    public function sign() {
        echo "Signing the contract.";
    }
}

class Manager {
    use Contract;

    public function sign() {
        echo "Signing a new player.";
    }
}
```

Both implement the `sign` method, which means that we have to apply the precedence rules defined previously. The method defined in the class takes precedence over the one from the trait, so in this case, the executed method will be the one from the class:

```php
$manager = new Manager();
$manager->sign(); // Signing a new player.
```

The most complicated scenario would be one where a class uses two traits with the same method. There are no rules that solve the conflict automatically, so you have to solve it explicitly. Check the following code:

```php
<?php

trait Contract {
    public function sign() {
        echo "Signing the contract.";
    }
}

trait Communicator {
    public function sign() {
        echo "Signing to the waitress.";
    }
```

```
}

class Manager {
    use Contract, Communicator;
}

$manager = new Manager();
$manager->sign();
```

The preceding code throws a fatal error, as both traits implement the same method. To choose the one you want to use, you have to use the operator `insteadof`. To use it, state the trait name and the method that you want to use, followed by `insteadof` and the trait that you are rejecting for use. Optionally, use the keyword `as` to add an alias like we did with namespaces so that you can use both the methods:

```
class Manager {
    use Contract, Communicator {
        Contract::sign insteadof Communicator;
        Communicator::sign as makeASign;
    }
}

$manager = new Manager();
$manager->sign(); // Signing the contract.
$manager->makeASign(); // Signing to the waitress.
```

You can see how we decided to use the method of `Contract` instead of `Communicator`, but added the alias so that both methods are available. Hopefully, you can see that even the conflicts can be solved, and there are specific cases where there is nothing to do but deal with them; in general, they look like a bad sign—no pun intended.

Handling exceptions

It does not matter how easy and intuitive your application is designed to be, there will be bad usage from the user or just random errors of connectivity, and your code has to be ready to handle these scenarios so that the user experience is a good as possible. We call these scenarios **exceptions**: an element of the language that identifies a case that is not as we expected.

The try...catch block

Your code can throw exceptions manually whenever you think it necessary. For example, take the `setId` method from the `Unique` trait. Thanks to type hinting, we are enforcing the ID to be a numeric one, but that is as far as it goes. What would happen if someone tries to set an ID that is a negative number? The code right now allows it to go through, but depending on your preferences, you would like to avoid it. That would be a good place for an exception to happen. Let's see how we would add this check and consequent exception:

```
public function setId($id) {
    if ($id < 0) {
        throw new \Exception('Id cannot be negative.');
    }
    if (empty($id)) {
        $this->id = ++self::$lastId;
    } else {
        $this->id = $id;
        if ($id > self::$lastId) {
            self::$lastId = $id;
        }
    }
}
```

As you can see, exceptions are objects of the class exception. Remember adding the backslash to the name of the class, unless you want to include it with `use Exception;` at the top of the file. The constructor of the `Exception` class takes some optional arguments, the first one of them being the message of the exception. Instances of the class `Exception` do nothing by themselves; they have to be thrown in order to be noticed by the program.

Let's try forcing our program to throw this exception. In order to do that, let's try to create a customer with a negative ID. In your `init.php` file, add the following:

```
$basic = new Basic(-1, "name", "surname", "email");
```

If you try it now in your browser, PHP will throw a fatal error saying that there was an uncaught exception, which is the expected behavior. For PHP, an exception is something from what it cannot recover, so it will stop execution. That is far from ideal, as you would like to just display an error message to the user, and let them try again.

You can—and should—capture exceptions using the `try...catch` blocks. You insert the code that might throw an exception in the `try` block and if an exception happens, PHP will jump to the `catch` block. Let's see how it works:

```
public function setId(int $id) {
    try {
        if ($id < 0) {
            throw new Exception('Id cannot be negative.');
        }
        if (empty($id)) {
            $this->id = ++self::$lastId;
        } else {
            $this->id = $id;
            if ($id > self::$lastId) {
                self::$lastId = $id;
            }
        }
    } catch (Exception $e) {
        echo $e->getMessage();
    }
}
```

If we test the last code snippet in our browser, we will see the message printed from the `catch` block. Calling the `getMessage` method on an exception instance will give us the message—the first argument when creating the object. But remember that the argument of the constructor is optional; so, do not rely on the message of the exception too much if you are not sure how it is generated, as it might be empty.

Note that after the exception is thrown, nothing else inside the `try` block is executed; PHP goes straight to the `catch` block. Additionally, the block gets an argument, which is the exception thrown. Here, type hinting is mandatory—you will see why very soon. Naming the argument as `$e` is a widely used convention, even though it is not a good practice to use poor descriptive names for variables.

Being a bit critical, so far, there is not any real advantage to be seen in using exceptions in this example. A simple `if...else` block would do exactly the same job, right? But the real power of exceptions lies in the ability to be propagated across methods. That is, the exception thrown on the `setId` method, if not captured, will be propagated to wherever the method was invoked, allowing us to capture it there. This is very useful, as different places in the code might want to handle the exception in a different way. To see how this is done, let's remove the `try...catch` inserted in `setId`, and place the following piece of code in your `init.php` file, instead:

```
try {
    $basic = new Basic(-1, "name", "surname", "email");
} catch (Exception $e) {
```

```
        echo 'Something happened when creating the basic customer: '
            . $e->getMessage();
    }
```

The preceding example shows how useful it is to catch propagated exceptions: we can be more specific of what happens, as we know what the user was trying to do when the exception was thrown. In this case, we know that we were trying to create the customer, but this exception might have been thrown when trying to update the ID of an existing customer, which would need a different error message.

The finally block

There is a third block that you can use when dealing with exceptions: the `finally` block. This block is added after the `try...catch` one, and it is optional. In fact, the `catch` block is optional too; the restriction is that a `try` must be followed by at least one of them. So you could have these three scenarios:

```
// scenario 1: the whole try-catch-finally
try {
    // code that might throw an exception
} catch (Exception $e) {
    // code that deals with the exception
} finally {
    // finally block
}

// scenario 2: try-finally without catch
try {
    // code that might throw an exception
} finally {
    // finally block
}

// scenario 3: try-catch without finally
try {
    // code that might throw an exception
} catch (Exception $e) {
    // code that deals with the exception
}
```

The code inside the `finally` block is executed when either the `try` or the `catch` blocks are executed completely. So, if we have a scenario where there is no exception, after all the code inside the `try` block is executed, PHP will execute the code inside `finally`. On the other hand, if there is an exception thrown inside the `try` block, PHP will jump to the `catch` block, and after executing everything there, it will execute the `finally` block too.

In order to test this functionality, let's implement a function that contains a `try`... `catch`...`finally` block, trying to create a customer with a given ID (through an argument), and logging all the actions that take place. You can add the following code snippet into your `init.php` file:

```php
function createBasicCustomer($id)
{
    try {
        echo "\nTrying to create a new customer.\n";
        return new Basic($id, "name", "surname", "email");
    } catch (Exception $e) {
        echo "Something happened when creating the basic customer: "
            . $e->getMessage() . "\n";
    } finally {
        echo "End of function.\n";
    }
}

createBasicCustomer(1);
createBasicCustomer(-1);
```

If you try this, your browser will show you the following output—remember to display the source code of the page to see it formatted prettily:

```
● ● ●                    Source of: http://localhost:8000/init.php
1
2 Trying to create a new customer.
3 End of function.
4
5 Trying to create a new customer.
6 Something happened when creating the basic customer: Id cannot be a negative number.
7 End of function.
```

The result might not be the one you expected. The first time we invoke the function, we are able to create the object without an issue, and that means we execute the `return` statement. In a normal function, this should be the end of it, but since we are inside the `try`...`catch`...`finally` block, we still need to execute the `finally` code! The second example looks more intuitive, jumping from the `try` to the `catch`, and then to the `finally` block.

The `finally` block is very useful when dealing with expensive resources like database connections. In *Chapter 5, Using Databases*, you will see how to use them. Depending on the type of connection, you will have to close it after use for allowing other users to connect. The `finally` block is used for closing those connections, regardless of whether the function throws an exception or not.

Catching different types of exceptions

Exceptions have already been proven useful, but there is still one important feature to show: catching different types of exceptions. As you already know, exceptions are instances of the class `Exception`, and as with any other class, they can be extended. The main goal of extending from this class is to create different types of exceptions, but we will not add any logic inside—even though you can, of course. Let's create a class that extends from `Exception`, and which identifies exceptions related to invalid IDs. Put this code inside the `src/Exceptions/InvalidIdException.php` file:

```php
<?php

namespace Bookstore\Exceptions;

use Exception;

class InvalidIdException extends Exception {
    public function __construct($message = null) {
        $message = $message ?: 'Invalid id provided.';
        parent::__construct($message);
    }
}
```

The `InvalidIdException` class extends from the class `Exception`, and so it can be thrown as one. The constructor of the class takes an optional argument, `$message`. The following two lines inside it contain interesting code:

- The `?:` operator is a shorter version of a conditional, and works like this: the expression on the left is returned if it does not evaluate to `false`, otherwise, the expression on the right will be returned. What we want here is to use the message given by the user, or a default one in case the user does not provide any. For more information and usages, you can visit the PHP documentation at `http://php.net/manual/en/language.operators.comparison.php`.

- `parent::__construct` will invoke the parent's constructor, that is, the constructor of the class `Exception`. As you already know, this constructor gets the message of the exception as the first argument. You could argue that, as we are extending from the `Exception` class, we do not really need to call any functions, as we can edit the properties of the class straightaway. The reason for avoiding this is to let the parent class manage its own properties. Imagine that, for some reason, in a future version of PHP, `Exception` changes the name of the property for the message. If you modify it directly, you will have to change that in your code, but if you use the constructor, you have nothing to fear. Internal implementations are more likely to change than external interfaces.

We can use this new exception instead of the generic one. Replace it in your `Unique` trait as follows:

```
throw new InvalidIdException('Id cannot be a negative number.');
```

You can see that we are still sending a message: that is because we want to be even more specific. But the exception would work as well without one. Try your code again, and you will see that nothing changes.

Now imagine that we have a very small database and we cannot allow more than 50 users. We can create a new exception that identifies this case, let's say, as `src/Exceptions/ExceededMaxAllowedException.php`:

```php
<?php

namespace Bookstore\Exceptions;

use Exception;

class ExceededMaxAllowedException extends Exception {
    public function __construct($message = null) {
        $message = $message ?: 'Exceeded max allowed.';
        parent::__construct($message);
    }
}
```

Let's modify our trait in order to check for this case. When setting an ID, if this ID is greater than 50, we can assume that we've reached the maximum number of users:

```php
public function setId(int $id) {
        if ($id < 0) {
            throw new InvalidIdException(
                'Id cannot be a negative number.'
            );
```

```
    }
    if (empty($id)) {
        $this->id = ++self::$lastId;
    } else {
        $this->id = $id;
        if ($id > self::$lastId) {
            self::$lastId = $id;
        }
    }
    if ($this->id > 50) {
        throw new ExceededMaxAllowedException(
            'Max number of users is 50.'
        );
    }
}
```

Now the preceding function throws two different exceptions: `InvalidIdException` and `ExceededMaxAllowedException`. When catching them, you might want to behave in a different way depending on the type of exception caught. Remember how you have to declare an argument in your `catch` block? Well, you can add as many `catch` blocks as needed, specifying a different exception class in each of them. The code could look like this:

```
function createBasicCustomer(int $id)
{
    try {
        echo "\nTrying to create a new customer with id $id.\n";
        return new Basic($id, "name", "surname", "email");
    } catch (InvalidIdException $e) {
        echo "You cannot provide a negative id.\n";
    } catch (ExceededMaxAllowedException $e) {
        echo "No more customers are allowed.\n";
    } catch (Exception $e) {
        echo "Unknown exception: " . $e->getMessage();
    }
}

createBasicCustomer(1);
createBasicCustomer(-1);
createBasicCustomer(55);
```

If you try this code, you should see the following output:

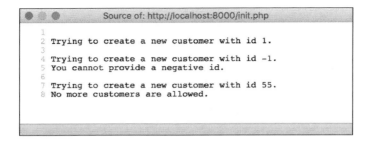

Note that we catch three exceptions here: our two new exceptions and the generic one. The reason for doing this is that it might happen that some other piece of code throws an exception of a different type than the ones we defined, and we need to define a `catch` block with the generic `Exception` class to get it, as all exceptions will extend from it. Of course, this is absolutely optional, and if you do not do it, the exception will be just propagated.

Bear in mind the order of the `catch` blocks. PHP tries to use the `catch` blocks in the order that you defined them. So, if your first catch is for `Exception`, the rest of the blocks will be never executed, as all exceptions extend from that class. Try it with the following code:

```
try {
    echo "\nTrying to create a new customer with id $id.\n";
    return new Basic($id, "name", "surname", "email");
} catch (Exception $e) {
    echo 'Unknown exception: ' . $e->getMessage() . "\n";
} catch (InvalidIdException $e) {
    echo "You cannot provide a negative id.\n";
} catch (ExceededMaxAllowedException $e) {
    echo "No more customers are allowed.\n";
}
```

The result that you get from the browser will always be from the first catch:

```
Source of: http://localhost:8000/init.php
1
2  Trying to create a new customer with id 1.
3
4  Trying to create a new customer with id -1.
5  Unkown exception: Id cannot be a negative number.
6
7  Trying to create a new customer with id 55.
8  Unkown exception: Max number of users is 50.
```

Design patterns

Developers have been creating code since way before the appearance of with Internet, and they have been working on a number of different areas, not just web applications. Because of that, a lot of people have already had to confront similar scenarios, carrying the experience of previous attempts for fixing the same thing. In short, it means that almost surely, someone has already designed a good way of solving the problem that you are facing now.

A lot of books have been written trying to group solutions to common problems, also known as **design patterns**. Design patterns are not algorithms that you copy and paste into your program, showing how to fix something step-by-step, but rather recipes that show you, in a heuristic way, how to look for the answer.

Studying them is essential if you want to become a professional developer, not only for solving problems, but also for communicating with other developers. It is very common to get an answer like "You could use a factory here", when discussing your program design. It saves a lot of time knowing what a factory is, rather than explaining the pattern each time someone mentions it.

As we said, there are entire books that talk about design patterns, and we highly recommend you to have a look at some of them. The goal of this section is to show you what a design pattern is and how you can use it. Additionally, we will show you some of the most common design patterns used with PHP when writing web applications, excluding the MVC pattern, which we will study in *Chapter 6, Adapting to MVC*.

Other than books, you could also visit the open source project **DesignPatternsPHP** at `http://designpatternsphp.readthedocs.org/en/latest/README.html`. There is a good collection of them, and they are implemented in PHP, so it would be easier for you to adapt.

Factory

A **factory** is a design pattern of the creational group, which means that it allows you to create objects. You might think that we do not need such a thing, as creating an object is as easy as using the `new` keyword, the class, and its arguments. But letting the user do that is dangerous for different reasons. Apart from the increased difficulty caused by using `new` when unit testing our code (you will learn about unit testing in *Chapter 7, Testing Web Applications*), a lot of coupling too gets added into our code.

When we discussed encapsulation, you learned that it is better to hide the internal implementation of a class, and you could consider the constructor as part of it. The reason is that the user needs to know at all times how to create objects, including what the arguments of the constructor are. And what if we want to change our constructor to accept different arguments? We need to go one by one to all the places where we have created objects and update them.

Another reason for using factories is to manage different classes that inherit a super class or implement the same interface. As you know, thanks to polymorphism, you can use one object without knowing the specific class that it instantiates, as long as you know the interface being implemented. It might so happen that your code needs to instantiate an object that implements an interface and use it, but the concrete class of the object may not be important at all.

Think about our bookstore example. We have two types of customers: basic and premium. But for most of the code, we do not really care what type of customer a specific instance is. In fact, we should implement our code to use objects that implement the `Customer` interface, being unaware of the specific type. So, if we decide in the future to add a new type, as long as it implements the correct interface, our code will work without an issue. But, if that is the case, what do we do when we need to create a new customer? We cannot instantiate an interface, so let's use the factory pattern. Add the following code into `src/Domain/Customer/CustomerFactory.php`:

```php
<?php

namespace Bookstore\Domain\Customer;

use Bookstore\Domain\Customer;

class CustomerFactory {
    public static function factory(
        string $type,
        int $id,
        string $firstname,
        string $surname,
        string $email
    ): Customer {
        switch ($type) {
            case 'basic':
                return new Basic($id, $firstname, $surname, $email);
            case 'premium':
                return new Premium($id, $firstname, $surname, $email);
        }
    }
}
```

The factory in the preceding code is less than ideal for different reasons. In the first one, we use a `switch`, and add a case for all the existing customer types. Two types do not make much difference, but what if we have 19? Let's try to make this factory method a bit more dynamic.

```
public static function factory(
        string $type,
        int $id,
        string $firstname,
        string $surname,
        string $email
    ): Customer {
    $classname = __NAMESPACE__ . '\\' . ucfirst($type);
    if (!class_exists($classname)) {
        throw new \InvalidArgumentException('Wrong type.');
    }
    return new $classname($id, $firstname, $surname, $email);
}
```

Yes, you can do what we did in the preceding code in PHP. Instantiating classes dynamically, that is, using the content of a variable as the name of the class, is one of the things that makes PHP so flexible… and dangerous. Used wrongly, it will make your code horribly difficult to read and maintain, so be careful about it. Note too the constant __NAMESPACE__, which contains the namespace of the current file.

Now this factory looks cleaner, and it is also very dynamic. You could add more customer types and, as long as they are inside the correct namespace and implement the interface, there is nothing to change on the factory side, nor in the usage of the factory.

In order to use it, let's change our `init.php` file. You can remove all our tests, and just leave the autoloader code. Then, add the following:

```
CustomerFactory::factory('basic', 2, 'mary', 'poppins', 'mary@poppins.com');
CustomerFactory::factory('premium', null, 'james', 'bond', 'james@bond.com');
```

The factory design pattern can be as complex as you need. There are different variants of it, and each one has its own place and time, but the general idea is always the same.

Singleton

If someone with a bit of experience with design patterns, or web development in general, reads the title of this section, they will probably start tearing their hair out and claiming that singleton is the worst example of a design pattern. But just bear with me.

When explaining interfaces, I added a note about how developers tend to complicate their code too much just so they can use all the tools they know. Using design patterns is one of the cases where this happens. They have been so famous, and people claimed that good use of them is directly linked to great developers, that everybody that learns them tries to use them absolutely everywhere.

The singleton pattern is probably the most infamous of the design patterns used in PHP for web development. This pattern has a very specific purpose, and when that is the case, the pattern proves to be very useful. But this pattern is so easy to implement that developers continuously try to add singletons everywhere, turning their code into something unmaintainable. It is for this reason that people call this an anti-pattern, something that should be avoided rather than used.

I do agree with this point of view, but I still think that you should be very familiar with this design pattern. Even though you should avoid its overuse, people still use it everywhere, and they refer to it countless times, so you should be in a position to either agree with them or rather have enough reasons to discourage them to use it. Having said that, let's see what the aim of the singleton pattern is.

The idea is simple: singletons are used when you want one class to always have one unique instance. Every time, and everywhere you use that class, it has to be through the same instance. The reason is to avoid having too many instances of some heavy resource, or to keep always the same state everywhere—to be global. Examples of this are database connections or configuration handlers.

Imagine that in order to run, our application needs some configuration, such as credentials for the database, URLs of special endpoints, directory paths for finding libraries or important files, and so on. When you receive a request, the first thing you do is to load this configuration from the filesystem, and then you store it as an array or some other data structure. Save the following code as your `src/Utils/Config.php` file:

```php
<?php

namespace Bookstore\Utils;

use Bookstore\Exceptions\NotFoundException;
```

```
class Config {
    private $data;

    public function __construct() {
    $json = file_get_contents(__DIR__ . '/../../config/app.json');
        $this->data = json_decode($json, true);
    }

    public function get($key) {
        if (!isset($this->data[$key])) {
            throw new NotFoundException("Key $key not in config.");
        }
        return $this->data[$key];
    }
}
```

As you can see, this class uses a new exception. Create it under src/Utils/ NotFoundException.php:

```php
<?php

namespace Bookstore\Exceptions;

use Exception;

class NotFoundException extends Exception {
}
```

Also, the class reads a file, config/app.json. You could add the following JSON map inside it:

```
{
  "db": {
    "user": "Luke",
    "password": "Skywalker"
  }
}
```

In order to use this configuration, let's add the following code into your init.php file.

```
$config = new Config();
$dbConfig = $config->get('db');
var_dump($dbConfig);
```

That seems a very good way to read configuration, right? But pay attention to the highlighted line. We instantiate the `Config` object, hence, we read a file, transform its contents from JSON to array, and store it. What if the file contains hundreds of lines instead of just six? You should notice then that instantiating this class is very expensive.

You do not want to read the files and transform them into arrays each time you ask for some data from your configuration. That is way too expensive! But, for sure, you will need the configuration array in very different places of your code, and you cannot carry this array everywhere you go. If you understood static properties and methods, you could argue that implementing a static array inside the object should fix the problem. You instantiate it once, and then just call a static method that will access an already populated static property. Theoretically, we skip the instantiation, right?

```php
<?php

namespace Bookstore\Utils;

use Bookstore\Exceptions\NotFoundException;

class Config {
    private static $data;

    public function __construct() {
        $json = file_get_contents(__DIR__ . '/../config/app.json');
        self::$data = json_decode($json, true);
    }

    public static function get($key) {
        if (!isset(self::$data[$key])) {
            throw new NotFoundException("Key $key not in config.");
        }
        return self::$data[$key];
    }
}
```

This seems to be a good idea, but it is highly dangerous. How can you be absolutely sure that the array has already been populated? And how can you be sure that, even using a static context, the user will not keep instantiating this class again and again? That is where singletons come in handy.

Implementing a singleton implies the following points:

1. Make the constructor of the class private, so absolutely no one from outside the class can ever instantiate that class.

2. Create a static property named $instance, which will contain an instance of itself—that is, in our Config class, the $instance property will contain an instance of the class Config.

3. Create a static method, getInstance, which will check if $instance is null, and if it is, it will create a new instance using the private constructor. Either way, it will return the $instance property.

Let's see what the singleton class would look like:

```php
<?php

namespace Bookstore\Utils;

use Bookstore\Exceptions\NotFoundException;

class Config {
    private $data;
    private static $instance;

    private function __construct() {
        $json = file_get_contents(__DIR__ . '/../config/app.json');
        $this->data = json_decode($json, true);
    }

    public static function getInstance(){
        if (self::$instance == null) {
            self::$instance = new Config();
        }
        return self::$instance;
    }

    public function get($key) {
        if (!isset($this->data[$key])) {
            throw new NotFoundException("Key $key not in config.");
        }
        return $this->data[$key];
    }
}
```

If you run this code right now, it will throw you an error, as the constructor of this class is private. First achievement unlocked! Let's use this class properly:

```
$config = Config::getInstance();
$dbConfig = $config->get('db');
var_dump($dbConfig);
```

Does it convince you? It proves to be very handy indeed. But I cannot emphasize this enough: be careful when you use this design pattern, as it has very, very, specific use cases. Avoid falling into the trap of implementing it everywhere!

Anonymous functions

Anonymous functions, or **lambda functions**, are functions without a name. As they do not have a name, in order to be able to invoke them, we need to store them as variables. It might be strange at the beginning, but the idea is quite simple. At this point of time, we do not really need any anonymous function, so let's just add the code into init.php, and then remove it:

```
$addTaxes = function (array &$book, $index, $percentage) {
    $book['price'] += round($percentage * $book['price'], 2);
};
```

This preceding anonymous function gets assigned to the variable $addTaxes. It expects three arguments: $book (an array as a reference), $index (not used), and $percentage. The function adds taxes to the price key of the book, rounded to 2 decimal places (round is a native PHP function). Do not mind the argument $index, it is not used in this function, but forced by how we will use it, as you will see.

You could instantiate a list of books as an array, iterate them, and then call this function each time. An example could be as follows:

```
$books = [
    ['title' => '1984', 'price' => 8.15],
    ['title' => 'Don Quijote', 'price' => 12.00],
    ['title' => 'Odyssey', 'price' => 3.55]
];
foreach ($books as $index => $book) {
    $addTaxes($book, $index, 0.16);
}
var_dump($books);
```

In order to use the function, you just invoke it as if $addTaxes contained the name of the function to be invoked. The rest of the function works as if it was a normal function: it receives arguments, it can return a value, and it has a scope. What is the benefit of defining it in this way? One possible application would be to use it as a **callable**. A callable is a variable type that identifies a function that PHP can call. You send this callable variable as an argument, and the function that receives it can invoke it. Take the PHP native function, array_walk. It gets an array, a callable, and some extra arguments. PHP will iterate the array, and for each element, it will invoke the callable function (just like the foreach loop). So, you can replace the whole loop by just the following:

```
array_walk($books, $addTaxes, 0.16);
```

The callable that array_walk receives needs to take at least two arguments: the value and the index of the current element of the array, and thus, the $index argument that we were forced to implement previously. It can optionally take extra arguments, which will be the extra arguments sent to array_walk—in this case, the 0.16 as $percentage.

Actually, anonymous functions are not the only callable in PHP. You can send normal functions and even class methods. Let's see how:

```
function addTaxes(array &$book, $index, $percentage) {
    if (isset($book['price'])) {
        $book['price'] += round($percentage * $book['price'], 2);
    }
}

class Taxes {
    public static function add(array &$book, $index, $percentage)
    {
        if (isset($book['price'])) {
            $book['price'] += round($percentage * $book['price'], 2);
        }
    }
    public function addTaxes(array &$book, $index, $percentage)
    {
        if (isset($book['price'])) {
            $book['price'] += round($percentage * $book['price'], 2);
        }
    }
}

// using normal function
array_walk($books, 'addTaxes', 0.16);
```

```
var_dump($books);

// using static class method
array_walk($books, ['Taxes', 'add'], 0.16);
var_dump($books);

// using class method
array_walk($books, [new Taxes(), 'addTaxes'], 0.16);
var_dump($books);
```

In the preceding example, you can see how we can use each case as a callable. For normal methods, just send the name of the method as a string. For static methods of a class, send an array with the name of the class in a way that PHP understands (either the full name including namespace, or adding the use keyword beforehand), and the name of the method, both as strings. To use a normal method of a class, you need to send an array with an instance of that class and the method name as a string.

OK, so anonymous functions can be used as callable, just as any other function or method can. So what is so special about them? One of the things is that anonymous functions are variables, and so they have all the advantages — or disadvantages — that a variable has. That includes scope — that is, the function is defined inside a scope, and as soon as this scope ends, the function will no longer be accessible. That can be useful if your function is extremely specific to that bit of code, and there is no way you will want to reuse it somewhere else. Moreover, as it is nameless, you will not have conflicts with any other existing function.

There is another benefit in using anonymous functions: inheriting variables from the parent scope. When you define an anonymous function, you can specify some variable from the scope where it is defined with the keyword use, and use it inside the function. The value of the variable will be the one it had at the moment of declaring the function, even if it is updated later. Let's see an example:

```
$percentage = 0.16;
$addTaxes = function (array &$book, $index) use ($percentage) {
    if (isset($book['price'])) {
        $book['price'] += round($percentage * $book['price'], 2);
    }
};
$percentage = 100000;
array_walk($books, $addTaxes);
var_dump($books);
```

The preceding example shows you how to use the keyword `use`. Even when we update `$percentage` after defining the function, the result shows you that the taxes were only 16%. This is useful, as it liberates you from having to send `$percentage` everywhere you want to use the function `$addTaxes`. If there is a scenario where you really need to have the updated value of the used variables, you can declare them as a reference as you would with a normal function's argument:

```
$percentage = 0.16;
$addTaxes = function (array &$book, $index) use (&$percentage) {
    if (isset($book['price'])) {
        $book['price'] += round($percentage * $book['price'], 2);
    }
};

array_walk($books, $addTaxes, 0.16);
var_dump($books);

$percentage = 100000;
array_walk($books, $addTaxes, 0.16);
var_dump($books);
```

In this last example, the first `array_walk` used the original value 0.16, as that was still the value of the variable. But on the second call, `$percentage` had already changed, and it affected the result of the anonymous function.

Summary

In this chapter, you have learned what object-oriented programming is, and how to apply it to our web application for creating a clean code, which is easy to maintain. You also know how to manage exceptions properly, the design patterns that are used the most, and how to use anonymous functions when necessary.

In the next chapter, we will explain how to manage the data of your application using databases so that you can completely separate data from code.

5
Using Databases

Data is probably the cornerstone of most web applications. Sure, your application has to be pretty, fast, error-free, and so on, but if something is essential to users, it is what data you can manage for them. From this, we can extract that managing data is one of the most important things you have to consider when designing your application.

Managing data implies not only storing read-only files and reading them when needed, as we were doing so far, but also adding, fetching, updating, and removing individual pieces of information. For this, we need a tool that categorizes our data and makes these tasks easier for us, and this is when databases come into play.

In this chapter, you will learn about:

- Schemas and tables
- Manipulating and querying data
- Using PDO to connect your database with PHP
- Indexing your data
- Constructing complex queries in joining tables

Introducing databases

Databases are tools to manage data. The basic functions of a database are inserting, searching, updating, and deleting data, even though most database systems do more than this. Databases are classified into two different categories depending on how they store data: relational and nonrelational databases.

Relational databases structure data in a very detailed way, forcing the user to use a defined format and allowing the creation of connections—that is, relations—between different pieces of information. Nonrelational databases are systems that store data in a more relaxed way, as though there were no apparent structure. Even though with these very vague definitions you could assume that everybody would like to use relational databases, both systems are very useful; it just depends on how you want to use them.

In this book, we will focus on relational databases as they are widely used in small web applications, in which there are not huge amounts of data. The reason is that usually the application contains data that is interrelated; for example, our application could store sales, which are composed of customers and books.

MySQL

MySQL has been the favorite choice of PHP developers for quite a long time. It is a relational database system that uses SQL as the language to communicate with the system. SQL is used in quite a few other systems, which makes things easier in case you need to switch databases or just need to understand an application with a different database than the one you are used to. The rest of the chapter will be focused on MySQL, but it will be helpful for you even if you choose a different SQL system.

In order to use MySQL, you need to install two applications: the server and the client. You might remember server-client applications from *Chapter 2, Web Applications with PHP*. The MySQL server is a program that listens for instructions or queries from clients, executes them, and returns a result. You need to start the server in order to access the database; take a look at *Chapter 1, Setting Up the Environment*, on how to do this. The client is an application that allows you to construct instructions and send them to the server, and it is the one that you will use.

GUI versus command line

The Graphical User Interface (GUI) is very common when using a database. It helps you in constructing instructions, and you can even manage data without them using just visual tables. On the other hand, command-line clients force you to write all the commands by hand, but they are lighter than GUIs, faster to start, and force you to remember how to write SQL, which you need when you write your applications in PHP. Also, in general, almost any machine with a database will have a MySQL client but might not have a graphical application.

You can choose the one that you are more comfortable with as you will usually work with your own machine. However, keep in mind that a basic knowledge of the command line will save your life on several occasions.

In order to connect the client with a server, you need to provide some information on where to connect and the credentials for the user to use. If you do not customize your MySQL installation, you should at least have a root user with no password, which is the one we will use. You could think that this seems to be a horrible security hole, and it might be so, but you should not be able to connect using this user if you do not connect from the same machine on which the server is. The most common arguments that you can use to provide information when starting the client are:

- `-u <name>`: This specifies the user—in our case, `root`.

- `-p<password>`: Without a space, this specifies the password. As we do not have a password for our user, we do not need to provide this.

- `-h <host>`: This specifies where to connect. By default, the client connects to the same machine. As this is our case, there is no need to specify any. If you had to, you could specify either an IP address or a hostname.

- `<schema name>`: This specifies the name of the schema to use. We will explain in a bit what this means.

With these rules, you should be able to connect to your database with the `mysql -u root` command. You should get an output very similar to the following one:

```
$ mysql -u root
Welcome to the MySQL monitor.  Commands end with ; or \g.
Your MySQL connection id is 2
Server version: 5.1.73 Source distribution


Copyright (c) 2000, 2013, Oracle and/or its affiliates. All rights
reserved.


Oracle is a registered trademark of Oracle Corporation and/or its
affiliates. Other names may be trademarks of their respective
owners.


Type 'help;' or '\h' for help. Type '\c' to clear the current input
statement.


mysql>
```

The terminal will show you the version of the server and some useful information about how to use the client. From now on, the command line will start with `mysql>` instead of your normal prompt, showing you that you are using the MySQL client. In order to execute queries, just type the query, end it with a semicolon, and press *Enter*. The client will send the query to the server and will show the result of it. To exit the client, you can either type \q and press *Enter* or press *Ctrl* + *D*, even though this last option will depend on your operating system.

Schemas and tables

Relational database systems usually have the same structure. They store data in different databases or **schemas**, which separate the data from different applications. These schemas are just collections of **tables**. Tables are definitions of specific data structures and are composed of **fields**. A field is a basic data type that defines the smallest component of information as though they were the atoms of the data. So, schemas are group of tables that are composed of fields. Let's look at each of these elements.

Understanding schemas

As defined before, schemas or databases— in MySQL, they are synonyms—are collections of tables with a common context, usually belonging to the same application. Actually, there are no restrictions around this, and you could have several schemas belonging to the same application if needed. However, for small web applications, as it is our case, we will have just one schema.

Your server probably already has some schemas. They usually contain the metadata needed for MySQL in order to operate, and we highly recommend that you do not modify them. Instead, let's just create our own schema. Schemas are quite simple elements, and they only have a mandatory name and an optional charset. The name identifies the schema, and the charset defines which type of codification or "alphabet" the strings should follow. As the default charset is `latin1`, if you do not need to change it, you do not need to specify it.

Use CREATE SCHEMA followed by the name of the schema in order to create the schema that we will use for our bookstore. The name has to be representative, so let's name it `bookstore`. Remember to end your line with a semicolon. Take a look at the following:

```
mysql> CREATE SCHEMA bookstore;
Query OK, 1 row affected (0.00 sec)
```

If you need to remember how a schema was created, you can use SHOW CREATE
SCHEMA to see its description, as follows:

```
mysql> SHOW CREATE SCHEMA bookstore \G
*************************** 1. row ***************************
        Database: bookstore
Create Database: CREATE DATABASE `bookstore` /*!40100 DEFAULT CHARACTER
SET latin1 */
1 row in set (0.00 sec)
```

As you can see, we ended the query with \G instead of a semicolon. This tells the
client to format the response in a different way than the semicolon does. When using
a command of the SHOW CREATE family, we recommend that you end it with \G to
get a better understanding.

Should you use uppercase or lowercase?

When writing queries, you might note that we used uppercase for
keywords and lowercase for identifiers, such as names of schemas.
This is just a convention widely used in order to make it clear what is
part of SQL and what is your data. However, MySQL keywords are
case-insensitive, so you could use any case indistinctively.

All data must belong to a schema. There cannot be data floating around outside
all schemas. This way, you cannot do anything unless you specify the schema you
want to use. In order to do this, just after starting your client, use the USE keyword
followed by the name of the schema. Optionally, you could tell the client which
schema to use when connecting to it, as follows:

```
mysql> USE bookstore;
Database changed
```

If you do not remember what the name of your schema is or want to check which
other schemas are in your server, you can run the SHOW SCHEMAS; command to get a
list of them, as follows:

```
mysql> SHOW SCHEMAS;
+--------------------+
| Database           |
+--------------------+
| information_schema |
| bookstore          |
```

```
| mysql              |
| test               |
+--------------------+
4 rows in set (0.00 sec)
```

Database data types

As in PHP, MySQL also has data types. They are used to define which kind of data a field can contain. As in PHP, MySQL is quite flexible with data types, transforming them from one type to the other if needed. There are quite a few of them, but we will explain the most important ones. We highly recommend that you visit the official documentation related to data types at `http://dev.mysql.com/doc/refman/5.7/en/data-types.html` if you want to build applications with more complex data structures.

Numeric data types

Numeric data can be categorized as integers or decimal numbers. For integers, MySQL uses the INT data type even though there are versions to store smaller numbers, such as TINYINT, SMALLINT, or MEDIUMINT, or bigger numbers, such as BIGINT. The following table shows what the sizes of the different numeric types are, so you can choose which one to use depending on your situation:

Type	Size/precision
TINYINT	-128 to 127
SMALLINT	-32,768 to 32,767
MEDIUMINT	-8,388,608 to 8,388,607
INT	-2,147,483,648 to 2,147,483,647
BIGINT	-9,223,372,036,854,775,808 to 9,223,372,036,854,775,807

Numeric types can be defined as signed by default or unsigned; that is, you can allow or not allow them to contain negative values. If a numeric type is defined as UNSIGNED, the range of numbers that it can take is doubled as it does not need to save space for negative numbers.

For decimal numbers we have two types: approximate values, which are faster to process but are not exact sometimes, and exact values that give you exact precision on the decimal value. For approximate values or the floating-point type, we have FLOAT and DOUBLE. For exact values or the fixed-point type we have DECIMAL.

MySQL allows you to specify the number of digits and decimal positions that the number can take. For example, to specify a number that can contains five digits and up to two of them can be decimal, we will use the FLOAT(5,2) notation. This is useful as a constraint, as you will note when we create tables with prices.

String data types

Even though there are several data types that allow you to store from single characters to big chunks of text or binary code, it is outside the scope of this chapter. In this section, we will introduce you to three types: CHAR, VARCHAR, and TEXT.

CHAR is a data type that allows you to store an exact number of characters. You need to specify how long the string will be once you define the field, and from this point on, all values for this field have to be of this length. One possible usage in our applications could be when storing the ISBN of the book as we know it is always 13 characters long.

VARCHAR or variable char is a data type that allows you to store strings up to 65,535 characters long. You do not need to specify how long they need to be, and you can insert strings of different lengths without an issue. Of course, the fact that this type is dynamic makes it slower to process compared with the previous one, but after a few times you know how long a string will always be. You could tell MySQL that even if you want to insert strings of different lengths, the maximum length will be a determined number. This will help its performance. For example, names are of different lengths, but you can safely assume that no name will be longer than 64 characters, so your field could be defined as VARCHAR(64).

Finally, TEXT is a data type for really big strings. You could use it if you want to store long comments from users, articles, and so on. As with INT, there are different versions of this data type: TINYTEXT, TEXT, MEDIUMTEXT, and LONGTEXT. Even if they are very important in almost any web application with user interaction, we will not use them in ours.

List of values

In MySQL, you can force a field to have a set of valid values. There are two types of them: ENUM, which allows exactly one of the possible predefined values, and SET, which allows any number of the predefined values.

For example, in our application, we have two types of customers: basic and premium. If we want to store our customers in a database, there is a chance that one of the fields will be the type of customer. As a customer has to be either basic or premium, a good solution would be to define the field as an enum as ENUM("basic", "premium"). In this way, we will make sure that all customers stored in our database will be of a correct type.

Although enums are quite common to use, the use of sets is less widespread. It is usually a better idea to use an extra table to define the values of the list, as you will note when we talk about foreign keys in this chapter.

Date and time data types

Date and time types are the most complex data types in MySQL. Even though the idea is simple, there are several functions and edge cases around these types. We cannot go through all of them, so we will just explain the most common uses, which are the ones we will need for our application.

DATE stores dates—that is, a combination of day, month, and year. TIME stores times—that is, a combination of hour, minute, and second. DATETIME are data types for both date and time. For any of these data types, you can provide just a string specifying what the value is, but you need to be careful with the format that you use. Even though you can always specify the format that you are entering the data in, you can just enter the dates or times in the default format—for example, 2014-12-31 for dates, 14:34:50 for time, and 2014-12-31 14:34:50 for the date and time.

A fourth type is TIMESTAMP. This type stores an integer, which is the representation of the seconds from January 1, 1970, which is also known as the Unix timestamp. This is a very useful type as in PHP, it is really easy to get the current Unix timestamp with the now() function, and the format for this data type is always the same, so it is safer to work with it. The downside is that the range of dates that it can represent is limited as compared to other types.

There are some functions that help you manage these types. These functions extract specific parts of the whole value, return the value with a different format, add or subtract dates, and so on. Let's take a look at a short list of them:

Function name	Description
DAY(), MONTH(), and YEAR()	Extracts the specific value for the day, month, or year from the DATE or DATETIME provided value.
HOUR(), MINUTE(), and SECOND()	Extracts the specific value for the hour, minute, or second from the TIME or DATETIME provided value.
CURRENT_DATE() and CURRENT_TIME()	Returns the current date or current time.
NOW()	Returns the current date and time.
DATE_FORMAT()	Returns the DATE, TIME or DATETIME value with the specified format.
DATE_ADD()	Adds the specified interval of time to a given date or time type.

Do not worry if you are confused on how to use any of these functions; we will use them during the rest of the book as part of our application. Also, an extensive list of all the types can be found at `http://dev.mysql.com/doc/refman/5.7/en/date-and-time-functions.html`.

Managing tables

Now that you understand the different types of data that fields can take, it is time to introduce tables. As defined in the *Schemas and tables* section, a table is a collection of fields that defines a type of information. You could compare it with OOP and think of tables as classes, fields being their properties. Each instance of the class would be a row on the table.

When defining a table, you have to declare the list of fields that the table contains. For each field, you need to specify its name, its type, and some extra information depending on the type of the field. The most common are:

- NOT NULL: This is used if the field cannot be null—that is, if it needs a concrete valid value for each row. By default, a field can be null.
- UNSIGNED: As mentioned earlier, this is used to forbid the use of negative numbers in this field. By default, a numeric field accepts negative numbers.
- DEFAULT <value>: This defines a default value in case the user does not provide any. Usually, the default value is null if this clause is not specified.

Table definitions also need a name, as with schemas, and some optional attributes. You can define the charset of the table or its engine. Engines can be a quite large topic to cover, but for the scope of this chapter, let's just note that we should use the InnoDB engine if we need strong relationships between tables. For more advanced readers, you can read more about MySQL engines at `https://dev.mysql.com/doc/refman/5.0/en/storage-engines.html`.

Knowing this, let's try to create a table that will keep our books. The name of the table should be `book`, as each row will define a book. The fields could have the same properties the `Book` class has. Let's take a look at how the query to construct the table would look:

```
mysql> CREATE TABLE book(
    -> isbn CHAR(13) NOT NULL,
    -> title VARCHAR(255) NOT NULL,
    -> author VARCHAR(255) NOT NULL,
    -> stock SMALLINT UNSIGNED NOT NULL DEFAULT 0,
    -> price FLOAT UNSIGNED
    -> ) ENGINE=InnoDb;
Query OK, 0 rows affected (0.01 sec)
```

As you can note, we can add more new lines until we end the query with a semicolon. With this, we can format the query in a way that looks more readable. MySQL will let us know that we are still writing the same query showing the `->` prompt. As this table contains five fields, it is very likely that we will need to refresh our minds from time to time as we will forget them. In order to display the structure of the table, you could use the DESC command, as follows:

```
mysql> DESC book;
+--------+----------------------+------+-----+---------+-------+
| Field  | Type                 | Null | Key | Default | Extra |
+--------+----------------------+------+-----+---------+-------+
| isbn   | char(13)             | NO   |     | NULL    |       |
| title  | varchar(255)         | NO   |     | NULL    |       |
| author | varchar(255)         | NO   |     | NULL    |       |
| stock  | smallint(5) unsigned | NO   |     | 0       |       |
| price  | float unsigned       | YES  |     | NULL    |       |
+--------+----------------------+------+-----+---------+-------+
5 rows in set (0.00 sec)
```

We used SMALLINT for `stock` as it is very unlikely that we will have more than thousands of copies of the same book. As we know that ISBN is 13 characters long, we enforced this when defining the field. Finally, both `stock` and `price` are unsigned as negative values do not make sense. Let's now create our `customer` table via the following script:

```
mysql> CREATE TABLE customer(
    -> id INT UNSIGNED NOT NULL,
    -> firstname VARCHAR(255) NOT NULL,
    -> surname VARCHAR(255) NOT NULL,
    -> email VARCHAR(255) NOT NULL,
    -> type ENUM('basic', 'premium')
    -> ) ENGINE=InnoDb;
Query OK, 0 rows affected (0.00 sec)
```

We already anticipated the use of enum for the field type as when designing classes, we could draw a diagram identifying the content of our database. On this, we could show the tables and their fields. Let's take a look at how the diagram of tables would look so far:

book		customer	
isbn varchar(13)		id int(10)	
title varchar(255)		firstname varchar(255)	
author varchar(255)		surname varchar(255)	
stock smallint(5)		email varchar(255)	
price float		type enum('basic' , 'premium')	

Note that even if we create tables similar to our classes, we will not create a table for Person. The reason is that databases store data, and there isn't any data that we could store for this class as the customer table already contains everything we need. Also, sometimes, we may create tables that do not exist as classes on our code, so the class-table relationship is a very flexible one.

Keys and constraints

Now that we have our main tables defined, let's try to think about how the data inside would look. Each row inside a table would describe an object, which may be either a book or a customer. What would happen if our application has a bug and allows us to create books or customers with the same data? How will the database differentiate them? In theory, we will assign IDs to customers in order to avoid these scenarios, but how do we enforce that the ID not be repeated?

MySQL has a mechanism that allows you to enforce certain restrictions on your data. Other than attributes such as NOT NULL or UNSIGNED that you already saw, you can tell MySQL that certain fields are more special than others and instruct it to add some behavior to them. These mechanisms are called **keys**, and there are four types: primary key, unique key, foreign key, and index. Let's take a closer look at them.

Primary keys

Primary keys are fields that identify a unique row from a table. There cannot be two of the same value in the same table, and they cannot be null. Adding a primary key to a table that defines *objects* is almost a must as it will assure you that you will always be able to differentiate two rows by this field.

Another part that makes primary keys so attractive is their ability to set the primary key as an autoincremental numeric value; that is, you do not have to assign a value to the ID, and MySQL will just pick up the latest inserted ID and increment it by 1, as we did with our Unique trait. Of course, for this to happen, your field has to be an integer data type. In fact, we highly recommend that you always define your primary key as an integer, even if the real-life object does not really have this ID at all. The reason is that you should search a row by this numeric ID, which is unique, and MySQL will add some performance improvements that come by setting the field as a key.

Then, let's add an ID to our book table. In order to add a new field, we need to alter our table. There is a command that allows you to do this: ALTER TABLE. With this command, you can modify the definition of any existing field, add new ones, or remove existing ones. As we add the field that will be our primary key and be autoincremental, we can add all these modifiers to the field definition. Execute the following code:

```
mysql> ALTER TABLE book
    -> ADD id INT UNSIGNED NOT NULL AUTO_INCREMENT
    -> PRIMARY KEY FIRST;
Query OK, 0 rows affected (0.02 sec)
Records: 0  Duplicates: 0  Warnings: 0
```

Note FIRST at the end of the command. When adding new fields, if you want them to appear on a different position than at the end of the table, you need to specify the position. It could be either FIRST or AFTER <other field>. For convenience, the primary key of a table is the first of its fields.

As the table customer already has an ID field, we do not have to add it again but rather modify it. In order to do this, we will just use the ALTER TABLE command with the MODIFY option, specifying the new definition of an already existing field, as follows:

```
mysql> ALTER TABLE customer
    -> MODIFY id INT UNSIGNED NOT NULL
    -> AUTO_INCREMENT PRIMARY KEY;
Query OK, 0 rows affected (0.00 sec)
Records: 0  Duplicates: 0  Warnings: 0
```

Foreign keys

Let's imagine that we need to keep track of the borrowed books. The table should contain the borrowed book, who borrowed it, and when it was borrowed. So, what kind of data would you use to identify the book or the customer? Would you use the title or the name? Well, we should use something that identifies a unique row from these tables, and this "something" is the primary key. With this action, we will eliminate the change of using a reference that can potentially point to two or more rows at the same time.

We could then create a table that contains `book_id` and `customer_id` as numeric fields, containing the IDs that reference these two tables. As the first approach, it makes sense, but we can find some weaknesses. For example, what happens if we insert wrong IDs and they do not exist in `book` or `customer`? We could have some code in our PHP side to make sure that when fetching information from `borrowed_books`, we only displayed the information that is correct. We could even have a routine that periodically checks for wrong rows and removes them, solving the issue of having wrong data wasting space in the disk. However, as with the `Unique` trait versus adding primary keys in MySQL, it is usually better to allow the database system to manage these things as the performance will usually be better, and you do not need to write extra code.

MySQL allows you to create keys that enforce references to other tables. These are called **foreign keys**, and they are the primary reason for which we were forced to use the InnoDB table engine instead of any other. A foreign key defines and enforces a reference between this field and another row of a different table. If the ID supplied for the field with a foreign key does not exist in the referenced table, the query will fail. Furthermore, if you have a valid `borrowed_books` row pointing to an existing book and you remove the entry from the book table, MySQL will complain about it—even though you will be able to customize this behavior soon—as this action would leave wrong data in the system. As you can note, this is way more useful than having to write code to manage these cases.

Let's create the `borrowed_books` table with the book, customer references, and dates. Note that we have to define the foreign keys after the definition of the fields as opposed to when we defined primary keys, as follows:

```
mysql> CREATE TABLE borrowed_books(
    -> book_id INT UNSIGNED NOT NULL,
    -> customer_id INT UNSIGNED NOT NULL,
    -> start DATETIME NOT NULL,
    -> end DATETIME DEFAULT NULL,
    -> FOREIGN KEY (book_id) REFERENCES book(id),
```

```
    -> FOREIGN KEY (customer_id) REFERENCES customer(id)

    -> ) ENGINE=InnoDb;
Query OK, 0 rows affected (0.00 sec)
```

As with SHOW CREATE SCHEMA, you can also check how the table looks. This command will also show you information about the keys as opposed to the DESC command. Let's take a look at how it would work:

```
mysql> SHOW CREATE TABLE borrowed_books \G
*************************** 1. row ***************************
       Table: borrowed_books
Create Table: CREATE TABLE `borrowed_books` (
  `book_id` int(10) unsigned NOT NULL,
  `customer_id` int(10) unsigned NOT NULL,
  `start` datetime NOT NULL,
  `end` datetime DEFAULT NULL,
  KEY `book_id` (`book_id`),
  KEY `customer_id` (`customer_id`),
  CONSTRAINT `borrowed_books_ibfk_1` FOREIGN KEY (`book_id`) REFERENCES
`book` (`id`),
  CONSTRAINT `borrowed_books_ibfk_2` FOREIGN KEY (`customer_id`)
REFERENCES `customer` (`id`)
) ENGINE=InnoDB DEFAULT CHARSET=latin1
1 row in set (0.00 sec)
```

Note two important things here. On one hand, we have two extra keys that we did not define. The reason is that when defining a foreign key, MySQL also defines the field as a key that will be used to improve performance on the table; we will look into this in a moment. The other element to note is the fact that MySQL defines names to the keys by itself. This is necessary as we need to be able to reference them in case we want to change or remove this key. You can let MySQL name the keys for you, or you can specify the names you prefer when creating them.

We are running a bookstore, and even if we allow customers to borrow books, we want to be able to sell them. A sale is a very important element that we need to track down as customers may want to review them, or you may just need to provide this information for taxation purposes. As opposed to borrowing, in which knowing the book, customer, and date was more than enough, here, we need to set IDs to the sales in order to identify them to the customers.

However, this table is more difficult to design than the other ones and not just because of the ID. Think about it: do customers buy books one by one? Or do they rather buy any number of books at once? Thus, we need to allow the table to contain an undefined amount of books. With PHP, this is easy as we would just use an array, but we do not have arrays in MySQL. There are two options to this problem.

One solution could be to set the ID of the sale as a normal integer field and not as a primary key. In this way, we would be able to insert several rows to the sales table, one for each borrowed book. However, this solution is less than ideal as we miss the opportunity of defining a very good primary key because it has the sales ID. Also, we are duplicating the data about the customer and date since they will always be the same.

The second solution, the one that we will implement, is the creation of a separated table that acts as a "list". We will still have our sales table, which will contain the ID of the sale as a primary key, the customer ID as a foreign key, and the dates. However, we will create a second table that we could name sale_book, and we will define there the ID of the sale, the ID of the book, and the amount of books of the same copy that the customer bought. In this way, we will have at once the information about the customer and date, and we will be able to insert as many rows as needed in our sale_book list-table without duplicating any data. Let's take a look at how we would create these:

```
mysql> CREATE TABLE sale(
    -> id INT UNSIGNED NOT NULL AUTO_INCREMENT PRIMARY KEY,
    -> customer_id INT UNSIGNED NOT NULL,
    -> date DATETIME NOT NULL,
    -> FOREIGN KEY (customer_id) REFERENCES customer(id)
    -> ) ENGINE=InnoDb;
Query OK, 0 rows affected (0.00 sec)


mysql> CREATE TABLE sale_book(
    -> sale_id INT UNSIGNED NOT NULL,
    -> book_id INT UNSIGNED NOT NULL,
    -> amount SMALLINT UNSIGNED NOT NULL DEFAULT 1,
    -> FOREIGN KEY (sale_id) REFERENCES sale(id),
    -> FOREIGN KEY (book_id) REFERENCES book(id)
    -> ) ENGINE=InnoDb;
Query OK, 0 rows affected (0.00 sec)
```

Keep in mind that you should always create the `sales` table first because if you create the `sale_book` table with a foreign key first, referencing a table that does not exist yet, MySQL will complain.

We created three new tables in this section, and they are interrelated. It is a good time to update the diagram of tables. Note that we link the fields with the tables when there is a foreign key defined. Take a look:

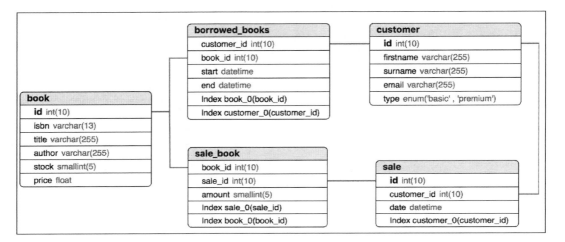

Unique keys

As you know, primary keys are extremely useful as they provide several features with them. One of these is that the field has to be unique. However, you can define only one primary key per table, even though you might have several fields that are unique. In order to amend this limitation, MySQL incorporates **unique keys**. Their job is to make sure that the field is not repeated in multiple rows, but they do not come with the rest of the functionalities of primary keys, such as being autoincremental. Also, unique keys can be null.

Our `book` and `customer` tables contain good candidates for unique keys. Books can potentially have the same title, and surely, there will be more than one book by the same author. However, they also have an ISBN which is unique; two different books should not have the same ISBN. In the same way, even if two customers were to have the same name, their e-mail addresses will be always different. Let's add the two keys with the ALTER TABLE command, though you can also add them when creating the table as we did with foreign keys, as follows:

```
mysql> ALTER TABLE book ADD UNIQUE KEY (isbn);
Query OK, 0 rows affected (0.01 sec)
Records: 0  Duplicates: 0  Warnings: 0


mysql> ALTER TABLE customer ADD UNIQUE KEY (email);
Query OK, 0 rows affected (0.01 sec)
Records: 0  Duplicates: 0  Warnings: 0
```

Indexes

Indexes, which are a synonym for keys, are fields that do not need any special behavior as do the rest of the keys but they are important enough in our queries. So, we will ask MySQL to do some work with them in order to perform better when querying by this field. Do you remember when adding a foreign key that MySQL added extra keys to the table? Those were indexes too.

Think about how the application will use the database. We want to show the catalog of books to our customers, but we cannot show all of them at once for sure. The customer will want to filter the results, and one of the most common ways of filtering is by specifying the title of the book that they are looking for. From this, we can extract that the title will be used to filter books quite often, so we want to add an index to this field. Let's add the index via the following code:

```
mysql> ALTER TABLE book ADD INDEX (title);
Query OK, 0 rows affected (0.01 sec)
Records: 0  Duplicates: 0  Warnings: 0
```

Remember that all other keys also provide indexing. IDs of books, customers and sales, ISBNs, and e-mails are already indexed, so there is no need to add another index here. Also, try not to add indexes to every single field as in doing so you will be **overindexing**, which would make some types of queries even slower than if they were without indexes!

Inserting data

We have created the perfect tables to hold our data, but so far they are empty. It is time that we populate them. We delayed this moment as altering tables with data is more difficult than when they are empty.

In order to insert this data, we will use the INSERT INTO command. This command will take the name of the table, the fields that you want to populate, and the data for each field. Note that you can choose not to specify the value for a field, and there are different reasons to do this, which are as follows:

- The field has a default value, and we are happy using it for this specific row

- Even though the field does not have an explicit default value, the field can take null values; so, by not specifying the field, MySQL will automatically insert a null here

- The field is a primary key and is autoincremental, and we want to let MySQL take the next ID for us

There are different reasons that can cause an INSERT INTO command to fail:

- If you do not specify the value of a field and MySQL cannot provide a valid default value

- If the value provided is not of the type of the field and MySQL fails to find a valid conversion

- If you specify that you want to set the value for a field but you fail to provide a value

- If you provide a foreign key with an ID but the ID does not exist in the referenced table

Let's take a look at how to add rows. Let's start with our customer table, adding one basic and one premium, as follows:

```
mysql> INSERT INTO customer (firstname, surname, email, type)
    -> VALUES ("Han", "Solo", "han@tatooine.com", "premium");
Query OK, 1 row affected (0.00 sec)

mysql> INSERT INTO customer (firstname, surname, email, type)
    -> VALUES ("James", "Kirk", "enter@prise", "basic");
Query OK, 1 row affected (0.00 sec)
```

Note that MySQL shows you some return information; in this case, it shows that there was one row affected, which is the row that we inserted. We did not provide an ID, so MySQL just added the next ones in the list. As it is the first time that we are adding data, MySQL used the IDs 1 and 2.

Let's try to trick MySQL and add another customer, repeating the e-mail address field that we set as unique in the previous section:

```
mysql> INSERT INTO customer (firstname, surname, email, type)
    -> VALUES ("Mr", "Spock", "enter@prise", "basic");
ERROR 1062 (23000): Duplicate entry 'enter@prise' for key 'email'
```

An error is returned with an error code and an error message, and the row was not inserted, of course. The error message usually contains enough information in order to understand the issue and how to fix it. If this is not the case, we can always try to search on the Internet using the error code and note what either the official documentation or other users have to say about it.

In case you need to introduce multiple rows to the same table and they contain the same fields, there is a shorter version of the command, in which you can specify the fields and then provide the groups of values for each row. Let's take a look at how to use it when adding books to our book table, as follows:

```
mysql> INSERT INTO book (isbn,title,author,stock,price) VALUES
    -> ("9780882339726","1984","George Orwell",12,7.50),
    -> ("9789724621081","1Q84","Haruki Murakami",9,9.75),
    -> ("9780736692427","Animal Farm","George Orwell",8,3.50),
    -> ("9780307350169","Dracula","Bram Stoker",30,10.15),
    -> ("9780753179246","19 minutes","Jodi Picoult",0,10);
Query OK, 5 rows affected (0.01 sec)
Records: 5  Duplicates: 0  Warnings: 0
```

As with customers, we will not specify the ID and let MySQL choose the appropriate one. Note also that now the amount of affected rows is 5 as we inserted five rows.

How can we take advantage of the explicit defaults that we defined in our tables? Well, we can do this in the same way as we did with the primary keys: do not specify them in the fields list or in the values list, and MySQL will just use the default value. For example, we defined a default value of 1 for our book.stock field, which is a useful notation for the book table and the stock field. Let's add another row using this default, as follows:

```
mysql> INSERT INTO book (isbn,title,author,price) VALUES
    -> ("9781416500360", "Odyssey", "Homer", 4.23);
Query OK, 1 row affected (0.00 sec)
```

Now that we have books and customers, let's add some historic data about customers borrowing books. For this, use the numeric IDs from book and customer, as in the following code:

```
mysql> INSERT INTO borrowed_books(book_id,customer_id,start,end)
    -> VALUES
    -> (1, 1, "2014-12-12", "2014-12-28"),
    -> (4, 1, "2015-01-10", "2015-01-13"),
    -> (4, 2, "2015-02-01", "2015-02-10"),
    -> (1, 2, "2015-03-12", NULL);
Query OK, 3 rows affected (0.00 sec)
Records: 3  Duplicates: 0  Warnings: 0
```

Querying data

It took quite a lot of time, but we are finally in the most exciting—and useful—section related to databases: querying data. Querying data refers to asking MySQL to return rows from the specified table and optionally filtering these results by a set of rules. You can also choose to get specific fields instead of the whole row. In order to query data, we will use the SELECT command, as follows:

```
mysql> SELECT firstname, surname, type FROM customer;
+-----------+---------+---------+
| firstname | surname | type    |
+-----------+---------+---------+
| Han       | Solo    | premium |
| James     | Kirk    | basic   |
+-----------+---------+---------+
2 rows in set (0.00 sec)
```

One of the simplest ways to query data is to specify the fields of interest after SELECT and specify the table with the FROM keyword. As we did not add any filters—mostly known as conditions—to the query, we got all the rows there. Sometimes, this is the desired behavior, but the most common thing to do is to add conditions to the query to retrieve only the rows that we need. Use the WHERE keyword to achieve this.

```
mysql> SELECT firstname, surname, type FROM customer
    -> WHERE id = 1;
+-----------+---------+---------+
| firstname | surname | type    |
```

```
+-----------+---------+---------+
| Han       | Solo    | premium |
+-----------+---------+---------+
```
1 row in set (0.00 sec)

Adding conditions is very similar to when we created Boolean expressions in PHP. We will specify the name of the field, an operator, and a value, and MySQL will retrieve only the rows that return `true` to this expression. In this case, we asked for the customers that had the ID 1, and MySQL returned one row: the one that had an ID of exactly 1.

A common query would be to get the books that start with some text. We cannot construct this expression with any comparison operand that you know, such as = and < or >, since we want to match only a part of the string. For this, MySQL has the `LIKE` operator, which takes a string that can contain wildcards. A wildcard is a character that represents a rule, matching any number of characters that follows the rule. For example, the % wildcard represents any number of characters, so using the 1% string would match any string that starts with 1 and is followed by any number or characters, matching strings such as 1984 or 1Q84. Let's consider the following example:

```
mysql> SELECT title, author, price FROM book
    -> WHERE title LIKE "1%";
+------------+-----------------+-------+
| title      | author          | price |
+------------+-----------------+-------+
| 1984       | George Orwell   |   7.5 |
| 1Q84       | Haruki Murakami |  9.75 |
| 19 minutes | Jodi Picoult    |    10 |
+------------+-----------------+-------+
3 rows in set (0.00 sec)
```

We asked for all the books whose title starts with 1, and we got three rows. You can imagine how useful this operator is, especially when we implement a search utility in our application.

As in PHP, MySQL also allows you to add logical operators—that is, operators that take operands and perform a logical operation, returning Boolean values as a result. The most common logical operators are, as in PHP, AND and OR. AND returns true if both the expressions are true and OR returns true if either of the operands is true. Let's consider an example, as follows:

```
mysql> SELECT title, author, price FROM book
    -> WHERE title LIKE "1%" AND stock > 0;
+------------+------------------+-------+
| title      | author           | price |
+------------+------------------+-------+
| 1984       | George Orwell     |   7.5 |
| 1Q84       | Haruki Murakami  |  9.75 |
+------------+------------------+-------+
2 rows in set (0.00 sec)
```

This example is very similar to the previous one, but we added an extra condition. We asked for all titles starting with 1 and whether there is stock available. This is why one of the books does not show as it does not satisfy both conditions. You can add as many conditions as you need with logical operators but bear in mind that AND operators take precedence over OR. If you want to change this precedence, you can always wrap expressions with a parenthesis, as in PHP.

So far, we have retrieved specific fields when querying for data, but we could ask for all the fields in a given table. To do this, we will just use the * wildcard in SELECT. Let's select all the fields for the customers via the following code:

```
mysql> SELECT * FROM customer \G
*************************** 1. row ***************************
       id: 1
firstname: Han
  surname: Solo
    email: han@tatooine.com
     type: premium
*************************** 2. row ***************************
       id: 2
firstname: James
  surname: Kirk
    email: enter@prise
     type: basic
2 rows in set (0.00 sec)
```

You can retrieve more information than just fields. For example, you can use COUNT to retrieve the amount of rows that satisfy the given conditions instead of retrieving all the columns. This way is faster than retrieving all the columns and then counting them because you save time in reducing the size of the response. Let's consider how it would look:

```
mysql> SELECT COUNT(*) FROM borrowed_books
    -> WHERE customer_id = 1 AND end IS NOT NULL;
+----------+
| COUNT(*) |
+----------+
|        1 |
+----------+
1 row in set (0.00 sec)
```

As you can note, the response says 1, which means that there is only one borrowed book that satisfies the conditions. However, check the conditions; you will note that we used another familiar logical operator: NOT. NOT negates the expression, as ! does in PHP. Note also that we do not use the equal sign to compare with null values. In MySQL, you have to use IS instead of the equals sign in order to compare with NULL. So, the second condition would be satisfied when a borrowed book has an end date that is not null.

Let's finish this section by adding two more features when querying data. The first one is the ability to specify in what order the rows should be returned. To do this, just use the keyword ORDER BY followed by the name of the field that you want to order by. You could also specify whether you want to order in ascending mode, which is by default, or in the descending mode, which can be done by appending DESC. The other feature is the ability to limit the amount of rows to return using LIMIT and the amount of rows to retrieve. Now, run the following:

```
mysql> SELECT id, title, author, isbn FROM book
    -> ORDER BY title LIMIT 4;
+----+-------------+-----------------+----------------+
| id | title       | author          | isbn           |
+----+-------------+-----------------+----------------+
|  5 | 19 minutes  | Jodi Picoult    | 9780753179246  |
|  1 | 1984        | George Orwell   | 9780882339726  |
|  2 | 1Q84        | Haruki Murakami | 9789724621081  |
|  3 | Animal Farm | George Orwell   | 9780736692427  |
+----+-------------+-----------------+----------------+
4 rows in set (0.00 sec)
```

Using PDO

So far, we have worked with MySQL, and you already have a good idea of what you can do with it. However, connecting to the client and performing queries manually is not our goal. What we want to achieve is that our application can take advantage of the database in an automatic way. In order to do this, we will use a set of classes that comes with PHP and allows you to connect to the database and perform queries from the code.

PHP Data Objects (PDO) is the class that connects to the database and allows you to interact with it. This is the popular way to work with databases for PHP developers, even though there are other ways that we will not discuss here. PDO allows you to work with different database systems, so you are not tied to MySQL only. In the following sections, we will consider how to connect to a database, insert data, and retrieve it using this class.

Connecting to the database

In order to connect to the database, it is good practice to keep the credentials—that is, the user and password—separated from the code in a configuration file. We already have this file as config/app.json from when we worked with the Config class. Let's add the correct credentials for our database. If you have the configuration by default, the configuration file should look similar to this:

```
{
  "db": {
    "user": "root",
    "password": ""
  }
}
```

Developers usually specify other information related to the connection, such as the host, port, or name of the database. This will depend on how your application is installed, whether MySQL is running on a different server, and so on, and it is up to you how much information you want to keep on your code and in your configuration files.

In order to connect to the database, we need to instantiate an object from the PDO class. The constructor of this class expects three arguments: **Data Source Name** (**DSN**), which is a string that represents the type of database to use; the name of the user; and the password. We already have the username and password from the Config class, but we still need to build DSN.

One of the formats for MySQL databases is `<database type>:host=<host>;dbname =<schema name>`. As our database system is MySQL, it runs on the same server, and the schema name is `bookstore`, DSN will be `mysql:host=127.0.0.1;dbname=book store`. Let's take a look at how we will put everything together:

```
$dbConfig = Config::getInstance()->get('db');
$db = new PDO(
    'mysql:host=127.0.0.1;dbname=bookstore',
    $dbConfig['user'],
    $dbConfig['password']
);
$db->setAttribute(PDO::ATTR_DEFAULT_FETCH_MODE, PDO::FETCH_ASSOC);
```

Note also that we will invoke the `setAttribute` method from the `PDO` instance. This method allows you to set some options to the connection; in this case, it sets the format of the results coming from MySQL. This option forces MySQL to return the arrays whose keys are the names of the fields, which is way more useful than the default one, returning numeric keys based on the order of the fields. Setting this option now will affect all the queries performed with the `$db` instance, rather than setting the option each time we perform a query.

Performing queries

The easiest way to retrieve data from your database is to use the `query` method. This method accepts the query as a string and returns a list of rows as arrays. Let's consider an example: write the following after the initialization of the database connection—for example, in the `init.php` file:

```
$rows = $db->query('SELECT * FROM book ORDER BY title');
foreach ($rows as $row) {
    var_dump($row);
}
```

This query tries to get all the books in the database, ordering them by the title. This could be the content of a function such as `getAllBooks`, which is used when we display our catalog. Each row is an array that contains all the fields as keys and the data as values.

If you run the application on your browser, you will get the following result:

```
Source of: http://localhost:8000/init.php
 1  array(6) {
 2    'id' =>
 3    string(1) "5"
 4    'isbn' =>
 5    string(13) "9780753179246"
 6    'title' =>
 7    string(10) "19 minutes"
 8    'author' =>
 9    string(12) "Jodi Picoult"
10    'stock' =>
11    string(1) "3"
12    'price' =>
13    string(2) "10"
14  }
15  array(6) {
16    'id' =>
17    string(1) "1"
18    'isbn' =>
19    string(13) "9780882339726"
20    'title' =>
21    string(4) "1984"
22    'author' =>
23    string(13) "George Orwell"
24    'stock' =>
25    string(2) "12"
26    'price' =>
27    string(3) "7.5"
```

The `query` function is useful when we want to retrieve data, but in order to execute queries that insert rows, PDO provides the `exec` function. This function also expects the first parameter as a string, defining the query to execute, but it returns a Boolean specifying whether the execution was successful or not. A good example would be to try to insert books. Type the following:

```
$query = <<<SQL
INSERT INTO book (isbn, title, author, price)
VALUES ("9788187981954", "Peter Pan", "J. M. Barrie", 2.34)
SQL;
$result = $db->exec($query);
var_dump($result); // true
```

This code also uses a new way of representing strings: heredoc. We will enclose the string between `<<<SQL` and `SQL;`, both in different lines, instead of quotes. The benefit of this is the ability to write strings in multiple lines with tabulations or any other blank space, and PHP will respect it. We can construct queries that are easy to read rather than writing them on a single line or having to concatenate the different strings. Note that `SQL` is a token to represent the start and end of the string, but you could use any text that you consider.

The first time you run the application with this code, the query will be executed successfully, and thus, the result will be the Boolean `true`. However, if you run it again, it will return `false` as the ISBN that we inserted is the same but we set its restriction to be unique.

It is useful to know that a query failed, but it is better if we know why. The PDO instance has the `errorInfo` method that returns an array with the information of the last error. The key 2 contains the description, so it is probably the one that we will use more often. Update the previous code with the following:

```
$query = <<<SQL
INSERT INTO book (isbn, title, author, price)
VALUES ("9788187981954", "Peter Pan", "J. M. Barrie", 2.34)
SQL;
$result = $db->exec($query);
var_dump($result); // false
$error = $db->errorInfo()[2];
var_dump($error); // Duplicate entry '9788187981954' for key 'isbn'
```

The result is that the query failed because the ISBN entry was duplicated. Now, we can build more meaningful error messages for our customers or just for debugging purposes.

Prepared statements

The previous two functions are very useful when you need to run quick queries that are always the same. However, in the second example you might note that the string of the query is not very useful as it always inserts the same book. Although it is true that you could just replace the values by variables, it is not good practice as these variables usually come from the user side and can contain malicious code. It is always better to first sanitize these values.

PDO provides the ability to prepare a statement—that is, a query that is parameterized. You can specify parameters for the fields that will change in the query and then assign values to these parameters. Let's consider first an example, as follows:

```
$query = 'SELECT * FROM book WHERE author = :author';
$statement = $db->prepare($query);
$statement->bindValue('author', 'George Orwell');
$statement->execute();
$rows = $statement->fetchAll();
var_dump($rows);
```

The query is a normal one except that it has `:author` instead of the string of the author that we want to find. This is a parameter, and we will identify them using the prefix `:`. The `prepare` method gets the query as an argument and returns a `PDOStatement` instance. This class contains several methods to bind values, execute statements, fetch results, and more. In this piece of code, we use only three of them, as follows:

- `bindValue`: This takes two arguments: the name of the parameter as described in the query and the value to assign. If you provide a parameter name that is not in the query, this will throw an exception.

- `execute`: This will send the query to MySQL with the replacement of the parameters by the provided values. If there is any parameter that is not assigned to a value, the method will throw an exception. As its brother `exec`, `execute` will return a Boolean, specifying whether the query was executed successfully or not.

- `fetchAll`: This will retrieve the data from MySQL in case it was a SELECT query. As a query, `fetchAll` will return a list of all rows as arrays.

If you try this code, you will note that the result is very similar to when using `query`; however, this time, the code is much more dynamic as you can reuse it for any author that you need.

```
Source of: http://localhost:8000/init.php
 1 array(2) {
 2   [0] =>
 3   array(6) {
 4     'id' =>
 5     string(1) "1"
 6     'isbn' =>
 7     string(13) "9780882339726"
 8     'title' =>
 9     string(4) "1984"
10     'author' =>
11     string(13) "George Orwell"
12     'stock' =>
13     string(2) "12"
14     'price' =>
15     string(3) "7.5"
16   }
17   [1] =>
18   array(6) {
19     'id' =>
20     string(1) "3"
21     'isbn' =>
22     string(13) "9780736692427"
23     'title' =>
24     string(11) "Animal Farm"
25     'author' =>
26     string(13) "George Orwell"
27     'stock' =>
28     string(1) "8"
29     'price' =>
30     string(3) "3.5"
31   }
32 }
```

There is another way to bind values to parameters of a query than using the bindValue method. You could prepare an array where the key is the name of the parameter and the value is the value you want to assign to it, and then you can send it as the first argument of the execute method. This way is quite useful as usually you already have this array prepared and do not need to call bindValue several times with its content. Add this code in order to test it:

```
$query = <<<SQL
INSERT INTO book (isbn, title, author, price)
VALUES (:isbn, :title, :author, :price)
SQL;
$statement = $db->prepare($query);
$params = [
    'isbn' => '9781412108614',
    'title' => 'Iliad',
    'author' => 'Homer',
    'price' => 9.25
];
$statement->execute($params);
echo $db->lastInsertId(); // 8
```

In this last example, we created a new book with almost all the parameters, but we did not specify the ID, which is the desired behavior as we want MySQL to choose a valid one for us. However, what happens if you want to know the ID of the inserted row? Well, you could query MySQL for the book with the same ISBN and the returned row would contain the ID, but this seems like a lot of work. Instead, PDO has the lastInsertId method, which returns the last ID inserted by a primary key, saving us from one extra query.

Joining tables

Even though querying MySQL is quite fast, especially if it is in the same server as our PHP application, we should try to reduce the number of queries that we will execute to improve the performance of our application. So far, we have queried data from just one table, but this is rarely the case. Imagine that you want to retrieve information about borrowed books: the table contains only IDs and dates, so if you query it, you will not get very meaningful data, right? One approach would be to query the data in borrowed_books, and based on the returning IDs, query the book and customer tables by filtering by the IDs we are interested in. However, this approach consists of at least three queries to MySQL and a lot of work with arrays in PHP. It seems as though there should be a better option!

In SQL, you can execute **join queries**. A join query is a query that joins two or more tables through a common field and, thus, allows you to retrieve data from these tables, reducing the amount of queries needed. Of course, the performance of a join query is not as good as the performance of a normal query, but if you have the correct keys and relationships defined, this option is way better than querying separately.

In order to join tables, you need to link them using a common field. Foreign keys are very useful in this matter as you know that both the fields are the same. Let's take a look at how we would query for all the important info related to the borrowed books:

```
mysql> SELECT CONCAT(c.firstname, ' ', c.surname) AS name,
    ->      b.title,
    ->      b.author,
    ->      DATE_FORMAT(bb.start, '%d-%m-%y') AS start,
    ->      DATE_FORMAT(bb.end, '%d-%m-%y') AS end
    -> FROM borrowed_books bb
    ->      LEFT JOIN customer c ON bb.customer_id = c.id
    ->      LEFT JOIN book b ON b.id = bb.book_id
    -> WHERE bb.start >= "2015-01-01";
```

name	title	author	start	end
Han Solo	Dracula	Bram Stoker	10-01-15	13-01-15
James Kirk	Dracula	Bram Stoker	01-02-15	10-02-15
James Kirk	1984	George Orwell	12-03-15	NULL

```
3 rows in set (0.00 sec)
```

There are several new concepts introduced in this last query. Especially with joining queries, as we joined the fields of different tables, it might occur that two tables have the same field name, and MySQL needs us to differentiate them. The way we will differentiate two fields of two different tables is by prepending the name of the table. Imagine that we want to differentiate the ID of a customer from the ID of the book; we should use them as customer.id and book.id. However, writing the name of the table each time would make our queries endless.

MySQL has the ability to add an alias to a table by just writing next to the table's real name, as we did in `borrowed_books` (bb), `customer` (c) or `book` (b). Once you add an alias, you can use it to reference this table, allowing us to write things such as `bb.customer_id` instead of `borrowed_books.customer_id`. It is also good practice to write the table of the field even if the field is not duplicated anywhere else as joining tables makes it a bit confusing to know where each field comes from.

When joining tables, you need to write them in the FROM clause using LEFT JOIN, followed by the name of the table, an optional alias, and the fields that connect both tables. There are different joining types, but let's focus on the most useful for our purposes. **Left joins** take each row from the first table—the one on the left-hand side of the definition—and search for the equivalent field in the right-hand side table. Once it finds it, it will concatenate both rows as if they were one. For example, when joining `borrowed_books` with `customer` for each `borrowed_books` row, MySQL will search for an ID in `customer` that matches the current `customer_id`, and then it will add all the information of this row in our current row in `borrowed_books` as if they were only one big table. As `customer_id` is a foreign key, we are certain that there will always be a customer to match.

You can join several tables, and MySQL will just resolve them from left to right; that is, it will first join the two first tables as one, then try to join this resulting one with the third table, and so on. This is, in fact, what we did in our example: we first joined `borrowed_books` with `customer` and then joined these two with `book`.

As you can note, there are also aliases for fields. Sometimes, we do more than just getting a field; an example was when we got how many rows a query matched with COUNT(*). However, the title of the column when retrieving this information was also COUNT(*), which is not always useful. At other times, we used two tables with colliding field names, and it makes everything confusing. When this happens, just add an alias to the field in the same way we did with table names; AS is optional, but it helps to understand what you are doing.

Let's move now to the usage of dates in this query. On one hand, we will use DATE_FORMAT for the first time. It accepts the date/time/datetime value and the string with the format. In this case, we used %d-%m-%y, which means day-month-year, but we could use %h-%i-%s to specify hours-minutes-seconds or any other combination.

Note also how we compared dates in the WHERE clause. Given two dates or time values of the same type, you can use the comparison operators as if they were numbers. In this case, we will do `bb.start >= "2015-01-01"`, which will give us the borrowed books from January 1, 2015, onward.

The final thing to note about this complex query is the use of the CONCAT function. Instead of returning two fields, one for the name and one for the surname, we want to get the full name. To do this, we will concatenate the fields using this function, sending as many strings as we want as arguments of the function and getting back the concatenated string. As you can see, you can send both fields and strings enclosed by single quotes.

Well, if you fully understood this query, you should feel satisfied with yourself; this was the most complex query we will see in this chapter. We hope you can get a sense of how powerful a database system can be and that from now on, you will try to process the data as much as you can on the database side instead of the PHP side. If you set the correct indexes, it will perform better.

Grouping queries

The last feature that we will discuss about querying is the GROUP BY clause. This clause allows you to group rows of the same table with a common field. For example, let's say we want to know how many books each author has in just one query. Try the following:

```
mysql> SELECT
    -> author,
    -> COUNT(*) AS amount,
    -> GROUP_CONCAT(title SEPARATOR ', ') AS titles
    -> FROM book
    -> GROUP BY author
    -> ORDER BY amount DESC, author;
+-----------------+--------+-------------------+
| author          | amount | titles            |
+-----------------+--------+-------------------+
| George Orwell   |      2 | 1984, Animal Farm |
| Homer           |      2 | Odyssey, Iliad    |
| Bram Stoker     |      1 | Dracula           |
| Haruki Murakami |      1 | 1Q84              |
| J. M. Barrie    |      1 | Peter Pan         |
| Jodi Picoult    |      1 | 19 minutes        |
+-----------------+--------+-------------------+
5 rows in set (0.00 sec)
```

The GROUP BY clause, always after the WHERE clause, gets a field—or many, separated by a coma—and treats all the rows with the same value for this field, as though they were just one. Thus, selecting by author will group all the rows that contain the same author. The feature might not seem very useful, but there are several functions in MySQL that take advantage of it. In this example:

- COUNT(*) is used in queries with GROUP BY and shows how many rows this field groups. In this case, we will use it to know how many books each author has. In fact, it always works like this; however, for queries without GROUP BY, MySQL treats the whole set of rows as one group.

- GROUP_CONCAT is similar to CONCAT, which we discussed earlier. The only difference is that this time the function will concatenate the fields of all the rows of a group. If you do not specify SEPARATOR, MySQL will use a single coma. However, in our case, we needed a coma and a space to make it readable, so we added SEPARATOR ', ' at the end. Note that you can add as many things to concatenate as you need in CONCAT, the separator will just separate the concatenations by rows.

Even though it is not about grouping, note the ORDER clause that we added. We ordered by two fields instead of one. This means that MySQL will order all the rows by the amount field; note that this is an alias, but you can use it here as well. Then, MySQL will order each group of rows with the same amount value by the title field.

There is one last thing to remember as we already presented all the important clauses that a SELECT query can contain: MySQL expects the clauses of the query to be always in the same order. If you write the same query but change this order, you will get an error. The order is as follows:

1. SELECT
2. FROM
3. WHERE
4. GROUP BY
5. ORDER BY

Updating and deleting data

We already know quite a lot about inserting and retrieving data, but if applications could only do this, they would be quite static. Editing this data as we need is what makes an application dynamic and what gives to the user some value. In MySQL, and in most database systems, you have two commands to change data: UPDATE and DELETE. Let's discuss them in detail.

Updating data

When updating data in MySQL, the most important thing is to have a unique reference of the row that you want to update. For this, primary keys are very useful; however, if you have a table with no primary keys, which should not be the case most of the time, you can still update the rows based on other fields. Other than the reference, you will need the new value and, of course, the table name and field to update. Let's take a look at a very simple example:

```
mysql> UPDATE book SET price = 12.75 WHERE id = 2;
Query OK, 1 row affected (0.00 sec)
Rows matched: 1  Changed: 1  Warnings: 0
```

In this UPDATE query, we set the price of the book with the ID 2 to 12.75. The SET clause does not need to specify only one change; you can specify several changes on the same row as soon as you separate them by commas—for example, SET price = 12.75, stock = 14. Also, note the WHERE clause, in which we specify which rows we want to change. MySQL gets all the rows of this table based on these conditions as though it were a SELECT query and apply the change to this set of rows.

What MySQL will return is very important: the number of rows matched and the number of rows changed. The first one is the number of rows that match the conditions in the WHERE clause. The second one specifies the amount of rows that can be changed. There are different reasons not to change a row—for example when the row already has the same value. To see this, let's run the same query again:

```
mysql> UPDATE book SET price = 12.75 WHERE id = 2;
Query OK, 0 rows affected (0.00 sec)
Rows matched: 1  Changed: 0  Warnings: 0
```

The same row now says that there was 1 row matched, as expected, but 0 rows were changed. The reason is that we already set the price of this book to 12.75, so MySQL does not need to do anything about this now.

As mentioned before, the WHERE clause is the most important bit in this query. Way too many times, we find developers that run a priori innocent UPDATE queries end up changing the whole table because they miss the WHERE clause; thus, MySQL matches the whole table as valid rows to update. This is usually not the intention of the developer, and it is something not very pleasant, so try to make sure you always provide a valid set of conditions. It is good practice to first write down the SELECT query that returns the rows you need to edit, and once you are sure that the conditions match the desired set of rows, you can write the UPDATE query.

However, sometimes, affecting multiple rows is the intended scenario. Imagine that we are going through tough times and need to increase the price of all our books. We decide that we want to increase the price by 16%, which is the same as the current price times 1.16. We can run the following query to perform these changes:

```
mysql> UPDATE book SET price = price * 1.16;
Query OK, 8 rows affected (0.00 sec)
Rows matched: 8   Changed: 8   Warnings: 0
```

This query does not contain any WHERE clause as we want to match all our books. Also note that the SET clause uses the `price` field to get the current value for the price, which is perfectly valid. Finally, note the number of rows matched and changed, which is 8 — the whole set of rows for this table.

To finish with this subsection, let's consider how we can use UPDATE queries from PHP through PDO. One very common scenario is when we want to add copies of the already existing books to our inventory. Given a book ID and an optional amount of books — by default, this value will be 1 — we will increase the stock value of this book by these many copies. Write this function in your init.php file:

```
function addBook(int $id, int $amount = 1): void {
    $db = new PDO(
        'mysql:host=127.0.0.1;dbname=bookstore',
        'root',
        ''
    );

    $query = 'UPDATE book SET stock = stock + :n WHERE id = :id';
    $statement = $db->prepare($query);
    $statement->bindValue('id', $id);
    $statement->bindValue('n', $amount);

    if (!$statement->execute()) {
        throw new Exception($statement->errorInfo()[2]);
    }
}
```

There are two arguments: $id and $amount. The first one will always be mandatory, whereas the second one can be omitted, and the default value will be 1. The function first prepares a query similar to the first one of this section, in which we increased the amount of stock of a given book, then binds both parameters to the statement, and finally executes the query. If something happens and execute returns false, we will throw an exception with the content of the error message from MySQL.

This function is very useful when we either buy more stock or a customer returns a book. We could even use it to remove books by providing a negative value to `$amount`, but this is very bad practice. The reason is that even if we forced the stock field to be unsigned, setting it to a negative value will not trigger any error, only a warning. MySQL will not set the row to a negative value, but the `execute` invocation will return `true`, and we will not know about it. It is better to just create a second method, `removeBook`, and verify first that the amount of books to remove is lower than or equal to the current stock.

Foreign key behaviors

One tricky thing to manage when updating or deleting rows is when the row that we update is part of a foreign key somewhere else. For example, our `borrowed_books` table contains the IDs of customers and books, and as you already know, MySQL enforces that these IDs are always valid and exist on these respective tables. What would happen, then, if we changed the ID of the book itself on the `book` table? Or even worse, what would happen if we removed one of the books from `book`, and there is a row in `borrowed_books` that references this ID?

MySQL allows you to set the desired reaction when one of these scenarios takes place. It has to be defined when adding the foreign key; so, in our case, we will need to first remove the existing ones and then add them again. To remove or drop a key, you need to know the name of this key, which we can find using the SHOW CREATE TABLE command, as follows:

```
mysql> SHOW CREATE TABLE borrowed_books \G
*************************** 1. row ***************************
       Table: borrowed_books
Create Table: CREATE TABLE `borrowed_books` (
  `book_id` int(10) unsigned NOT NULL,
  `customer_id` int(10) unsigned NOT NULL,
  `start` datetime NOT NULL,
  `end` datetime DEFAULT NULL,
  KEY `book_id` (`book_id`),
  KEY `customer_id` (`customer_id`),
  CONSTRAINT `borrowed_books_ibfk_1` FOREIGN KEY (`book_id`) REFERENCES `book` (`id`),
  CONSTRAINT `borrowed_books_ibfk_2` FOREIGN KEY (`customer_id`) REFERENCES `customer` (`id`)
) ENGINE=InnoDB DEFAULT CHARSET=latin1
1 row in set (0.00 sec)
```

The two foreign keys that we want to remove are borrowed_books_ibfk_1 and borrowed_books_ibfk_2. Let's remove them using the ALTER TABLE command, as we did before:

```
mysql> ALTER TABLE borrowed_books
    -> DROP FOREIGN KEY borrowed_books_ibfk_1;
Query OK, 4 rows affected (0.02 sec)
Records: 4  Duplicates: 0  Warnings: 0


mysql> ALTER TABLE borrowed_books
    -> DROP FOREIGN KEY borrowed_books_ibfk_2;
Query OK, 4 rows affected (0.01 sec)
Records: 4  Duplicates: 0  Warnings: 0
```

Now, we need to add the foreign keys again. The format of the command will be the same as when we added them, but appending the new desired behavior. In our case, if we remove a customer or book from our tables, we want to remove the rows referencing these books and customers from borrowed_books; so, we need to use the CASCADE option. Let's consider what they would look like:

```
mysql> ALTER TABLE borrowed_books
    -> ADD FOREIGN KEY (book_id) REFERENCES book (id)
    -> ON DELETE CASCADE ON UPDATE CASCADE,
    -> ADD FOREIGN KEY (customer_id) REFERENCES customer (id)
    -> ON DELETE CASCADE ON UPDATE CASCADE;
Query OK, 4 rows affected (0.01 sec)
Records: 4  Duplicates: 0  Warnings: 0
```

Note that we can define the CASCADE behavior for both actions: when updating and when deleting rows. There are other options instead of CASCADE—for example SET NULL, which sets the foreign keys columns to NULL and allows the original row to be deleted, or the default one, RESTRICT, which rejects the update/delete commands.

Deleting data

Deleting data is almost the same as updating it. You need to provide a WHERE clause that will match the rows that you want to delete. Also, as with when updating data, it is highly recommended to first build the SELECT query that will retrieve the rows that you want to delete before performing the DELETE command. Do not think that you are wasting time with this methodology; as the saying goes, measure twice, cut once. Not always is it possible to recover data after deleting rows!

Let's try to delete a book by observing how the CASCADE option we set earlier behaves. For this, let's first query for the existing borrowed books list via the following:

```
mysql> SELECT book_id, customer_id FROM borrowed_books;
+---------+-------------+
| book_id | customer_id |
+---------+-------------+
|       1 |           1 |
|       4 |           1 |
|       4 |           2 |
|       1 |           2 |
+---------+-------------+
4 rows in set (0.00 sec)
```

There are two different books, 1 and 4, with each of them borrowed twice. Let's try to delete the book with the ID 4. First, build a query such as SELECT * FROM book WHERE id = 4 to make sure that the condition in the WHERE clause is the appropriate one. Once you are sure, perform the following query:

```
mysql> DELETE FROM book WHERE id = 4;
Query OK, 1 row affected (0.02 sec)
```

As you can note, we only specified the DELETE FROM command followed by the name of the table and the WHERE clause. MySQL tells us that there was 1 row affected, which makes sense, given the previous SELECT statement we made.

If we go back to our borrowed_books table and query for the existing ones, we will note that all the rows referencing the book with the ID 4 are gone. This is because when deleting them from the book table, MySQL noticed the foreign key reference, checked what it needed to do while deleting—in this case, CASCADE—and deleted also the rows in borrowed_books. Take a look at the following:

```
mysql> SELECT book_id, customer_id FROM borrowed_books;
+---------+-------------+
| book_id | customer_id |
+---------+-------------+
|       1 |           1 |
|       1 |           2 |
+---------+-------------+
2 rows in set (0.00 sec)
```

Working with transactions

In the previous section, we reiterated how important it is to make sure that an update or delete query contain the desirable matching set of rows. Even though this will always apply, there is a way to revert the changes that you just made, which is working with **transactions**.

A transaction is a state where MySQL keeps track of all the changes that you make in your data in order to be able to revert all of them if needed. You need to explicitly start a transaction, and before you close the connection to the server, you need to commit your changes. This means that MySQL does not really perform these changes until you tell it to do so. If during a transaction you want to revert the changes, you should roll back instead of making a commit.

PDO allows you to do this with three functions:

- `beginTransaction`: This will start the transaction.
- `commit`: This will commit your changes. Keep in mind that if you do not commit and the PHP script finishes or you close the connection explicitly, MySQL will reject all the changes you made during this transaction.
- `rollBack`: This will roll back all the changes that were made during this transaction.

One possible use of transactions in your application is when you need to perform multiple queries and all of them have to be successful and the whole set of queries should not be performed otherwise. This would be the case when adding a sale into the database. Remember that our sales are stored in two tables: one for the sale itself and one for the list of books related to this sale. When adding a new one, you need to make sure that all the books are added to this database; otherwise, the sale will be corrupted. What you should do is execute all the queries, checking for their returning values. If any of them returns `false`, the whole sale should be rolled back.

Let's create an `addSale` function in your `init.php` file in order to emulate this behavior. The content should be as follows:

```php
function addSale(int $userId, array $bookIds): void {
    $db = new PDO(
        'mysql:host=127.0.0.1;dbname=bookstore',
        'root',
        ''
    );

    $db->beginTransaction();
    try {
        $query = 'INSERT INTO sale (customer_id, date) '
```

```
                   . 'VALUES(:id, NOW())';
        $statement = $db->prepare($query);
        if (!$statement->execute(['id' => $userId])) {
            throw new Exception($statement->errorInfo()[2]);
        }
        $saleId = $db->lastInsertId();

        $query = 'INSERT INTO sale_book (book_id, sale_id) '
               . 'VALUES(:book, :sale)';
        $statement = $db->prepare($query);
        $statement->bindValue('sale', $saleId);
        foreach ($bookIds as $bookId) {
            $statement->bindValue('book', $bookId);
            if (!$statement->execute()) {
                throw new Exception($statement->errorInfo()[2]);
            }
        }

        $db->commit();
    } catch (Exception $e) {
        $db->rollBack();
        throw $e;
    }
}
```

This function is quite complex. It gets as arguments the ID of the customer and the list of books as we assume that the date of the sale is the current date. The first thing we will do is connect to the database, instantiating the PDO class. Right after this, we will begin our transaction, which will last only during the course of this function. Once we begin the transaction, we will open a try...catch block that will enclose the rest of the code of the function. The reason is that if we throw an exception, the catch block will capture it, rolling back the transaction and propagating the exception. The code inside the try block just adds first the sale and then iterates the list of books, inserting them into the database too. At all times, we will check the response of the execute function, and if it's false, we will throw an exception with the information of the error.

Let's try to use this function. Write the following code that tries to add a sale for three books; however, one of them does not exist, which is the one with the ID 200:

```
try {
    addSale(1, [1, 2, 200]);
} catch (Exception $e) {
    echo 'Error adding sale: ' . $e->getMessage();
}
```

This code will echo the error message, complaining about the nonexistent book. If you check in MySQL, there will be no rows in the `sales` table as the function rolled back when the exception was thrown.

Finally, let's try the following code instead. This one will add three valid books so that the queries are always successful and the `try` block can go until the end, where we will commit the changes:

```
try {
    addSale(1, [1, 2, 3]);
} catch (Exception $e) {
    echo 'Error adding sale: ' . $e->getMessage();
}
```

Test it, and you will see how there is no message printed on your browser. Then, go to your database to make sure that there is a new `sales` row and there are three books linked to it.

Summary

In this chapter, we learned the importance of databases and how to use them from our web application: from setting up the connection using PDO and creating and fetching data on demand to constructing more complex queries that fulfill our needs. With all of this, our application looks way more useful now than when it was completely static.

In the next chapter, we will discover how to apply the most important design patterns for web applications through **Model View Controller (MVC)**. You will gain a sense of clarity in your code when you organize your application in this way.

6
Adapting to MVC

Web applications are more complex than what we have built so far. The more functionality you add, the more difficult the code is to maintain and understand. It is for this reason that structuring your code in an organized way is crucial. You could design your own structure, but as with OOP, there already exist some design patterns that try to solve this problem.

MVC (model-view-controller) has been the favorite pattern for web developers. It helps us separate the different parts of a web application, leaving the code easy to understand even for beginners. We will try to refactor our bookstore example to use the MVC pattern, and you will realize how quickly you can add new functionality after that.

In this chapter, you will learn the following:

- Using Composer to manage dependencies
- Designing a router for your application
- Organizing your code into models, views, and controllers
- Twig as the template engine
- Dependency injection

The MVC pattern

So far, each time we have had to add a feature, we added a new PHP file with a mixture of PHP and HTML for that specific page. For chunks of code with a single purpose, and which we have to reuse, we created functions and added them to the functions file. Even for very small web applications like ours, the code starts becoming very confusing, and the ability to reuse code is not as helpful as it could be. Now imagine an application with a large number of features: that would be pretty much chaos itself.

The problems do not stop here. In our code, we have mixed HTML and PHP code in a single file. That will give us a lot of trouble when trying to change the design of the web application, or even if we want to perform a very small change across all pages, such as changing the menu or footer of the page. The more complex the application, the more problems we will encounter.

MVC came up as a pattern to help us divide the different parts of the application. These parts are known as models, views, and controllers. **Models** manage the data and/or the business logic, **views** contain the templates for our responses (for example, HTML pages), and **controllers** orchestrate requests, deciding what data to use and how to render the appropriate template. We will go through them in later sections of this chapter.

Using Composer

Even though this is not a necessary component when implementing the MVC pattern, Composer has been an indispensable tool for any PHP web application over the last few years. The main goal of this tool is to help you manage the dependencies of your application, that is, the third-party libraries (of code) that we need to use in our application. We can achieve that by just creating a configuration file that lists them, and by running a command in your command line.

You need to install Composer on your development machine (see *Chapter 1*, *Setting Up the Environment*). Make sure that you have it by executing the following command:

```
$ composer -version
```

This should return the version of your Composer installation. If it does not, return to the installation section to fix the problem.

Managing dependencies

As we stated earlier, the main goal of Composer is to manage dependencies. For example, we've already implemented our configuration reader, the `Config` class, but if we knew of someone that implemented a better version of it, we could just use theirs instead of reinventing the wheel; just make sure that they allow you to do so!

Open source

Open source refers to the code that developers write and share with the community in order to be used by others without restrictions. There are actually different types of licenses, and some give you more flexibility than others, but the basic idea is that we can reuse the libraries that other developers have written in our applications. That helps the community to grow in knowledge, as we can learn what others have done, improve it, and share it afterwards.

We've already implemented a decent configuration reader, but there are other elements of our application that need to be done. Let's take advantage of Composer to reuse someone else's libraries. There are a couple of ways of adding a dependency to our project: executing a command in our command line, or editing the configuration file manually. As we still do not have Composer's configuration file, let's use the first option. Execute the following command in the root directory of your application:

```
$ composer require monolog/monolog
```

This command will show the following result:

```
Using version ^1.17 for monolog/monolog
./composer.json has been created
Loading composer repositories with package information
Updating dependencies (including require-dev)
  - Installing psr/log (1.0.0)
    Downloading: 100%

  - Installing monolog/monolog (1.17.2)
    Downloading: 100%
...
Writing lock file
Generating autoload files
```

With this command, we asked Composer to add the library monolog/monolog as a dependency of our application. Having executed that, we can now see some changes in our directory:

- We have a new file named composer.json. This is the configuration file where we can add our dependencies.
- We have a new file named composer.lock. This is a file that Composer uses in order to track the dependencies that have already been installed and their versions.

- We have a new directory named vendor. This directory contains the code of the dependencies that Composer downloaded.

The output of the command also shows us some extra information. In this case, it says that it downloaded two libraries or packages, even though we asked for only one. The reason is that the package that we needed also contained other dependencies that were resolved by Composer. Also note the version that Composer downloaded; as we did not specify any version, Composer took the most recent one available, but you can always try to write the specific version that you need.

We will need another library, in this case twig/twig. Let's add it to our dependencies list with the following command:

```
$ composer require twig/twig
```

This command will show the following result:

```
Using version ^1.23 for twig/twig
./composer.json has been updated
Loading composer repositories with package information
Updating dependencies (including require-dev)
  - Installing twig/twig (v1.23.1)
    Downloading: 100%


Writing lock file
Generating autoload files
```

If we check the composer.json file, we will see the following content:

```
{
    "require": {
        "monolog/monolog": "^1.17",
        "twig/twig": "^1.23"
    }
}
```

The file is just a JSON map that contains the configuration of our application; in this case, the list of the two dependencies that we installed. As you can see, the dependencies' name follows a pattern: two words separated by a slash. The first of the words refers to the vendor that developed the library. The second of them is the name of the library itself. The dependency has a version, which could be the exact version number—as in this case—or it could contain wildcard characters or tag names. You can read more about this at https://getcomposer.org/doc/articles/aliases.md.

Finally, if you would like to add another dependency, or edit the `composer.json` file in any other way, you should run `composer update` in your command line, or wherever the `composer.json` file is, in order to update the dependencies.

Autoloader with PSR-4

In the previous chapters, we also added an autoloader to our application. As we are now using someone else's code, we need to know how to load their classes too. Soon, developers realized that this scenario without a standard would be virtually impossible to manage, and they came out with some standards that most developers follow. You can find a lot of information on this topic at `http://www.php-fig.org`.

Nowadays, PHP has two main standards for autoloading: **PSR-0** and **PSR-4**. They are very similar, but we will be implementing the latter, as it is the most recent standard published. This standard basically follows what we've already introduced when talking about namespaces: the namespace of a class must be the same as the directory where it is, and the name of the class should be the name of the file, followed by the extension `.php`. For example, the file in `src/Domain/Book.php` contains the class `Book` inside the namespace `Bookstore\Domain`.

Applications using Composer should follow one of those standards, and they should note in their respective `composer.json` file which one they are using. This means that Composer knows how to autoload its own application files, so we will not need to take care of it when we download external libraries. To specify that, we edit our `composer.json` file, and add the following content:

```
{
    "require": {
        "monolog/monolog": "^1.17",
        "twig/twig": "^1.23"
    },
    "autoload": {
        "psr-4": {
            "Bookstore\\": "src"
        }
    }
}
```

The preceding code means that we will use PSR-4 in our application, and that all the namespaces that start with `Bookstore` should be found inside the `src/` directory. This is exactly what our autoloader was doing already, but reduced to a couple of lines in a configuration file. We can safely remove our autoloader and any reference to it now.

Composer generates some mappings that help to speed up the loading of classes. In order to update those maps with the new information added to the configuration file, we need to run the `composer update` command that we ran earlier. This time, the output will tell us that there is no package to update, but the autoload files will be generated again:

```
$ composer update
Loading composer repositories with package information
Updating dependencies (including require-dev)
Nothing to install or update
Writing lock file
Generating autoload files
```

Adding metadata

In order to know where to find the libraries that you define as dependencies, Composer keeps a repository of packages and versions, known as **Packagist**. This repository keeps a lot of useful information for developers, such as all the versions available for a given package, the authors, some description of what the package does (or a website pointing to that information), and the dependencies that this package will download. You can also browse the packages, searching by name or categories.

But how does Packagist know about this? It is all thanks to the `composer.json` file itself. In there, you can define all the metadata of your application in a format that Composer understands. Let's see an example. Add the following content to your `composer.json` file:

```json
{
    "name": "picahielos/bookstore",
    "description": "Manages an online bookstore.",
    "minimum-stability": "stable",
    "license": "Apache-2.0",
    "type": "project",
    "authors": [
        {
            "name": "Antonio Lopez",
            "email": "antonio.lopez.zapata@gmail.com"
        }
    ],
    // ...
}
```

The configuration file now contains the name of the package following the Composer convention: vendor name, slash, and the package name—in this case, `picahielos/bookstore`. We also add a description, license, authors, and other metadata. If you have your code in a pubic repository such as GitHub, adding this `composer.json` file will allow you to go to Packagist and insert the URL of your repository. Packagist will add your code as a new package, extracting the info from your `composer.json` file. It will show the available versions based on your tags or branches. In order to learn more about it, we encourage you to visit the official documentation at `https://getcomposer.org/doc/04-schema.md`.

The index.php file

In MVC applications, we usually have one file that gets all the requests, and routes them to the specific controller depending on the URL. This logic can generally be found in the `index.php` file in our root directory. We already have one, but as we are adapting our features to the MVC pattern, we will not need the current `index.php` anymore. Hence, you can safely replace it with the following:

```php
<?php

require_once __DIR__ . '/vendor/autoload.php';
```

The only thing that this file will do now is include the file that handles all the autoloading from the Composer code. Later, we will initialize everything here, such as database connections, configuration readers, and so on, but right now, let's leave it empty.

Working with requests

As you might recall from previous chapters, the main purpose of a web application is to process HTTP requests coming from the client and return a response. If that is the main goal of your application, managing requests and responses should be an important part of your code.

PHP is a language that can be used for scripts, but its main usage is in web applications. Due to this, the language comes ready with a lot of helpers for managing requests and responses. Still, the native way is not ideal, and as good OOP developers, we should come up with a set of classes that help with that. The main elements for this small project—still inside your application—are the request and the router. Let's start!

The request object

As we start our mini framework, we need to change our directory structure a bit. We will create the src/Core directory for all the classes related to the framework. As the configuration reader from the previous chapters is also part of the framework (rather than functionality for the user), we should move the Config.php file to this directory too.

The first thing to consider is what a request looks like. If you remember *Chapter 2, Web Applications with PHP*, a request is basically a message that goes to a URL, and has a method—GET or POST for now. The URL is at the same time composed of two parts: the domain of the web application, that is, the name of your server, and the path of the request inside the server. For example, if you try to access http://bookstore. com/my-books, the first part, http://bookstore.com, would be the domain and /my-books would be the path. In fact, http would not be part of the domain, but we do not need that level of granularity for our application. You can get this information from the global array $_SERVER that PHP populates for each request.

Our Request class should have a property for each of those three elements, followed by a set of getters and some other helpers that will be useful for the user. Also, we should initialize all the properties from $_SERVER in the constructor. Let's see what it would look like:

```php
<?php

namespace Bookstore\Core;

class Request {
    const GET = 'GET';
    const POST = 'POST';

    private $domain;
    private $path;
    private $method;

    public function __construct() {
        $this->domain = $_SERVER['HTTP_HOST'];
        $this->path = $_SERVER['REQUEST_URI'];
        $this->method = $_SERVER['REQUEST_METHOD'];
    }

    public function getUrl(): string {
        return $this->domain . $this->path;
    }
}
```

```php
    public function getDomain(): string {
        return $this->domain;
    }

    public function getPath(): string {
        return $this->path;
    }

    public function getMethod(): string {
        return $this->method;
    }

    public function isPost(): bool {
        return $this->method === self::POST;
    }

    public function isGet(): bool {
        return $this->method === self::GET;
    }
}
```

We can see in the preceding code that other than the getters for each property, we added the methods `getUrl`, `isPost`, and `isGet`. The user could find the same information using the already existing getters, but as they will be needed a lot, it is always good to make it easier for the user. Also note that the properties are coming from the values of the `$_SERVER` array: `HTTP_HOST`, `REQUEST_URI`, and `REQUEST_METHOD`.

Filtering parameters from requests

Another important part of a request is the information that comes from the user, that is, the GET and POST parameters, and the cookies. As with the `$_SERVER` global array, this information comes from `$_POST`, `$_GET`, and `$_COOKIE`, but it is always good to avoid using them directly, without filtering, as the user could send malicious code.

We will now implement a class that will represent a map—key-value pairs—that can be filtered. We will call it `FilteredMap`, and will include it in our namespace, `Bookstore\Core`. We will use it to contain the parameters GET and POST and the cookies as two new properties in our `Request` class. The map will contain only one property, the array of data, and will have some methods to fetch information from it. To construct the object, we need to send the array of data as an argument to the constructor:

```php
<?php

namespace Bookstore\Core;
```

```php
class FilteredMap {
    private $map;

    public function __construct(array $baseMap) {
        $this->map = $baseMap;
    }

    public function has(string $name): bool {
        return isset($this->map[$name]);
    }

    public function get(string $name) {
        return $this->map[$name] ?? null;
    }
}
```

This class does not do much so far. We could have the same functionality with a normal array. The utility of this class comes when we add filters while fetching data. We will implement three filters, but you can add as many as you need:

```php
public function getInt(string $name) {
    return (int) $this->get($name);
}

public function getNumber(string $name) {
    return (float) $this->get($name);
}

public function getString(string $name, bool $filter = true) {
    $value = (string) $this->get($name);
    return $filter ? addslashes($value) : $value;
}
```

These three methods in the preceding code allow the user to get parameters of a specific type. Let's say that the developer needs to get the ID of the book from the request. The best option is to use the getInt method to make sure that the returned value is a valid integer, and not some malicious code that can mess up our database. Also note the function getString, where we use the addSlashed method. This method adds slashes to some of the suspicious characters, such as slashes or quotes, trying to prevent malicious code with it.

Now we are ready to get the GET and POST parameters as well as the cookies from our Request class using our FilteredMap. The new code would look like the following:

```php
<?php

namespace Bookstore\Core;

class Request {
    // ...
    private $params;
    private $cookies;

    public function __construct() {
        $this->domain = $_SERVER['HTTP_HOST'];
        $this->path = explode('?', $_SERVER['REQUEST_URI'])[0];
        $this->method = $_SERVER['REQUEST_METHOD'];
        $this->params = new FilteredMap(
            array_merge($_POST, $_GET)
        );
        $this->cookies = new FilteredMap($_COOKIE);
    }

    // ...

    public function getParams(): FilteredMap {
        return $this->params;
    }

    public function getCookies(): FilteredMap {
        return $this->cookies;
    }
}
```

With this new addition, a developer could get the POST parameter price with the following line of code:

```php
$price = $request->getParams()->getNumber('price');
```

This is way safer than the usual call to the global array:

```php
$price = $_POST['price'];
```

Mapping routes to controllers

If you can recall from any URL that you use daily, you will probably not see any PHP file as part of the path, like we have with `http://localhost:8000/init.php`. Websites try to format their URLs to make them easier to remember instead of depending on the file that should handle that request. Also, as we've already mentioned, all our requests go through the same file, `index.php`, regardless of their path. Because of this, we need to keep a map of the URL paths, and who should handle them.

Sometimes, we have URLs that contain parameters as part of their path, which is different from when they contain the GET or POST parameters. For example, to get the page that shows a specific book, we might include the ID of the book as part of the URL, such as `/book/12` or `/book/3`. The ID will change for each different book, but the same controller should handle all of these requests. To achieve this, we say that the URL contains an argument, and we could represent it by `/book/:id`, where `id` is the argument that identifies the ID of the book. Optionally, we could specify the kind of value this argument can take, for example, number, string, and so on.

Controllers, the ones in charge of processing requests, are defined by a method's class. This method takes as arguments all the arguments that the URL's path defines, such as the ID of the book. We group controllers by their functionality, that is, a `BookController` class will contain the methods related to requests about books.

Having defined all the elements of a route—a URL-controller relationship—we are ready to create our `routes.json` file, a configuration file that will keep this map. Each entry of this file should contain a route, the key being the URL, and the value, a map of information about the controller. Let's see an example:

```
{
  "books/:page": {
    "controller": "Book",
    "method": "getAllWithPage",
    "params": {
      "page": "number"
    }
  }
}
```

The route in the preceding example refers to all the URLs that follow the pattern `/books/:page`, with `page` being any number. Thus, this route will match URLs such as `/books/23` or `/books/2`, but it should not match `/books/one` or `/books`. The controller that will handle this request should be the `getAllWithPage` method from `BookController`; we will append `Controller` to all the class names. Given the parameters that we defined, the definition of the method should be something like the following:

```
public function getAllWithPage(int $page): string {
    //...
}
```

There is one last thing we should consider when defining a route. For some endpoints, we should enforce the user to be authenticated, such as when the user is trying to access their own sales. We could define this rule in several ways, but we chose to do it as part of the route, adding the entry `"login": true` as part of the controller's information. With that in mind, let's add the rest of the routes that define all the views that we expect to have:

```
{
//...
  "books": {
    "controller": "Book",
    "method": "getAll"
  },
  "book/:id": {
    "controller": "Book",
    "method": "get",
    "params": {
      "id": "number"
    }
  },
  "books/search": {
    "controller": "Book",
    "method": "search"
  },
  "login": {
    "controller": "Customer",
    "method": "login"
  },
  "sales": {
    "controller": "Sales",
    "method": "getByUser" ,
    "login": true
  },
  "sales/:id": {
    "controller": "Sales",
    "method": "get",
    "login": true,
    "params": {
      "id": "number"
    }
  },
```

```
    "my-books": {
      "controller": "Book",
      "method": "getByUser",
      "login": true
    }
  }
```

These routes define all the pages we need; we can get all the books in a paginated way or specific books by their ID, we can search books, list the sales of the user, show a specific sale by its ID, and list all the books that a certain user has borrowed. However, we are still lacking some of the endpoints that our application should be able to handle. For all those actions that are trying to modify data rather than requesting it, that is, borrowing a book or buying it, we need to add endpoints too. Add the following to your `routes.json` file:

```
{
  // ...
  "book/:id/buy": {
    "controller": "Sales",
    "method": "add",
    "login": true
    "params": {
      "id": "number"
    }
  },
  "book/:id/borrow": {
    "controller": "Book",
    "method": "borrow",
    "login": true
    "params": {
      "id": "number"
    }
  },
  "book/:id/return": {
    "controller": "Book",
    "method": "returnBook",
    "login": true
    "params": {
      "id": "number"
    }
  }
}
```

The router

The router will be by far the most complicated piece of code in our application. The main goal is to receive a `Request` object, decide which controller should handle it, invoke it with the necessary parameters, and return the response from that controller. The main goal of this section is to understand the importance of the router rather than its detailed implementation, but we will try to describe each of its parts. Copy the following content as your `src/Core/Router.php` file:

```php
<?php

namespace Bookstore\Core;

use Bookstore\Controllers\ErrorController;
use Bookstore\Controllers\CustomerController;

class Router {
    private $routeMap;
    private static $regexPatters = [
        'number' => '\d+',
        'string' => '\w'
    ];

    public function __construct() {
        $json = file_get_contents(
            __DIR__ . '/../../config/routes.json'
        );
        $this->routeMap = json_decode($json, true);
    }

    public function route(Request $request): string {
        $path = $request->getPath();

        foreach ($this->routeMap as $route => $info) {
            $regexRoute = $this->getRegexRoute($route, $info);
            if (preg_match("@^/$regexRoute$@", $path)) {
                return $this->executeController(
                    $route, $path, $info, $request
                );
            }
        }

        $errorController = new ErrorController($request);
        return $errorController->notFound();
    }
}
```

The constructor of this class reads from the `routes.json` file, and stores the content as an array. Its main method, `route`, takes a `Request` object and returns a string, which is what we will send as output to the client. This method iterates all the routes from the array, trying to match each with the path of the given request. Once it finds one, it tries to execute the controller related to that route. If none of the routes are a good match to the request, the router will execute the `notFound` method of the `ErrorController`, which will then return an error page.

URLs matching with regular expressions

While matching a URL with the route, we need to take care of the arguments for dynamic URLs, as they do not let us perform a simple string comparison. PHP—and other languages—has a very strong tool for performing string comparisons with dynamic content: regular expressions. Being an expert in regular expressions takes time, and it is outside the scope of this book, but we will give you a brief introduction to them.

A regular expression is a string that contains some wildcard characters that will match the dynamic content. Some of the most important ones are as follows:

- `^`: This is used to specify that the matching part should be the start of the whole string
- `$`: This is used to specify that the matching part should be the end of the whole string
- `\d`: This is used to match a digit
- `\w`: This is used to match a word
- `+`: This is used for following a character or expression, to let that character or expression to appear at least once or many times
- `*`: This is used for following a character or expression, to let that character or expression to appear zero or many times
- `.`: This is used to match any single character

Let's see some examples:

- The pattern `.*` will match anything, even an empty string
- The pattern `.+` will match anything that contains at least one character
- The pattern `^\d+$` will match any number that has at least one digit

In PHP, we have different functions to work with regular expressions. The easiest of them, and the one that we will use, is pregmatch. This function takes a pattern as its first argument (delimited by two characters, usually @ or /), the string that we are trying to match as the second argument, and optionally, an array where PHP stores the occurrences found. The function returns a Boolean value, being true if there was a match, false otherwise. We use it as follows in our Route class:

```
preg_match("@^/$regexRoute$@", $path)
```

The $path variable contains the path of the request, for example, /books/2. We match using a pattern that is delimited by @, has the ^ and $ wildcards to force the pattern to match the whole string, and contains the concatenation of / and the variable $regexRoute. The content of this variable is given by the following method; add this as well to your Router class:

```
private function getRegexRoute(
    string $route,
    array $info
): string {
    if (isset($info['params'])) {
        foreach ($info['params'] as $name => $type) {
            $route = str_replace(
                ':' . $name, self::$regexPatters[$type], $route
            );
        }
    }

    return $route;
}
```

The preceding method iterates the parameters list coming from the information of the route. For each parameter, the function replaces the name of the parameter inside the route by the wildcard character corresponding to the type of parameter—check the static array, $regexPatterns. To illustrate the usage of this function, let's see some examples:

- The route /books will be returned without a change, as it does not contain any argument
- The route books/:id/borrow will be changed to books/\d+/borrow, as the URL argument, id, is a number

Extracting the arguments of the URL

In order to execute the controller, we need three pieces of data: the name of the class to instantiate, the name of the method to execute, and the arguments that the method needs to receive. We already have the first two as part of the route $info array, so let's focus our efforts on finding the third one. Add the following method to the Router class:

```
private function extractParams(
    string $route,
    string $path
) : array {
    $params = [];

    $pathParts = explode('/', $path);
    $routeParts = explode('/', $route);

    foreach ($routeParts as $key => $routePart) {
        if (strpos($routePart, ':') === 0) {
            $name = substr($routePart, 1);
            $params[$name] = $pathParts[$key+1];
        }
    }

    return $params;
}
```

This last method expects that both the path of the request and the URL of the route follow the same pattern. With the explode method, we get two arrays that should match each of their entries. We iterate them, and for each entry in the route array that looks like a parameter, we fetch its value in the URL. For example, if we had the route /books/:id/borrow and the path /books/12/borrow, the result of this method would be the array *['id' => 12]*.

Executing the controller

We end this section by implementing the method that executes the controller in charge of a given route. We already have the name of the class, the method, and the arguments that the method needs, so we could make use of the call_user_func_array native function that, given an object, a method name, and the arguments for the method, invokes the method of the object passing the arguments. We have to make use of it as the number of arguments is not fixed, and we cannot perform a normal invocation.

But we are still missing a behavior introduced when creating our `routes.json` file. There are some routes that force the user to be logged in, which, in our case, means that the user has a cookie with the user ID. Given a route that enforces authorization, we will check whether our request contains the cookie, in which case we will set it to the controller class through `setCustomerId`. If the user does not have a cookie, instead of executing the controller for the current route, we will execute the `showLogin` method of the `CustomerController` class, which will render the template for the login form. Let's see how everything would look on adding the last method of our `Router` class:

```
private function executeController(
    string $route,
    string $path,
    array $info,
    Request $request
): string {
    $controllerName = '\Bookstore\Controllers\\'
        . $info['controller'] . 'Controller';
    $controller = new $controllerName($request);

    if (isset($info['login']) && $info['login']) {
        if ($request->getCookies()->has('user')) {
            $customerId = $request->getCookies()->get('user');
            $controller->setCustomerId($customerId);
        } else {
            $errorController = new CustomerController($request);
            return $errorController->login();
        }
    }

    $params = $this->extractParams($route, $path);
    return call_user_func_array(
        [$controller, $info['method']], $params
    );
}
```

We have already warned you about the lack of security in our application, as this is just a project with didactic purposes. So, avoid copying the authorization system implemented here.

M for model

Imagine for a moment that our bookstore website is quite successful, so we think of building a mobile app to increase our market. Of course, we would want to use the same database that we use for our website, as we need to sync the books that people borrow or buy from both apps. We do not want to be in a position where two people buy the same last copy of a book!

Not only the database, but the queries used to get books, update them, and so on, have to be the same too, otherwise we would end up with unexpected behavior. Of course, one apparently easy option would be to replicate the queries in both codebases, but that has a huge maintainability problem. What if we change one single field of our database? We need to apply the same change to at least two different codebases. That does not seem to be useful at all.

Business logic plays an important role here too. Think of it as decisions you need to take that affect your business. In our case, that a premium customer is able to borrow 10 books and a normal one only 3, is business logic. This logic should be put in a common place too, because, if we want to change it, we will have the same problems as with our database queries.

We hope that by now we've convinced you that data and business logic should be separated from the rest of the code in order to make it reusable. Do not worry if it is hard for you to define what should go as part of the model or as part of the controller; a lot of people struggle with this distinction. As our application is very simple, and it does not have a lot of business logic, we will just focus on adding all the code related to MySQL queries.

As you can imagine, for an application integrated with MySQL, or any other database system, the database connection is an important element of a model. We chose to use PDO in order to interact with MySQL, and as you might remember, instantiating that class was a bit of a pain. Let's create a singleton class that returns an instance of PDO to make things easier. Add this code to `src/Core/Db.php`:

```php
<?php

namespace Bookstore\Core;

use PDO;

class Db {
    private static $instance;

    private static function connect(): PDO {
        $dbConfig = Config::getInstance()->get('db');
```

```
        return new PDO(
            'mysql:host=127.0.0.1;dbname=bookstore',
            $dbConfig['user'],
            $dbConfig['password']
        );
    }

    public static function getInstance(){
        if (self::$instance == null) {
            self::$instance = self::connect();
        }
        return self::$instance;
    }
}
```

This class, defined in the preceding code snippet, just implements the singleton pattern and wraps the creation of a PDO instance. From now on, in order to get a database connection, we just need to write Db::getInstance().

Although it might not be true for all models, in our application, they will always have to access the database. We could create an abstract class where all models extend. This class could contain a $db protected property that will be set on the constructor. With this, we avoid duplicating the same constructor and property definition across all our models. Copy the following class into src/Models/ AbstractModel.php:

```php
<?php

namespace Bookstore\Models;

use PDO;

abstract class AbstractModel {
    private $db;

    public function __construct(PDO $db) {
        $this->db = $db;
    }
}
```

Finally, to finish the setup of the models, we could create a new exception (as we did with the NotFoundException class) that represents an error from the database. It will not contain any code, but we will be able to differentiate where an exception is coming from. We will save it in src/Exceptions/DbException.php:

```php
<?php

namespace Bookstore\Exceptions;

use Exception;

class DbException extends Exception {
}
```

Now that we've set the ground, we can start writing our models. It is up to you to organize your models, but it is a good idea to mimic the domain objects structure. In this case, we would have three models: CustomerModel, BookModel, and SalesModel. In the following sections, we will explain the contents of each of them.

The customer model

Let's start with the easiest one. As our application is still very primitive, we will not allow the creation of new costumers, and work with the ones we inserted manually into the database instead. That means that the only thing we need to do with customers is to query them. Let's create a CustomerModel class in src/Models/CustomerModel.php with the following content:

```php
<?php

namespace Bookstore\Models;

use Bookstore\Domain\Customer;
use Bookstore\Domain\Customer\CustomerFactory;
use Bookstore\Exceptions\NotFoundException;

class CustomerModel extends AbstractModel {
    public function get(int $userId): Customer {
        $query = 'SELECT * FROM customer WHERE customer_id = :user';
        $sth = $this->db->prepare($query);
        $sth->execute(['user' => $userId]);

        $row = $sth->fetch();

        if (empty($row)) {
```

```
                throw new NotFoundException();
        }

        return CustomerFactory::factory(
            $row['type'],
            $row['id'],
            $row['firstname'],
            $row['surname'],
            $row['email']
        );
    }

    public function getByEmail(string $email): Customer {
        $query = 'SELECT * FROM customer WHERE email = :user';
        $sth = $this->db->prepare($query);
        $sth->execute(['user' => $email]);

        $row = $sth->fetch();

        if (empty($row)) {
            throw new NotFoundException();
        }

        return CustomerFactory::factory(
            $row['type'],
            $row['id'],
            $row['firstname'],
            $row['surname'],
            $row['email']
        );
    }
}
```

The CustomerModel class, which extends from the AbstractModel class, contains two methods; both of them return a Customer instance, one of them when providing the ID of the customer, and the other one when providing the e-mail. As we already have the database connection as the $db property, we just need to prepare the statement with the given query, execute the statement with the arguments, and fetch the result. As we expect to get a customer, if the user provided an ID or an e-mail that does not belong to any customer, we will need to throw an exception—in this case, a NotFoundException is just fine. If we find a customer, we use our factory to create the object and return it.

The book model

Our `BookModel` class gives us a bit more of work. Customers had a factory, but it is not worth having one for books. What we use for creating them from MySQL rows is not the constructor, but a fetch mode that PDO has, and that allows us to map a row into an object. To do so, we need to adapt the `Book` domain object a bit:

- The names of the properties have to be the same as the names of the fields in the database

- There is no need for a constructor or setters, unless we need them for other purposes

- To go with encapsulation, properties should be private, so we will need getters for all of them

The new `Book` class should look like the following:

```php
<?php

namespace Bookstore\Domain;

class Book {
    private $id;
    private $isbn;
    private $title;
    private $author;
    private $stock;
    private $price;

    public function getId(): int {
        return $this->id;
    }

    public function getIsbn(): string {
        return $this->isbn;
    }

    public function getTitle(): string {
        return $this->title;
    }

    public function getAuthor(): string {
        return $this->author;
    }
```

```php
        public function getStock(): int {
            return $this->stock;
        }

        public function getCopy(): bool {
            if ($this->stock < 1) {
                return false;
            } else {
                $this->stock--;
                return true;
            }
        }

        public function addCopy() {
            $this->stock++;
        }

        public function getPrice(): float {
            return $this->price;
        }
    }
```

We retained the getCopy and addCopy methods even though they are not getters, as we will need them later. Now, when fetching a group of rows from MySQL with the fetchAll method, we can send two parameters: the constant PDO::FETCH_CLASS that tells PDO to map rows to a class, and the name of the class that we want to map to. Let's create the BookModel class with a simple get method that fetches a book from the database with a given ID. This method will return either a Book object or throw an exception in case the ID does not exist. Save it as src/Models/BookModel.php:

```php
<?php

namespace Bookstore\Models;

use Bookstore\Domain\Book;
use Bookstore\Exceptions\DbException;
use Bookstore\Exceptions\NotFoundException;
use PDO;

class BookModel extends AbstractModel {
    const CLASSNAME = '\Bookstore\Domain\Book';

    public function get(int $bookId): Book {
        $query = 'SELECT * FROM book WHERE id = :id';
        $sth = $this->db->prepare($query);
```

```
        $sth->execute(['id' => $bookId]);

        $books = $sth->fetchAll(
            PDO::FETCH_CLASS, self::CLASSNAME
        );
        if (empty($books)) {
            throw new NotFoundException();
        }

        return $books[0];
    }
}
```

There are advantages and disadvantages of using this fetch mode. On one hand, we avoid a lot of dull code when creating objects from rows. Usually, we either just send all the elements of the row array to the constructor of the class, or use setters for all its properties. If we add more fields to the MySQL table, we just need to add the properties to our domain class, instead of changing everywhere where we were instantiating the objects. On the other hand, you are forced to use the same names for the fields in both the table's as well as the class' properties, which means high coupling (always a bad idea). This also causes some conflicts when following conventions, because in MySQL, it is common to use book_id, but in PHP, the property is $bookId.

Now that we know how this fetch mode works, let's add three other methods that fetch data from MySQL. Add the following code to your model:

```
public function getAll(int $page, int $pageLength): array {
    $start = $pageLength * ($page - 1);

    $query = 'SELECT * FROM book LIMIT :page, :length';
    $sth = $this->db->prepare($query);
    $sth->bindParam('page', $start, PDO::PARAM_INT);
    $sth->bindParam('length', $pageLength, PDO::PARAM_INT);
    $sth->execute();

    return $sth->fetchAll(PDO::FETCH_CLASS, self::CLASSNAME);
}

public function getByUser(int $userId): array {
    $query = <<<SQL
SELECT b.*
FROM borrowed_books bb LEFT JOIN book b ON bb.book_id = b.id
WHERE bb.customer_id = :id
SQL;
```

```
    $sth = $this->db->prepare($query);
    $sth->execute(['id' => $userId]);

    return $sth->fetchAll(PDO::FETCH_CLASS, self::CLASSNAME);
}

public function search(string $title, string $author): array {
    $query = <<<SQL
SELECT * FROM book
WHERE title LIKE :title AND author LIKE :author
SQL;
    $sth = $this->db->prepare($query);
    $sth->bindValue('title', "%$title%");
    $sth->bindValue('author', "%$author%");
    $sth->execute();

    return $sth->fetchAll(PDO::FETCH_CLASS, self::CLASSNAME);
}
```

The methods added are as follows:

- getAll returns an array of all the books for a given page. Remember that LIMIT allows you to return a specific number of rows with an offset, which can work as a paginator.

- getByUser returns all the books that a given customer has borrowed—we will need to use a join query for this. Note that we return b.*, that is, only the fields of the book table, skipping the rest of the fields.

- Finally, there is a method to search by either title or author, or both. We can do that using the operator LIKE and enclosing the patterns with %. If we do not specify one of the parameters, we will try to match the field with %%, which matches everything.

So far, we have been adding methods to fetch data. Let's add methods that will allow us to modify the data in our database. For the book model, we will need to be able to borrow books and return them. Here is the code for those two actions:

```
public function borrow(Book $book, int $userId) {
    $query = <<<SQL
INSERT INTO borrowed_books (book_id, customer_id, start)
VALUES(:book, :user, NOW())
SQL;
    $sth = $this->db->prepare($query);
    $sth->bindValue('book', $book->getId());
    $sth->bindValue('user', $userId);
```

```
        if (!$sth->execute()) {
            throw new DbException($sth->errorInfo()[2]);
        }

        $this->updateBookStock($book);
    }

    public function returnBook(Book $book, int $userId) {
        $query = <<<SQL
UPDATE borrowed_books SET end = NOW()
WHERE book_id = :book AND customer_id = :user AND end IS NULL
SQL;
        $sth = $this->db->prepare($query);
        $sth->bindValue('book', $book->getId());
        $sth->bindValue('user', $userId);
        if (!$sth->execute()) {
            throw new DbException($sth->errorInfo()[2]);
        }

        $this->updateBookStock($book);
    }

    private function updateBookStock(Book $book) {
        $query = 'UPDATE book SET stock = :stock WHERE id = :id';
        $sth = $this->db->prepare($query);
        $sth->bindValue('id', $book->getId());
        $sth->bindValue('stock', $book->getStock());
        if (!$sth->execute()) {
            throw new DbException($sth->errorInfo()[2]);
        }
    }
}
```

When borrowing a book, you are adding a row to the `borrower_books` table. When returning books, you do not want to remove that row, but rather to set the end date in order to keep a history of the books that a user has been borrowing. Both methods need to change the stock of the borrowed book: when borrowing it, reducing the stock by one, and when returning it, increasing the stock. That is why, in the last code snippet, we created a private method to update the stock of a given book, which will be used from both the `borrow` and `returnBook` methods.

The sales model

Now we need to add the last model to our application: the `SalesModel`. Using the same fetch mode that we used with books, we need to adapt the domain class as well. We need to think a bit more in this case, as we will be doing more than just fetching. Our application has to be able to create new sales on demand, containing the ID of the customer and the books. We can already add books with the current implementation, but we need to add a setter for the customer ID. The ID of the sale will be given by the autoincrement ID in MySQL, so there is no need to add a setter for it. The final implementation would look as follows:

```php
<?php

namespace Bookstore\Domain;

class Sale {
    private $id;
    private $customer_id;
    private $books;
    private $date;

    public function setCustomerId(int $customerId) {
        $this->customer_id = $customerId;
    }

    public function getId(): int {
        return $this->id;
    }

    public function getCustomerId(): int {
        return $this->customer_id;
    }

    public function getBooks(): array {
        return $this->books;
    }

    public function getDate(): string {
        return $this->date;
    }

    public function addBook(int $bookId, int $amount = 1) {
        if (!isset($this->books[$bookId])) {
            $this->books[$bookId] = 0;
```

```
        }
        $this->books[$bookId] += $amount;
    }

    public function setBooks(array $books) {
        $this->books = $books;
    }
}
```

The `SalesModel` will be the most difficult one to write. The problem with this model is that it includes manipulating different tables: `sale` and `sale_book`. For example, when getting the information of a sale, we need to get the information from the `sale` table, and then the information of all the books in the `sale_book` table. You could argue about whether to have one unique method that fetches all the necessary information related to a sale, or to have two different methods, one to fetch the sale and the other to fetch the books, and let the controller to decide which one to use.

This actually starts a very interesting discussion. On one hand, we want to make things easier for the controller—having one unique method to fetch the entire `Sale` object. This makes sense as the controller does not need to know about the internal implementation of the `Sale` object, which lowers coupling. On the other hand, forcing the model to always fetch the whole object, even if we only need the information in the `sale` table, is a bad idea. Imagine if the sale contains a lot of books; fetching them from MySQL will decrease performance unnecessarily.

You should think how your controllers need to manage sales. If you will always need the entire object, you can have one method without being concerned about performance. If you only need to fetch the entire object sometimes, maybe you could add both methods. For our application, we will have one method to rule them all, since that is what we will always need.

Lazy loading

As with any other design challenge, other developers have already given a lot of thought to this problem. They came up with a design pattern named **lazy load**. This pattern basically lets the controller think that there is only one method to fetch the whole domain object, but we will actually be fetching only what we need from database.

The model fetches the most used information for the object and leaves the rest of the properties that need extra database queries empty. Once the controller uses a getter of a property that is empty, the model automatically fetches that data from the database. We get the best of both worlds: there is simplicity for the controller, but we do not spend more time than necessary querying unused data.

Add the following as your `src/Models/SaleModel.php` file:

```php
<?php
namespace Bookstore\Models;

use Bookstore\Domain\Sale;
use Bookstore\Exceptions\DbException;
use PDO;

class SaleModel extends AbstractModel {
    const CLASSNAME = '\Bookstore\Domain\Sale';

    public function getByUser(int $userId): array {
        $query = 'SELECT * FROM sale WHERE s.customer_id = :user';
        $sth = $this->db->prepare($query);
        $sth->execute(['user' => $userId]);

        return $sth->fetchAll(PDO::FETCH_CLASS, self::CLASSNAME);
    }

    public function get(int $saleId): Sale {
        $query = 'SELECT * FROM sale WHERE id = :id';
        $sth = $this->db->prepare($query);
        $sth->execute(['id' => $saleId]);
        $sales = $sth->fetchAll(PDO::FETCH_CLASS, self::CLASSNAME);

        if (empty($sales)) {
            throw new NotFoundException('Sale not found.');
        }
        $sale = array_pop($sales);

        $query = <<<SQL
SELECT b.id, b.title, b.author, b.price, sb.amount as stock, b.isbn
FROM sale s
LEFT JOIN sale_book sb ON s.id = sb.sale_id
LEFT JOIN book b ON sb.book_id = b.id
WHERE s.id = :id
SQL;
        $sth = $this->db->prepare($query);
        $sth->execute(['id' => $saleId]);
        $books = $sth->fetchAll(
            PDO::FETCH_CLASS, BookModel::CLASSNAME
        );

        $sale->setBooks($books);
        return $sale;
    }
}
```

Another tricky method in this model is the one that takes care of creating a sale in the database. This method has to create a sale in the `sale` table, and then add all the books for that sale to the `sale_book` table. What would happen if we have a problem when adding one of the books? We would leave a corrupted sale in the database. To avoid that, we need to use transactions, starting with one at the beginning of the model's or the controller's method, and either rolling back in case of error, or committing it at the end of the method.

In the same method, we also need to take care of the ID of the sale. We do not set the ID of the sale when creating the `sale` object, because we rely on the autoincremental field in the database. But when inserting the books into `sale_book`, we do need the ID of the sale. For that, we need to request the PDO for the last inserted ID with the `lastInsertId` method. Let's add then the `create` method into your `SaleModel`:

```php
public function create(Sale $sale) {
    $this->db->beginTransaction();

    $query = <<<SQL
INSERT INTO sale(customer_id, date)
VALUES(:id, NOW())
SQL;
    $sth = $this->db->prepare($query);
    if (!$sth->execute(['id' => $sale->getCustomerId()])) {
        $this->db->rollBack();
        throw new DbException($sth->errorInfo()[2]);
    }

    $saleId = $this->db->lastInsertId();
    $query = <<<SQL
INSERT INTO sale_book(sale_id, book_id, amount)
VALUES(:sale, :book, :amount)
SQL;
    $sth = $this->db->prepare($query);
    $sth->bindValue('sale', $saleId);
    foreach ($sale->getBooks() as $bookId => $amount) {
        $sth->bindValue('book', $bookId);
        $sth->bindValue('amount', $amount);
        if (!$sth->execute()) {
            $this->db->rollBack();
            throw new DbException($sth->errorInfo()[2]);
        }
    }

    $this->db->commit();
}
```

One last thing to note from this method is that we prepare a statement, bind a value to it (the sale ID), and then bind and execute the same statement as many times as the books in the array. Once you have a statement, you can bind the values as many times as you want. Also, you can execute the same statement as many times as you want, and the values stay the same.

V for view

The view is the layer that takes care of the... view. In this layer, you find all the templates that render the HTML that the user gets. Although the separation between views and the rest of the application is easy to see, that does not make views an easy part. In fact, you will have to learn a new technology in order to write views properly. Let's get into the details.

Introduction to Twig

In our first attempt at writing views, we mixed up PHP and HTML code. We already know that the logic should not be mixed in the same place as HTML, but that is not the end of the story. When rendering HTML, we need some logic there too. For example, if we want to print a list of books, we need to repeat a certain block of HTML for each book. And since a priori we do not know the number of books to print, the best option would be a `foreach` loop.

One option that a lot of people take is minimizing the amount of logic that you can include in a view. You could set some rules, such as *we should only include conditionals and loops*, which is a reasonable amount of logic needed to render basic views. The problem is that there is not a way of enforcing this kind of rule, and other developers can easily start adding heavy logic in there. While some people are OK with that, assuming that no one will do it, others prefer to implement more restrictive systems. That was the beginning of template engines.

You could think of a template engine as another language that you need to learn. Why would you do that? Because this new "language" is more limited than PHP. These languages usually allow you to perform conditionals and simple loops, and that is it. The developer is not able to add PHP to that file, since the template engine will not treat it as PHP code. Instead, it will just print the code to the output—the response' body—as if it was plain text. Also, as it is specially oriented to write templates, the syntax is usually easier to read when mixed with HTML. Almost everything is an advantage.

The inconvenience of using a template engine is that it takes some time to translate the new language to PHP, and then to HTML. This can be quite time consuming, so it is very important that you choose a good template engine. Most of them also allow you to cache templates, improving the performance. Our choice is a quite light and widely used one: **Twig**. As we've already added the dependency in our Composer file, we can use it straight away.

Setting up Twig is quite easy. On the PHP side, you just need to specify the location of the templates. A common convention is to use the `views` directory for that. Create the directory, and add the following two lines into your `index.php`:

```php
$loader = new Twig_Loader_Filesystem(__DIR__ . '/views');
$twig = new Twig_Environment($loader);
```

The book view

In these sections, as we work with templates, it would be nice to see the result of your work. We have not yet implemented any controllers, so we will force our `index.php` to render a specific template, regardless of the request. We can start rendering the view of a single book. For that, let's add the following code at the end of your `index.php`, after creating your `twig` object:

```php
$bookModel = new BookModel(Db::getInstance());
$book = $bookModel->get(1);

$params = ['book' => $book];
echo $twig->loadTemplate('book.twig')->render($params);
```

In the preceding code, we request the book with ID 1 to the `BookModel`, get the book object, and create an array where the `book` key has the value of the `book` object. After that, we tell Twig to load the template `book.twig` and to render it by sending the array. This takes the template and injects the `$book` object, so that you are able to use it inside the template.

Let's now create our first template. Write the following code into `view/book.twig`. By convention, all Twig templates should have the `.twig` extension:

```twig
<h2>{{ book.title }}</h2>
<h3>{{ book.author }}</h3>

<hr>

<p>
    <strong>ISBN</strong> {{ book.isbn }}
</p>
```

```
<p>
    <strong>Stock</strong> {{ book.stock }}
</p>
<p>
    <strong>Price</strong> {{ book.price|number_format(2) }} €
</p>

<hr>

<h3>Actions</h3>

<form method="post" action="/book/{{ book.id }}/borrow">
    <input type="submit" value="Borrow">
</form>

<form method="post" action="/book/{{ book.id }}/buy">
    <input type="submit" value="Buy">
</form>
```

Since this is your first Twig template, let's go step by step. You can see that most of the content is HTML: some headers, a couple of paragraphs, and two forms with two buttons. You can recognize the Twig part, since it is enclosed by {{ }}. In Twig, everything that is between those curly brackets will be printed out. The first one that we find contains book.title. Do you remember that we injected the book object when rendering the template? We can access it here, just not with the usual PHP syntax. To access an object's property, use . instead of ->. So, this book.title will return the value of the title property of the book object, and the {{ }} will make Twig print it out. The same applies to the rest of the template.

There is one that does a bit more than just access an object's property. The book.price|number_format(2) gets the price of the book and sends it as an argument (using the pipe symbol) to the function number_format, which has already got 2 as another argument. This bit of code basically formats the price to two digital figures. In Twig, you also have some functions, but they are mostly reduced to formatting the output, which is an acceptable amount of logic.

Are you convinced now about how clean it is to use a template engine for your views? You can try it in your browser: accessing any path, your web server should execute the index.php file, forcing the template book.twig to be rendered.

Layouts and blocks

When you design your web application, usually you would want to share a common layout across most of your views. In our case, we want to always have a menu at the top of the view that allows us to go to the different sections of the website, or even to search books from wherever the user is. As with models, we want to avoid code duplication, since if we were to copy and paste the layout everywhere, updating it would be a nightmare. Instead, Twig comes with the ability to define layouts.

A **layout** in Twig is just another template file. Its content is just the common HTML code that we want to display across all views (in our case, the menu and search bar), and contains some tagged gaps (blocks in Twig's world), where you will be able to inject the specific HTML of each view. You can define one of those blocks with the tag `{% block %}`. Let's see what our `views/layout.twig` file would look like:

```
<html>
<head>
    <title>{% block title %}{% endblock %}</title>
</head>
<body>
    <div style="border: solid 1px">
        <a href="/books">Books</a>
        <a href="/sales">My Sales</a>
        <a href="/my-books">My Books</a>
        <hr>
        <form action="/books/search" method="get">
            <label>Title</label>
            <input type="text" name="title">
            <label>Author</label>
            <input type="text" name="author">
            <input type="submit" value="Search">
        </form>
    </div>
    {% block content %}{% endblock %}
</body>
</html>
```

As you can see in the preceding code, blocks have a name so that templates using the layout can refer to them. In our layout, we defined two blocks: one for the title of the view and the other for the content itself. When a template uses the layout, we just need to write the HTML code for each of the blocks defined in the layout, and Twig will do the rest. Also, to let Twig know that our template wants to use the layout, we use the tag `{% extends %}` with the layout filename. Let's update `views/book.twig` to use our new layout:

```
{% extends 'layout.twig' %}

{% block title %}
    {{ book.title }}
{% endblock %}

{% block content %}
<h2>{{ book.title }}</h2>
//...
</form>
{% endblock %}
```

At the top of the file, we add the layout that we need to use. Then, we open a block tag with the reference name, and we write inside it the HTML that we want to use. You can use anything valid inside a block, either Twig code or plain HTML. In our template, we used the title of the book as the `title` block, which refers to the title of the view, and we put all the previous HTML inside the `content` block. Note that everything in the file is inside a block now. Try it in your browser now to see the changes.

Paginated book list

Let's add another view, this time for a paginated list of books. In order to see the result of your work, update the content of `index.php`, replacing the code of the previous section with the following:

```
$bookModel = new BookModel(Db::getInstance());
$books = $bookModel->getAll(1, 3);

$params = ['books' => $books, 'currentPage' => 2];
echo $twig->loadTemplate('books.twig')->render($params);
```

In the preceding snippet, we force the application to render the `books.twig` template, sending an array of books from page number 1, and showing 3 books per page. This array, though, might not always return 3 books, maybe because there are only 2 books in the database. We should then use a loop to iterate the list instead of assuming the size of the array. In Twig, you can emulate a `foreach` loop using `{% for <element> in <array> %}` in order to iterate an array. Let's use it for your `views/books.twig`:

```
{% extends 'layout.twig' %}

{% block title %}
    Books
{% endblock %}
```

```
{% block content %}
<table>
    <thead>
        <th>Title</th>
        <th>Author</th>
        <th></th>
    </thead>
{% for book in books %}
    <tr>
        <td>{{ book.title }}</td>
        <td>{{ book.author }}</td>
        <td><a href="/book/{{ book.id }}">View</a></td>
    </tr>
{% endfor %}
</table>
{% endblock %}
```

We can also use conditionals in a Twig template, which work the same as the conditionals in PHP. The syntax is `{% if <boolean expression> %}`. Let's use it to decide if we should show the previous and/or following links on our page. Add the following code at the end of the content block:

```
{% if currentPage != 1 %}
    <a href="/books/{{ currentPage - 1 }}">Previous</a>
{% endif %}
{% if not lastPage %}
    <a href="/books/{{ currentPage + 1 }}">Next</a>
{% endif %}
```

The last thing to note from this template is that we are not restricted to using only variables when printing out content with `{{ }}`. We can add any valid Twig expression that returns a value, as we did with `{{ currentPage + 1 }}`.

The sales view

We have already shown you everything that you will need for using templates, and now we just have to finish adding all of them. The next one in the list is the template that shows the list of sales for a given user. Update your `index.php` file with the following hack:

```
$saleModel = new SaleModel(Db::getInstance());
$sales = $saleModel->getByUser(1);

$params = ['sales' => $sales];
echo $twig->loadTemplate('sales.twig')->render($params);
```

The template for this view will be very similar to the one listing the books: a table populated with the content of an array. The following is the content of views/ sales.twig:

```
{% extends 'layout.twig' %}

{% block title %}
    My sales
{% endblock %}

{% block content %}
<table>
    <thead>
        <th>Id</th>
        <th>Date</th>
    </thead>
{% for sale in sales %}
    <tr>
        <td>{{ sale.id}}</td>
        <td>{{ sale.date }}</td>
        <td><a href="/sales/{{ sale.id }}">View</a></td>
    </tr>
{% endfor %}
</table>
{% endblock %}
```

The other view related to sales is where we want to display all the content of a specific one. This sale, again, will be similar to the books list, as we will be listing the books related to that sale. The hack to force the rendering of this template is as follows:

```
$saleModel = new SaleModel(Db::getInstance());
$sale = $saleModel->get(1);

$params = ['sale' => $sale];
echo $twig->loadTemplate('sale.twig')->render($params);
```

And the Twig template should be placed in views/sale.twig:

```
{% extends 'layout.twig' %}

{% block title %}
    Sale {{ sale.id }}
{% endblock %}

{% block content %}
```

```
<table>
    <thead>
        <th>Title</th>
        <th>Author</th>
        <th>Amount</th>
        <th>Price</th>
        <th></th>
    </thead>
    {% for book in sale.books %}
        <tr>
            <td>{{ book.title }}</td>
            <td>{{ book.author }}</td>
            <td>{{ book.stock }}</td>
            <td>{{ (book.price * book.stock)|number_format(2) }} €<//
td>
            <td><a href="/book/{{ book.id }}">View</a></td>
        </tr>
    {% endfor %}
</table>
{% endblock %}
```

The error template

We should add a very simple template that will be shown to the user when there is an error in our application, rather than showing a PHP error message. This template will just expect the `errorMessage` variable, and it could look like the following. Save it as `views/error.twig`:

```
{% extends 'layout.twig' %}

{% block title %}
    Error
{% endblock %}

{% block content %}
    <h2>Error: {{ errorMessage }}</h2>
{% endblock %}
```

Note that even the error page extends from the layout, as we want the user to be able to do something else when this happens.

The login template

Our last template will be the one that allows the user to log in. This template is a bit different from the others, as it will be used in two different scenarios. In the first one, the user accesses the login view for the first time, so we need to show the form. In the second one, the user has already tried to log in, and there was an error when doing so, that is, the e-mail address was not found. In this case, we will add an extra variable to the template, `errorMessage`, and we will add a conditional to show its contents only when this variable is defined. You can use the operator `is defined` to check that. Add the following template as `views/login.twig`:

```
{% extends 'layout.twig' %}

{% block title %}
    Login
{% endblock %}

{% block content %}
    {% if errorMessage is defined %}
        <strong>{{ errorMessage }}</strong>
    {% endif %}
    <form action="/login" method="post">
        <label>Email</label>
        <input type="text" name="email">
        <input type="submit">
    </form>
{% endblock %}
```

C for controller

It is finally time for the director of the orchestra. Controllers represent the layer in our application that, given a request, talks to the models and builds the views. They act like the manager of a team: they decide what resources to use depending on the situation.

As we stated when explaining models, it is sometimes difficult to decide if some piece of logic should go into the controller or the model. At the end of the day, MVC is a pattern, like a recipe that guides you, rather than an exact algorithm that you need to follow step by step. There will be scenarios where the answer is not straightforward, so it will be up to you; in these cases, just try to be consistent. The following are some common scenarios that might be difficult to localize:

- The request points to a path that we do not support. This scenario is already covered in our application, and it is the router that should take care of it, not the controller.

- The request tries to access an element that does not exist, for example, a book ID that is not in the database. In this case, the controller should ask the model if the book exists, and depending on the response, render a template with the book's contents, or another with a "Not found" message.

- The user tries to perform an action, such as buying a book, but the parameters coming from the request are not valid. This is a tricky one. One option is to get all the parameters from the request without checking them, sending them straight to the model, and leaving the task of sanitizing the information to the model. Another option is that the controller checks that the parameters provided make sense, and then gives them to the model. There are other solutions, like building a class that checks if the parameters are valid, which can be reused in different controllers. In this case, it will depend on the amount of parameters and logic involved in the sanitization. For requests receiving a lot of data, the third option looks like the best of them, as we will be able to reuse the code in different endpoints, and we are not writing controllers that are too long. But in requests where the user sends one or two parameters, sanitizing them in the controller might be good enough.

Now that we've set the ground, let's prepare our application to use controllers. The first thing to do is to update our index.php, which has been forcing the application to always render the same template. Instead, we should be giving this task to the router, which will return the response as a string that we can just print with echo. Update your index.php file with the following content:

```php
<?php

use Bookstore\Core\Router;
use Bookstore\Core\Request;

require_once __DIR__ . '/vendor/autoload.php';

$router = new Router();
$response = $router->route(new Request());
echo $response;
```

As you might remember, the router instantiates a controller class, sending the request object to the constructor. But controllers have other dependencies as well, such as the template engine, the database connection, or the configuration reader. Even though this is not the best solution (you will improve it once we cover dependency injection in the next section), we could create an AbstractController that would be the parent of all controllers, and will set those dependencies. Copy the following as src/Controllers/AbstractController.php:

```php
<?php

namespace Bookstore\Controllers;

use Bookstore\Core\Config;
use Bookstore\Core\Db;
use Bookstore\Core\Request;
use Monolog\Logger;
use Twig_Environment;
use Twig_Loader_Filesystem;
use Monolog\Handler\StreamHandler;

abstract class AbstractController {
    protected $request;
    protected $db;
    protected $config;
    protected $view;
    protected $log;

    public function __construct(Request $request) {
        $this->request = $request;
        $this->db = Db::getInstance();
        $this->config = Config::getInstance();

        $loader = new Twig_Loader_Filesystem(
            __DIR__ . '/../../views'
        );
        $this->view = new Twig_Environment($loader);

        $this->log = new Logger('bookstore');
        $logFile = $this->config->get('log');
        $this->log->pushHandler(
            new StreamHandler($logFile, Logger::DEBUG)
        );
    }

    public function setCustomerId(int $customerId) {
        $this->customerId = $customerId;
    }
}
```

When instantiating a controller, we will set some properties that will be useful when handling requests. We already know how to instantiate the database connection, the configuration reader, and the template engine. The fourth property, `$log`, will allow the developer to write logs to a given file when necessary. We will use the Monolog library for that, but there are many other options. Notice that in order to instantiate the logger, we get the value of log from the configuration, which should be the path to the log file. The convention is to use the `/var/log/` directory, so create the `/var/log/bookstore.log` file, and add `"log": "/var/log/bookstore.log"` to your configuration file.

Another thing that is useful to some controllers — but not all of them — is the information about the user performing the action. As this is only going to be available for certain routes, we should not set it when constructing the controller. Instead, we have a setter for the router to set the customer ID when available; in fact, the router does that already.

Finally, a handy helper method that we could use is one that renders a given template with parameters, as all the controllers will end up rendering one template or the other. Let's add the following protected method to the `AbstractController` class:

```
protected function render(string $template, array $params): string {
    return $this->view->loadTemplate($template)->render($params);
}
```

The error controller

Let's start by creating the easiest of the controllers: the `ErrorController`. This controller does not do much; it just renders the `error.twig` template sending the "Page not found!" message. As you might remember, the router uses this controller when it cannot match the request to any of the other defined routes. Save the following class in `src/Controllers/ErrorController.php`:

```php
<?php

namespace Bookstore\Controllers;

class ErrorController extends AbstractController {
    public function notFound(): string {
        $properties = ['errorMessage' => 'Page not found!'];
        return $this->render('error.twig', $properties);
    }
}
```

The login controller

The second controller that we have to add is the one that manages the login of the customers. If we think about the flow when a user wants to authenticate, we have the following scenarios:

- The user wants to get the login form in order to submit the necessary information and log in.

- The user tries to submit the form, but we could not get the e-mail address. We should render the form again, letting them know about the problem.

- The user submits the form with an e-mail, but it is not a valid one. In this case, we should show the login form again with an error message explaining the situation.

- The user submits a valid e-mail, we set the cookie, and we show the list of books so the user can start searching. This is absolutely arbitrary; you could choose to send them to their borrowed books page, their sales, and so on. The important thing here is to notice that we will be redirecting the request to another controller.

There are up to four possible paths. We will use the `request` object to decide which of them to use in each case, returning the corresponding response. Let's create, then, the `CustomerController` class in `src/Controllers/CustomerController.php` with the `login` method, as follows:

```php
<?php

namespace Bookstore\Controllers;

use Bookstore\Exceptions\NotFoundException;
use Bookstore\Models\CustomerModel;

class CustomerController extends AbstractController {
    public function login(string $email): string {
        if (!$this->request->isPost()) {
            return $this->render('login.twig', []);
        }

        $params = $this->request->getParams();

        if (!$params->has('email')) {
            $params = ['errorMessage' => 'No info provided.'];
            return $this->render('login.twig', $params);
        }

        $email = $params->getString('email');
```

```
$customerModel = new CustomerModel($this->db);

try {
    $customer = $customerModel->getByEmail($email);
} catch (NotFoundException $e) {
    $this->log->warn('Customer email not found: ' . $email);
    $params = ['errorMessage' => 'Email not found.'];
    return $this->render('login.twig', $params);
}

setcookie('user', $customer->getId());

$newController = new BookController($this->request);
return $newController->getAll();
    }
}
```

As you can see, there are four different returns for the four different cases. The controller itself does not do anything, but orchestrates the rest of the components, and makes decisions. First, we check if the request is a POST, and if it is not, we will assume that the user wants to get the form. If it is, we will check for the e-mail in the parameters, returning an error if the e-mail is not there. If it is, we will try to find the customer with that e-mail, using our model. If we get an exception saying that there is no such customer, we will render the form with a "Not found" error message. If the login is successful, we will set the cookie with the ID of the customer, and will execute the getAll method of BookController (still to be written), returning the list of books.

At this point, you should be able to test the login feature of your application end to end with the browser. Try to access http://localhost:8000/login to see the form, adding random e-mails to get the error message, and adding a valid e-mail (check your customer table in MySQL) to log in successfully. After this, you should see the cookie with the customer ID.

The book controller

The BookController class will be the largest of our controllers, as most of the application relies on it. Let's start by adding the easiest methods, the ones that just retrieve information from the database. Save this as src/Controllers/BookController.php:

```php
<?php

namespace Bookstore\Controllers;

use Bookstore\Models\BookModel;
```

```php
class BookController extends AbstractController {
    const PAGE_LENGTH = 10;

    public function getAllWithPage($page): string {
        $page = (int)$page;
        $bookModel = new BookModel($this->db);

        $books = $bookModel->getAll($page, self::PAGE_LENGTH);

        $properties = [
            'books' => $books,
            'currentPage' => $page,
            'lastPage' => count($books) < self::PAGE_LENGTH
        ];
        return $this->render('books.twig', $properties);
    }

    public function getAll(): string {
        return $this->getAllWithPage(1);
    }

    public function get(int $bookId): string {
        $bookModel = new BookModel($this->db);

        try {
            $book = $bookModel->get($bookId);
        } catch (\Exception $e) {
            $this->log->error(
                'Error getting book: ' . $e->getMessage()
            );
            $properties = ['errorMessage' => 'Book not found!'];
            return $this->render('error.twig', $properties);
        }

        $properties = ['book' => $book];
        return $this->render('book.twig', $properties);
    }

    public function getByUser(): string {
        $bookModel = new BookModel($this->db);

        $books = $bookModel->getByUser($this->customerId);
```

```
        $properties = [
            'books' => $books,
            'currentPage' => 1,
            'lastPage' => true
        ];
        return $this->render('books.twig', $properties);
    }
}
```

There's nothing too special in this preceding code so far. The `getAllWithPage` and `getAll` methods do the same thing, one with the page number given by the user as a URL argument, and the other setting the page number as 1 — the default case. They ask the model for the list of books to be displayed and passed to the view. The information of the current page — and whether or not we are on the last page — is also sent to the template in order to add the "previous" and "next" page links.

The `get` method will get the ID of the book that the customer is interested in. It will try to fetch it using the model. If the model throws an exception, we will render the error template with a "Book not found" message. Instead, if the book ID is valid, we will render the book template as expected.

The `getByUser` method will return all the books that the authenticated customer has borrowed. We will make use of the `customerId` property that we set from the router. There is no sanity check here, since we are not trying to get a specific book, but rather a list, which could be empty if the user has not borrowed any books yet — but that is not an issue.

Another getter controller is the one that searches for a book by its title and/or author. This method will be triggered when the user submits the form in the layout template. The form sends both the `title` and the `author` fields, so the controller will ask for both. The model is ready to use the arguments that are empty, so we will not perform any extra checking here. Add the method to the `BookController` class:

```
public function search(): string {
    $title = $this->request->getParams()->getString('title');
    $author = $this->request->getParams()->getString('author');

    $bookModel = new BookModel($this->db);
    $books = $bookModel->search($title, $author);

    $properties = [
        'books' => $books,
        'currentPage' => 1,
        'lastPage' => true
    ];
    return $this->render('books.twig', $properties);
}
```

Your application cannot perform any actions, but at least you can finally browse the list of books, and click on any of them to view the details. We are finally getting something here!

Borrowing books

Borrowing and returning books are probably the actions that involve the most logic, together with buying a book, which will be covered by a different controller. This is a good place to start logging the user's actions, since it will be useful later for debugging purposes. Let's see the code first, and then discuss it briefly. Add the following two methods to your `BookController` class:

```
public function borrow(int $bookId): string {
    $bookModel = new BookModel($this->db);

    try {
        $book = $bookModel->get($bookId);
    } catch (NotFoundException $e) {
        $this->log->warn('Book not found: ' . $bookId);
        $params = ['errorMessage' => 'Book not found.'];
        return $this->render('error.twig', $params);
    }

    if (!$book->getCopy()) {
        $params = [
            'errorMessage' => 'There are no copies left.'
        ];
        return $this->render('error.twig', $params);
    }

    try {
        $bookModel->borrow($book, $this->customerId);
    } catch (DbException $e) {
        $this->log->error(
            'Error borrowing book: ' . $e->getMessage()
        );
        $params = ['errorMessage' => 'Error borrowing book.'];
        return $this->render('error.twig', $params);
    }

    return $this->getByUser();
}

public function returnBook(int $bookId): string {
```

```
$bookModel = new BookModel($this->db);

try {
    $book = $bookModel->get($bookId);
} catch (NotFoundException $e) {
    $this->log->warn('Book not found: ' . $bookId);
    $params = ['errorMessage' => 'Book not found.'];
    return $this->render('error.twig', $params);
}

$book->addCopy();

try {
    $bookModel->returnBook($book, $this->customerId);
} catch (DbException $e) {
    $this->log->error(
        'Error returning book: ' . $e->getMessage()
    );
    $params = ['errorMessage' => 'Error returning book.'];
    return $this->render('error.twig', $params);
}

return $this->getByUser();
}
```

As we mentioned earlier, one of the new things here is that we are logging user actions, like when trying to borrow or return a book that is not valid. Monolog allows you to write logs with different priority levels: error, warning, and notices. You can invoke methods such as error, warn, or notice to refer to each of them. We use warnings when something unexpected, yet not critical, happens, for example, trying to borrow a book that is not there. Errors are used when there is an unknown problem from which we cannot recover, like an error from the database.

The modus operandi of these two methods is as follows: we get the book object from the 3database with the given book ID. As usual, if there is no such book, we return an error page. Once we have the book domain object, we make use of the helpers addCopy and getCopy in order to update the stock of the book, and send it to the model, together with the customer ID, to store the information in the database. There is also a sanity check when borrowing a book, just in case there are no more books available. In both cases, we return the list of books that the user has borrowed as the response of the controller.

The sales controller

We arrive at the last of our controllers: the `SalesController`. With a different model, it will end up doing pretty much the same as the methods related to borrowed books. But we need to create the `sale` domain object in the controller instead of getting it from the model. Let's add the following code, which contains a method for buying a book, `add`, and two getters: one that gets all the sales of a given user and one that gets the info of a specific sale, that is, `getByUser` and `get` respectively. Following the convention, the file will be `src/Controllers/SalesController.php`:

```php
<?php

namespace Bookstore\Controllers;

use Bookstore\Domain\Sale;
use Bookstore\Models\SaleModel;

class SalesController extends AbstractController {
    public function add($id): string {
        $bookId = (int)$id;
        $salesModel = new SaleModel($this->db);

        $sale = new Sale();
        $sale->setCustomerId($this->customerId);
        $sale->addBook($bookId);

        try {
            $salesModel->create($sale);
        } catch (\Exception $e) {
            $properties = [
                'errorMessage' => 'Error buying the book.'
            ];
            $this->log->error(
                'Error buying book: ' . $e->getMessage()
            );
            return $this->render('error.twig', $properties);
        }

        return $this->getByUser();
    }

    public function getByUser(): string {
```

```
        $salesModel = new SaleModel($this->db);

        $sales = $salesModel->getByUser($this->customerId);

        $properties = ['sales' => $sales];
        return $this->render('sales.twig', $properties);
    }

    public function get($saleId): string {
        $salesModel = new SaleModel($this->db);

        $sale = $salesModel->get($saleId);

        $properties = ['sale' => $sale];
        return $this->render('sale.twig', $properties);
    }
}
```

Dependency injection

At the end of the chapter, we will cover one of the most interesting and controversial of the topics that come with, not only the MVC pattern, but OOP in general: **dependency injection**. We will show you why it is so important, and how to implement a solution that suits our specific application, even though there are quite a few different implementations that can cover different necessities.

Why is dependency injection necessary?

We still need to cover the way to unit test your code, hence you have not experienced it by yourself yet. But one of the signs of a potential source of problems is when you use the new statement in your code to create an instance of a class that does not belong to your code base — also known as a dependency. Using new to create a domain object like Book or Sale is fine. Using it to instantiate models is also acceptable. But manually instantiating, which something else, such as the template engine, the database connection, or the logger, is something that you should avoid. There are different reasons that support this idea:

- If you want to use a controller from two different places, and each of these places needs a different database connection or log file, instantiating those dependencies inside the controller will not allow us to do that. The same controller will always use the same dependency.

- Instantiating the dependencies inside the controller means that the controller is fully aware of the concrete implementation of each of its dependencies, that is, the controller knows that we are using PDO with the MySQL driver and the location of the credentials for the connection. This means a high level of coupling in your application — so, bad news.

- Replacing one dependency with another that implements the same interface is not easy if you are instantiating the dependency explicitly everywhere, as you will have to search all these places, and change the instantiation manually.

For all these reasons, and more, it is always good to provide the dependencies that a class such as a controller needs instead of letting it create its own. This is something that everybody agrees with. The problem comes when implementing a solution. There are different options:

- We have a constructor that expects (through arguments) all the dependencies that the controller, or any other class, needs. The constructor will assign each of the arguments to the properties of the class.

- We have an empty constructor, and instead, we add as many setter methods as the dependencies of the class.

- A hybrid of both, where we set the main dependencies through a constructor, and set the rest of the dependencies via setters.

- Sending an object that contains all the dependencies as a unique argument for the constructor, and the controller gets the dependencies that it needs from that container.

Each solution has its pros and cons. If we have a class with a lot of dependencies, injecting all of them via the constructor would make it counterintuitive, so it would be better if we inject them using setters, even though a class with a lot of dependencies looks like bad design. If we have just one or two dependencies, using the constructor could be acceptable, and we will write less code. For classes with several dependencies, but not all of them mandatory, using the hybrid version could be a good solution. The fourth option makes it easier when injecting the dependencies as we do not need to know what each object expects. The problem is that each class should know how to fetch its dependency, that is, the dependency name, which is not ideal.

Implementing our own dependency injector

Open source solutions for dependency injectors are already available, but we think that it would be a good experience to implement a simple one by yourself. The idea of our dependency injector is a class that contains instances of the dependencies that your code needs. This class, which is basically a map of dependency names to dependency instances, will have two methods: a getter and a setter of dependencies. We do not want to use a static property for the dependencies array, as one of the goals is to be able to have more than one dependency injector with a different set of dependencies. Add the following class to `src/Utils/DependencyInjector.php`:

```php
<?php

namespace Bookstore\Utils;

use Bookstore\Exceptions\NotFoundException;

class DependencyInjector {
    private $dependencies = [];

    public function set(string $name, $object) {
        $this->dependencies[$name] = $object;
    }

    public function get(string $name) {
        if (isset($this->dependencies[$name])) {
            return $this->dependencies[$name];
        }
        throw new NotFoundException(
            $name . ' dependency not found.'
        );
    }
}
```

Having a dependency injector means that we will always use the same instance of a given class every time we ask for it, instead of creating one each time. That means that singleton implementations are not needed anymore; in fact, as mentioned in *Chapter 4, Creating Clean Code with OOP*, it is preferable to avoid them. Let's get rid of them, then. One of the places where we were using it was in our configuration reader. Replace the existing code with the following in the `src/Core/Config.php` file:

```php
<?php

namespace Bookstore\Core;

use Bookstore\Exceptions\NotFoundException;
```

```
class Config {
    private $data;

    public function __construct() {
        $json = file_get_contents(
            __DIR__ . '/../../config/app.json'
        );
        $this->data = json_decode($json, true);
    }

    public function get($key) {
        if (!isset($this->data[$key])) {
            throw new NotFoundException("Key $key not in config.");
        }
        return $this->data[$key];
    }
}
```

The other place where we were making use of the singleton pattern was in the DB class. In fact, the purpose of the class was only to have a singleton for our database connection, but if we are not making use of it, we can remove the entire class. So, delete your src/Core/DB.php file.

Now we need to define all these dependencies and add them to our dependency injector. The index.php file is a good place to have the dependency injector before we route the request. Add the following code just before instantiating the Router class:

```
$config = new Config();

$dbConfig = $config->get('db');
$db = new PDO(
    'mysql:host=127.0.0.1;dbname=bookstore',
    $dbConfig['user'],
    $dbConfig['password']
);

$loader = new Twig_Loader_Filesystem(__DIR__ . '/../../views');
$view = new Twig_Environment($loader);

$log = new Logger('bookstore');
$logFile = $config->get('log');
$log->pushHandler(new StreamHandler($logFile, Logger::DEBUG));

$di = new DependencyInjector();
$di->set('PDO', $db);
```

```
$di->set('Utils\Config', $config);
$di->set('Twig_Environment', $view);
$di->set('Logger', $log);

$router = new Router($di);
//...
```

There are a few changes that we need to make now. The most important of them refers to the AbstractController, the class that will make heavy use of the dependency injector. Add a property named $di to that class, and replace the constructor with the following:

```
public function __construct(
    DependencyInjector $di,
    Request $request
) {
    $this->request = $request;
    $this->di = $di;

    $this->db = $di->get('PDO');
    $this->log = $di->get('Logger');
    $this->view = $di->get('Twig_Environment');
    $this->config = $di->get('Utils\Config');

    $this->customerId = $_COOKIE['id'];
}
```

The other changes refer to the Router class, as we are sending it now as part of the constructor, and we need to inject it to the controllers that we create. Add a $di property to that class as well, and change the constructor to the following one:

```
public function __construct(DependencyInjector $di) {
    $this->di = $di;

    $json = file_get_contents(__DIR__ . '/../../config/routes.json');
    $this->routeMap = json_decode($json, true);
}
```

Also change the content of the executeController and route methods:

```
public function route(Request $request): string {
    $path = $request->getPath();

    foreach ($this->routeMap as $route => $info) {
        $regexRoute = $this->getRegexRoute($route, $info);
        if (preg_match("@^/$regexRoute$@", $path)) {
```

```
                return $this->executeController(
                    $route, $path, $info, $request
                );
            }
        }

        $errorController = new ErrorController(
            $this->di,
            $request
        );
        return $errorController->notFound();
    }

    private function executeController(
        string $route,
        string $path,
        array $info,
        Request $request
    ): string {
        $controllerName = '\Bookstore\Controllers\\'
            . $info['controller'] . 'Controller';
        $controller = new $controllerName($this->di, $request);

        if (isset($info['login']) && $info['login']) {
            if ($request->getCookies()->has('user')) {
                $customerId = $request->getCookies()->get('user');
                $controller->setCustomerId($customerId);
            } else {
                $errorController = new CustomerController(
                    $this->di,
                    $request
                );
                return $errorController->login();
            }
        }

        $params = $this->extractParams($route, $path);
        return call_user_func_array(
            [$controller, $info['method']], $params
        );
    }
```

There is one last place that you need to change. The `login` method of `CustomerController` was instantiating a controller too, so we need to inject the dependency injector there as well:

```
$newController = new BookController($this->di, $this->request);
```

Summary

In this chapter, you learned what MVC is, and how to write an application that follows that pattern. You also know how to use a router to route requests to controllers, Twig to write templates, and Composer to manage your dependencies and autoloader. You were introduced to dependency injection, and you even built your own implementation, even though it is a very controversial topic with many different points of view.

In the next chapter, we will go through one of the most important parts needed when writing good code and good applications: unit testing your code to get quick feedback from it.

Testing Web Applications

We are pretty sure you have heard the term "bug" when speaking about applications. Sentences such as "We found a bug in the application that..." followed by some very undesirable behavior are more common than you think. Writing code is not the only task of a developer; testing it is crucial too. You should not release a version of your application that has not been tested. However, could you imagine having to test your entire application every time you change a line? It would be a nightmare!

Well, we are not the first ones to have this issue, so, luckily enough, developers have already found a pretty good solution to this problem. In fact, they found more than one solution, turning testing into a very hot topic of discussion. Even being a test developer has become quite a common role. In this chapter, we will introduce you to one of the approaches of testing your code: unit tests.

In this chapter, you will learn about:

- How unit tests work
- Configuring PHPUnit to test your code
- Writing tests with assertions, data providers, and mocks
- Good and bad practices when writing unit tests

The necessity for tests

When you work on a project, chances are that you are not the only developer who will work with this code. Even in the case where you are the only one who will ever change it, if you do this a few weeks after creating it, you will probably not remember all the places that this piece of code is affected. Okay, let's assume that you are the only developer and your memory is beyond limits; would you be able to verify that a change on a frequently used object, such as a request, will always work as expected? More importantly, would you like to do it every single time you make a tiny change?

Types of tests

While writing your application, making changes to the existing code, or adding new features, it is very important to get good *feedback*. How do you know that the feedback you get is good enough? It should accomplish the AEIOU principles:

- **Automatic**: Getting the feedback should be as painless as possible. Getting it by running just one command is always preferable to having to test your application manually.

- **Extensive**: We should be able to cover as many use cases as possible, including edge cases that are difficult to foresee when writing code.

- **Immediate**: You should get it as soon as possible. This means that the feedback that you get just after introducing a change is way better than the feedback that you get after your code is in production.

- **Open**: The results should be transparent, and also, the tests should give us insight to other developers as to how to integrate or operate with the code.

- **Useful**: It should answer questions such as "Will this change work?", "Will it break the application unexpectedly?", or "Is there any edge case that does not work properly?".

So, even though the concept is quite weird at the beginning, the best way to test your code is… with more code. Exactly! We will write code with the goal of testing the code of our application. Why? Well, it is the best way we know to satisfy all the AEIU principles, and it has the following advantages:

- We can execute the tests by just running one command from our command line or even from our favorite IDE. There is no need to manually test your application via a browser continually.

- We need to write the test just once. At the beginning, it may be a bit painful, but once the code is written, you will not need to repeat it again and again. This means that after some work, we will be able to test every single case effortlessly. If we had to test it manually, along with all the use cases and edge cases, it would be a nightmare.

- You do not need to have the whole application working in order to know whether your code works. Imagine that you are writing your router: in order to know whether it works, you will have to wait until your application works in a browser. Instead, you can write your tests and run them as soon as you finish your class.

- When writing your tests, you will be provided with feedback on what is failing. This is very useful to know when a specific function of the router does not work and the reason for the failure, which is better than getting a 500 error on our browser.

We hope that by now we have sold you on the idea that writing tests is indispensable. This was the easy part, though. The problem is that we know several different approaches. Do we write tests that test the entire application or tests that test specific parts? Do we isolate the tested area from the rest? Do we want to interact with the database or with other external resources while testing? Depending on your answers, you will decide on which type of tests you want to write. Let's discuss the three main approaches that developers agree with:

- **Unit tests**: These are tests that have a very focused scope. Their aim is to test a single class or method, isolating them from the rest of code. Take your `Sale` domain class as an example: it has some logic regarding the addition of books, right? A unit test might just instantiate a new sale, add books to the object, and verify that the array of books is valid. Unit tests are super fast due to their reduced scope, so you can have several different scenarios of the same functionality easily, covering all the edge cases you can imagine. They are also isolated, which means that we will not care too much about how all the pieces of our application are integrated. Instead, we will make sure that each piece works perfectly fine.

- **Integration tests**: These are tests with a wider scope. Their aim is to verify that all the pieces of your application work together, so their scope is not limited to a class or function but rather includes a set of classes or the whole application. There is still some isolation in case we do not want to use a real database or depend on some other external web service. An example in our application would be to simulate a `Request` object, send it to the router, and verify that the response is as expected.

- **Acceptance tests**: These are tests with an even wider scope. They try to test a whole functionality from the user's point of view. In web applications, this means that we can launch a browser and simulate the clicks that the user would make, asserting the response in the browser each time. And yes, all of this through code! These tests are slower to run, as you can imagine, because their scope is larger and working with a browser slows them down quite a lot too.

So, with all these types of tests, which one should you write? The answer is all of them. The trick is to know when and how many of each type you should write. One good approach is to write a lot of unit tests, covering absolutely everything in your code, then writing fewer integration tests to make sure that all the components of your application work together, and finally writing acceptance tests but testing only the main flows of your application. The following test pyramid represents this idea:

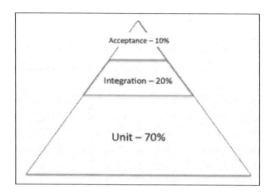

The reason is simple: your real feedback will come from your unit tests. They will tell you if you messed up something with your changes as soon as you finish writing them because executing unit tests is easy and fast. Once you know that all your classes and functions behave as expected, you need to verify that they can work together. However, for this, you do not need to test all the edge cases again; you already did this when writing unit tests. Here, you need to write just a few integration tests that confirm that all the pieces communicate properly. Finally, to make sure that not only that the code works but also the user experience is the desired one, we will write acceptance tests that emulate a user going through the different views. Here, tests are very slow and only possible once the flow is complete, so the feedback comes later. We will add acceptance tests to make sure that the main flows work, but we do not need to test every single scenario as we already did this with integration and unit tests.

Unit tests and code coverage

Now that you know what tests are, why we need them, and which types of tests we have, we will focus the rest of the chapter on writing good unit tests as they will be the ones that will occupy most of your time.

As we explained before, the idea of a unit test is to make sure that a piece of code, usually a class or method, works as expected. As the amount of code that a method contains should be small, running the test should take almost no time. Taking advantage of this, we will run several tests, trying to cover as many use cases as possible.

If this is not the first time you've heard about unit tests, you might know the concept of **code coverage**. This concept refers to the amount of code that our tests execute, that is, the percentage of tested code. For example, if your application has 10,000 lines and your tests test a total of 7,500 lines, your code coverage is 75%. There are tools that show marks on your code to indicate whether a certain line is tested or not, which is very useful in order to identify which parts of your application are not tested and thus warn you that it is more dangerous to change them.

However, code coverage is a double-edge sword. Why is this so? This is because developers tend to get obsessed with code coverage, aiming for a 100% coverage. However, you should be aware that code coverage is just a consequence, not your goal. Your goal is to write unit tests that verify all the use cases of certain pieces of code in order to make you feel safer each time that you have to change this code. This means that for a given method, it might not be enough to write one test because the same line with different input values may behave differently. However, if your focus was on code coverage, writing one test would satisfy it, and you might not need to write any more tests.

Integrating PHPUnit

Writing tests is a task that you could do by yourself; you just need to write code that throws exceptions when conditions are not met and then run the script any time you need. Luckily, other developers were not satisfied with this manual process, so they implemented tools to help us automate this process and get good feedback. The most used in PHP is **PHPUnit**. PHPUnit is a framework that provides a set of tools to write tests in an easier manner, gives us the ability to run tests automatically, and delivers useful feedback to the developer.

In order to use PHPUnit, traditionally, we installed it on our laptop. In doing so, we added the classes of the framework to include the path of PHP and also the executable to run the tests. This was less than ideal as we forced developers to install one more tool on their development machine. Nowadays, Composer (refer to *Chapter 6, Adapting to MVC*, in order to refresh your memory) helps us in including PHPUnit as a dependency of the project. This means that running Composer, which you will do for sure in order to get the rest of the dependencies, will get PHPUnit too. Add, then, the following into `composer.json`:

```
{
//...
    "require": {
        "monolog/monolog": "^1.17",
        "twig/twig": "^1.23"
    },
```

```
    "require-dev": {
        "phpunit/phpunit": "5.1.3"
    },
    "autoload": {
        "psr-4": {
            "Bookstore\\": "src"
        }
    }
}
```

Note that this dependency is added as `require-dev`. This means that the dependency will be downloaded only when we are on a development environment, but it will not be part of the application that we will deploy on production as we do not need to run tests there. To get the dependency, as always, run `composer update`.

A different approach is to install PHPUnit globally so that all the projects on your development environment can use it instead of installing it locally each time. You can read about how to install tools globally with Composer at `https://akrabat.com/global-installation-of-php-tools-with-composer/`.

The phpunit.xml file

PHPUnit needs a `phpunit.xml` file in order to define the way we want to run the tests. This file defines a set of rules like where the tests are, what code are the tests testing, and so on. Add the following file in your root directory:

```xml
<?xml version="1.0" encoding="UTF-8"?>

<phpunit backupGlobals="false"
         backupStaticAttributes="false"
         colors="true"
         convertErrorsToExceptions="true"
         convertNoticesToExceptions="true"
         convertWarningsToExceptions="true"
         processIsolation="false"
         stopOnFailure="false"
         syntaxCheck="false"
         bootstrap="vendor/autoload.php"
>
<testsuites>
<testsuite name="Bookstore Test Suite">
<directory>./tests/</directory>
</testsuite>
</testsuites>
```

```
<filter>
<whitelist>
<directory>./src</directory>
</whitelist>
</filter>
</phpunit>
```

This file defines quite a lot of things. The most important are explained as follows:

- Setting `convertErrorsToExceptions`, `convertNoticesToExceptions`, and `convertWarningsToExceptions` to `true` will make your tests fail if there is a PHP error, warning, or notice. The goal is to make sure that your code does not contain minor errors on edge cases, which are always the source of potential problems.

- The `stopOnFailure` tells PHPUnit whether it should continue executing the rest of tests or not when there is a failed test. In this case, we want to run all of them to know how many tests are failing and why.

- The `bootstrap` defines which file we should execute before starting to run the tests. The most common usage is to include the autoloader, but you could also include a file that initializes some dependencies, such as databases or configuration readers.

- The `testsuites` defines the directories where PHPUnit will look for tests. In our case, we defined `./tests`, but we could add more if we had them in different directories.

- The `whitelist` defines the list of directories that contain the code that we are testing. This can be useful to generate output related to the code coverage.

When running the tests with PHPUnit, just make sure that you run the command from the same directory where the `phpunit.xml` file is. We will show you how in the next section.

Your first test

Right, that's enough preparations and theory; let's write some code. We will write tests for the basic customer, which is a domain object with little logic. First of all, we need to refactor the `Unique` trait as it still contains some unnecessary code after integrating our application with MySQL. We are talking about the ability to assign the next available ID, which is now handled by the autoincremental field. Remove it, leaving the code as follows:

```
<?php

namespace Bookstore\Utils;

trait Unique {
```

```
    protected $id;

    public function setId(int $id) {
        $this->id = $id;
    }

    public function getId(): int {
        return $this->id;
    }
}
```

The tests will be inside the `tests/` directory. The structure of directories should be the same as in the `src/` directory so that it is easier to identify where each test should be. The file and the class names need to end with `Test` so that PHPUnit knows that a file contains tests. Knowing this, our test should be in `tests/Domain/Customer/BasicTest.php`, as follows:

```php
<?php

namespace Bookstore\Tests\Domain\Customer;

use Bookstore\Domain\Customer\Basic;
use PHPUnit_Framework_TestCase;

class BasicTest extends PHPUnit_Framework_TestCase {
    public function testAmountToBorrow() {
        $customer = new Basic(1, 'han', 'solo', 'han@solo.com');

        $this->assertSame(
            3,
            $customer->getAmountToBorrow(),
            'Basic customer should borrow up to 3 books.'
        );
    }
}
```

As you can note, the `BasicTest` class extends from `PHPUnit_Framework_TestCase`. All test classes have to extend from this class. This class comes with a set of methods that allow you to make assertions. An assertion in PHPUnit is just a check performed on a value. Assertions can be comparisons to other values, a verification of some attributes of the values, and so on. If an assertion is not true, the test will be marked as failed, outputting the proper error message to the developer. The example shows an assertion using the `assertSame` method, which will compare two values, expecting that both of them are exactly the same. The third argument is an error message that the assertion will show in case it fails.

Also, note that the function names that start with `test` are the ones executed with PHPUnit. In this example, we have one unique test named `testAmountToBorrow` that instantiates a basic customer and verifies that the amount of books that the customer can borrow is 3. In the next section, we will show you how to run this test and get feedback from it.

Optionally, you could use any function name if you add the `@test` annotation in the method's DocBlock, as follows:

```
/**
 * @test
 */
public function thisIsATestToo() {
  //...
}
```

Running tests

In order to run the tests you wrote, you need to execute the script that Composer generated in `vendor/bin`. Remember always to run from the root directory of the project so that PHPUnit can find your `phpunit.xml` configuration file. Then, type `./vendor/bin/phpunit`.

```
● ● ●          1. vagrant@vagrant-ubuntu-trusty-64: /vagrant (bash)
vagrant@vagrant-ubuntu-trusty-64:/vagrant$ ./vendor/bin/phpunit
PHPUnit 5.1.3 by Sebastian Bergmann and contributors.

.                                                              1 / 1 (100%)

Time: 192 ms, Memory: 4.00Mb

OK (1 test, 1 assertion)
vagrant@vagrant-ubuntu-trusty-64:/vagrant$
```

When executing this program, we will get the feedback given by the tests. The output shows us that there is one test (one method) and one assertion and whether these were satisfactory. This output is what you would like to see every time you run your tests, but you will get more failed tests than you would like. Let's take a look at them by adding the following test:

```
public function testFail() {
    $customer = new Basic(1, 'han', 'solo', 'han@solo.com');

    $this->assertSame(
        4,
```

```
                  $customer->getAmountToBorrow(),
                  'Basic customer should borrow up to 3 books.'
          );
    }
```

This test will fail as we are checking whether `getAmountToBorrow` returns 4, but you know that it always returns 3. Let's run the tests and take a look at what kind of output we get.

```
● ● ●              1. vagrant@vagrant-ubuntu-trusty-64: /vagrant (bash)
vagrant@vagrant-ubuntu-trusty-64:/vagrant$ ./vendor/bin/phpunit
PHPUnit 5.1.3 by Sebastian Bergmann and contributors.

.F                                                              2 / 2 (100%)

Time: 143 ms, Memory: 4.00Mb

There was 1 failure:

1) Bookstore\Tests\Domain\Customer\BasicTest::testFail
Basic customer should borrow up to 3 books.
Failed asserting that 3 is identical to 4.

/vagrant/tests/Domain/Customer/BasicTest.php:29

FAILURES!
Tests: 2, Assertions: 2, Failures: 1.
vagrant@vagrant-ubuntu-trusty-64:/vagrant$
```

We can quickly note that the output is not good due to the red color. It shows us that there is a failure, pointing to the class and test method that failed. The feedback points out the type of failure (as 3 is not identical to 4) and optionally, the error message we added when invoking the `assert` method.

Writing unit tests

Let's start digging into all the features that PHPUnit offers us in order to write tests. We will divide these features in different subsections: setting up a test, assertions, exceptions, and data providers. Of course, you do not need to use all of these tools each time you write a test.

The start and end of a test

PHPUnit gives you the opportunity to set up a common scenario for each test in a class. For this, you need to use the `setUp` method, which, if present, is executed each time that a test of this class is executed. The instance of the class that invokes the `setUp` and `test` methods is the same, so you can use the properties of the class to save the context. One common use would be to create the object that we will use for our tests in case this is always the same. For an example, write the following code in `tests/Domain/Customer/BasicTest.php`:

```php
<?php

namespace Bookstore\Tests\Domain\Customer;

use Bookstore\Domain\Customer\Basic;
use PHPUnit_Framework_TestCase;

class BasicTest extends PHPUnit_Framework_TestCase {
    private $customer;

    public function setUp() {
        $this->customer = new Basic(
            1, 'han', 'solo', 'han@solo.com'
        );
    }

    public function testAmountToBorrow() {
        $this->assertSame(
            3,
            $this->customer->getAmountToBorrow(),
            'Basic customer should borrow up to 3 books.'
        );
    }
}
```

When `testAmountToBorrow` is invoked, the `$customer` property is already initialized through the execution of the `setUp` method. If the class had more than one test, the `setUp` method would be executed each time.

Even though it is less common to use, there is another method used to clean up the scenario after the test is executed: `tearDown`. This works in the same way, but it is executed after each test of this class is executed. Possible uses would be to clean up database data, close connections, delete files, and so on.

Assertions

You have already been introduced to the concept of assertions, so let's just list the most common ones in this section. For the full list, we recommend you to visit the official documentation at `https://phpunit.de/manual/current/en/appendixes.` `assertions.html` as it is quite extensive; however, to be honest, you will probably not use many of them.

The first type of assertion that we will see is the Boolean assertion, that is, the one that checks whether a value is `true` or `false`. The methods are as simple as `assertTrue` and `assertFalse`, and they expect one parameter, which is the value to assert, and optionally, a text to display in case of failure. In the same `BasicTest` class, add the following test:

```
public function testIsExemptOfTaxes() {
    $this->assertFalse(
        $this->customer->isExemptOfTaxes(),
        'Basic customer should be exempt of taxes.'
    );
}
```

This test makes sure that a basic customer is never exempt of taxes. Note that we could do the same assertion by writing the following:

```
$this->assertSame(
    $this->customer->isExemptOfTaxes(),
    false,
    'Basic customer should be exempt of taxes.'
);
```

A second group of assertions would be the comparison assertions. The most famous ones are `assertSame` and `assertEquals`. You have already used the first one, but are you sure of its meaning? Let's add another test and run it:

```
public function testGetMonthlyFee() {
    $this->assertSame(
        5,
        $this->customer->getMonthlyFee(),
        'Basic customer should pay 5 a month.'
    );
}
```

The result of the test is shown in the following screenshot:

```
1. vagrant@vagrant-ubuntu-trusty-64: /vagrant (bash)
vagrant@vagrant-ubuntu-trusty-64:/vagrant$ ./vendor/bin/phpunit
PHPUnit 5.1.3 by Sebastian Bergmann and contributors.

..E                                                      3 / 3 (100%)

Time: 149 ms, Memory: 4.00Mb

There was 1 failure:

1) Bookstore\Tests\Domain\Customer\BasicTest::testGetMonthlyFee
Basic customer should pay 5 a month.
Failed asserting that 5.0 is identical to 5.

/vagrant/tests/Domain/Customer/BasicTest.php:37

FAILURES!
Tests: 3, Assertions: 3, Failures: 1.
vagrant@vagrant-ubuntu-trusty-64:/vagrant$
```

The test failed! The reason is that `assertSame` is the equivalent to comparing using identity, that is, without using type juggling. The result of the `getMonthlyFee` method is always a float, and we will compare it with an integer, so it will never be the same, as the error message tells us. Change the assertion to `assertEquals`, which compares using equality, and the test will pass now.

When working with objects, we can use an assertion to check whether a given object is an instance of the expected class or not. When doing so, remember to send the full name of the class as this is a quite common mistake. Even better, you could get the class name using `::class`, for example, `Basic::class`. Add the following test in `tests/Domain/Customer/CustomerFactoryTest.php`:

```php
<?php

namespace Bookstore\Tests\Domain\Customer;

use Bookstore\Domain\Customer\CustomerFactory;
use PHPUnit_Framework_TestCase;

class CustomerFactoryTest extends PHPUnit_Framework_TestCase {
    public function testFactoryBasic() {
        $customer = CustomerFactory::factory(
            'basic', 1, 'han', 'solo', 'han@solo.com'
        );
```

```
        $this->assertInstanceOf(
Basic::class,
            $customer,
            'basic should create a Customer\Basic object.'
        );
    }
}
```

This test creates a customer using the `customer` factory. As the type of customer was `basic`, the result should be an instance of `Basic`, which is what we are testing with `assertInstanceOf`. The first argument is the expected class, the second is the object that we are testing, and the third is the error message. This test also helps us to note the behavior of comparison assertions with objects. Let's create a basic `customer` object as expected and compare it with the result of the factory. Then, run the test, as follows:

```
$expectedBasicCustomer = new Basic(1, 'han', 'solo', 'han@solo.com');

$this->assertSame(
    $customer,
    $expectedBasicCustomer,
    'Customer object is not as expected.'
);
```

The result of this test is shown in the following screenshot:

```
● ● ●              1. vagrant@vagrant-ubuntu-trusty-64: /vagrant (bash)
vagrant@vagrant-ubuntu-trusty-64:/vagrant$ ./vendor/bin/phpunit
PHPUnit 5.1.3 by Sebastian Bergmann and contributors.

...F
                                                           4 / 4 (100%)

Time: 139 ms, Memory: 4.00Mb

There was 1 failure:

1) Bookstore\Tests\Domain\Customer\CustomerFactoryTest::testFactoryBasic
Customer object is not as expected.
Failed asserting that two variables reference the same object.

/vagrant/tests/Domain/Customer/CustomerFactoryTest.php:26

FAILURES!
Tests: 4, Assertions: 5, Failures: 1.
vagrant@vagrant-ubuntu-trusty-64:/vagrant$
```

The test failed because when you compare two objects with identity comparison, you comparing the object reference, and it will only be the same if the two objects are exactly the same instance. If you create two objects with the same properties, they will be equal but never identical. To fix the test, change the assertion as follows:

```
$expectedBasicCustomer = new Basic(1, 'han', 'solo', 'han@solo.com');

$this->assertEquals(
    $customer,
    $expectedBasicCustomer,
    'Customer object is not as expected.'
);
```

Let's now write the tests for the `sale` domain object at `tests/Domain/SaleTest.php`. This class is very easy to test and allows us to use some new assertions, as follows:

```
<?php

namespace Bookstore\Tests\Domain\Customer;

use Bookstore\Domain\Sale;
use PHPUnit_Framework_TestCase;

class SaleTest extends PHPUnit_Framework_TestCase {
    public function testNewSaleHasNoBooks() {
        $sale = new Sale();

        $this->assertEmpty(
            $sale->getBooks(),
            'When new, sale should have no books.'
        );
    }

    public function testAddNewBook() {
        $sale = new Sale();
        $sale->addBook(123);

        $this->assertCount(
            1,
            $sale->getBooks(),
            'Number of books not valid.'
        );
        $this->assertArrayHasKey(
            123,
```

```
            $sale->getBooks(),
            'Book id could not be found in array.'
        );
        $this->assertSame(
            $sale->getBooks()[123],
            1,
            'When not specified, amount of books is 1.'
        );
    }
}
```

We added two tests here: one makes sure that for a new `sale` instance, the list of books associated with it is empty. For this, we used the `assertEmpty` method, which takes an array as an argument and will assert that it is empty. The second test is adding a book to the sale and then making sure that the list of books has the correct content. For this, we will use the `assertCount` method, which verifies that the array, that is, the second argument, has as many elements as the first argument provided. In this case, we expect that the list of books has only one entry. The second assertion of this test is verifying that the array of books contains a specific key, which is the ID of the book, with the `assertArrayHasKey` method, in which the first argument is the key, and the second one is the array. Finally, we will check with the already known `assertSame` method that the amount of books inserted is 1.

Even though these two new assertion methods are useful sometimes, all the three assertions of the last test can be replaced by just an `assertSame` method, comparing the whole array of books with the expected one, as follows:

```
$this->assertSame(
    [123 => 1],
    $sale->getBooks(),
    'Books array does not match.'
);
```

The suite of tests for the `sale` domain object would not be enough if we were not testing how the class behaves when adding multiple books. In this case, using `assertCount` and `assertArrayHasKey` would make the test unnecessarily long, so let's just compare the array with an expected one via the following code:

```
public function testAddMultipleBooks() {
    $sale = new Sale();
    $sale->addBook(123, 4);
    $sale->addBook(456, 2);
    $sale->addBook(456, 8);

    $this->assertSame(
```

```
            [123 => 4, 456 => 10],
            $sale->getBooks(),
            'Books are not as expected.'
        );
    }
```

Expecting exceptions

Sometimes, a method is expected to throw an exception for certain unexpected use cases. When this happens, you could try to capture this exception inside the test or take advantage of another tool that PHPUnit offers: **expecting exceptions**. To mark a test to expect a given exception, just add the `@expectedException` annotation followed by the exception's class full name. Optionally, you can use `@expectedExceptionMessage` to assert the message of the exception. Let's add the following tests to our `CustomerFactoryTest` class:

```
    /**
     * @expectedException \InvalidArgumentException
     * @expectedExceptionMessage Wrong type.
     */
    public function testCreatingWrongTypeOfCustomer() {
        $customer = CustomerFactory::factory(
            'deluxe', 1, 'han', 'solo', 'han@solo.com'

        );
    }
```

In this test we will try to create a deluxe customer with our factory, but as this type of customer does not exist, we will get an exception. The type of the expected exception is `InvalidArgumentException`, and the error message is "Wrong type". If you run the tests, you will see that they pass.

If we defined an expected exception and the exception is never thrown, the test will fail; expecting exceptions is just another type of assertion. To see this happen, add the following to your test and run it; you will get a failure, and PHPUnit will complain saying that it expected the exception, but it was never thrown:

```
    /**
     * @expectedException \InvalidArgumentException
     */
    public function testCreatingCorrectCustomer() {
        $customer = CustomerFactory::factory(
            'basic', 1, 'han', 'solo', 'han@solo.com'
        );
    }
```

Data providers

If you think about the flow of a test, most of the time, we invoke a method with an input and expect an output. In order to cover all the edge cases, it is natural that we will repeat the same action with a set of inputs and expected outputs. PHPUnit gives us the ability to do so, thus removing a lot of duplicated code. This feature is called **data providing**.

A data provider is a public method defined in the test class that returns an array with a specific schema. Each entry of the array represents a test in which the key is the name of the test—optionally, you could use numeric keys—and the value is the parameter that the test needs. A test will declare that it needs a data provider with the @dataProvider annotation, and when executing tests, the data provider injects the arguments that the test method needs. Let's consider an example to make it easier. Write the following two methods in your CustomerFactoryTest class:

```
public function providerFactoryValidCustomerTypes() {
    return [
        'Basic customer, lowercase' => [
            'type' => 'basic',
            'expectedType' => '\Bookstore\Domain\Customer\Basic'
        ],
        'Basic customer, uppercase' => [
            'type' => 'BASIC',
            'expectedType' => '\Bookstore\Domain\Customer\Basic'
        ],
        'Premium customer, lowercase' => [
            'type' => 'premium',
            'expectedType' => '\Bookstore\Domain\Customer\Premium'
        ],
        'Premium customer, uppercase' => [
            'type' => 'PREMIUM',
            'expectedType' => '\Bookstore\Domain\Customer\Premium'
        ]
    ];
}

/**
 * @dataProvider providerFactoryValidCustomerTypes
 * @param string $type
 * @param string $expectedType
 */
public function testFactoryValidCustomerTypes(
    string $type,
    string $expectedType
```

```
    ) {
        $customer = CustomerFactory::factory(
            $type, 1, 'han', 'solo', 'han@solo.com'
        );
        $this->assertInstanceOf(
            $expectedType,
            $customer,
            'Factory created the wrong type of customer.'
        );
    }
}
```

The test here is `testFactoryValidCustomerTypes`, which expects two arguments: `$type` and `$expectedType`. The test uses them to create a customer with the factory and verify the type of the result, which we already did by hardcoding the types. The test also declares that it needs the `providerFactoryValidCustomerTypes` data provider. This data provider returns an array of four entries, which means that the test will be executed four times with four different sets of arguments. The name of each test is the key of each entry—for example, "Basic customer, lowercase". This is very useful in case a test fails because it will be displayed as part of the error messages. Each entry is a map with two values, `type` and `expectedType`, which are the names of the arguments of the `test` method. The values of these entries are the values that the `test` method will get.

The bottom line is that the code we wrote would be the same as if we wrote `testFactoryValidCustomerTypes` four times, hardcoding `$type` and `$expectedType` each time. Imagine now that the `test` method contains tens of lines of code or we want to repeat the same test with tens of datasets; do you see how powerful it is?

Testing with doubles

So far, we tested classes that are quite isolated; that is, they do not have much interaction with other classes. Nevertheless, we have classes that use several classes, such as controllers. What can we do with these interactions? The idea of unit tests is to test a specific method and not the whole code base, right?

PHPUnit allows you to mock these dependencies; that is, you can provide fake objects that look similar to the dependencies that the tested class needs, but they do not use code from those classes. The goal of this is to provide a dummy instance that the class can use and invoke its methods without the side effect of what these invocations might have. Imagine as an example the case of the models: if the controller uses a real model, then when invoking methods from it, the model would access the database each time, making the tests quite unpredictable.

If we use a mock as the model instead, the controller can invoke its methods as many times as needed without any side effect. Even better, we can make assertions of the arguments that the mock received or force it to return specific values. Let's take a look at how to use them.

Injecting models with DI

The first thing we need to understand is that if we create objects using new inside the controller, we will not be able to mock them. This means that we need to inject all the dependencies—for example, using a dependency injector. We will do this for all of the dependencies but one: the models. In this section, we will test the borrow method of the BookController class, so we will show the changes that this method needs. Of course, if you want to test the rest of the code, you should apply these same changes to the rest of the controllers.

The first thing to do is to add the BookModel instance to the dependency injector in our index.php file. As this class also has a dependency, PDO, use the same dependency injector to get an instance of it, as follows:

```
$di->set('BookModel', new BookModel($di->get('PDO')));
```

Now, in the borrow method of the BookController class, we will change the new instantiation of the model to the following:

```
public function borrow(int $bookId): string {
    $bookModel = $this->di->get('BookModel');

    try {
//...
```

Customizing TestCase

When writing your unit test's suite, it is quite common to have a customized TestCase class from which all tests extend. This class always extends from PHPUnit_Framework_TestCase, so we still get all the assertions and other methods. As all tests have to import this class, let's change our autoloader so that it can recognize namespaces from the tests directory. After this, run composer update, as follows:

```
"autoload": {
    "psr-4": {
        "Bookstore\\Tests\\": "tests",
        "Bookstore\\": "src"
    }
}
```

With this change, we will tell Composer that all the namespaces starting with `Bookstore\Tests` will be located under the `tests` directory, and the rest will follow the previous rules.

Let's add now our customized `TestCase` class. The only helper method we need right now is one to create mocks. It is not really necessary, but it makes things cleaner. Add the following class in `tests/AbstractTestClase.php`:

```php
<?php

namespace Bookstore\Tests;

use PHPUnit_Framework_TestCase;
use InvalidArgumentException;

abstract class AbstractTestCase extends PHPUnit_Framework_TestCase {
    protected function mock(string $className) {
        if (strpos($className, '\\') !== 0) {
            $className = '\\' . $className;
        }

        if (!class_exists($className)) {
            $className = '\Bookstore\\' . trim($className, '\\');

            if (!class_exists($className)) {
                throw new InvalidArgumentException(
                    "Class $className not found."
                );
            }
        }

        return $this->getMockBuilder($className)
            ->disableOriginalConstructor()
            ->getMock();
    }
}
```

This method takes the name of a class and tries to figure out whether the class is part of the `Bookstore` namespace or not. This will be handy when mocking objects of our own codebase as we will not have to write `Bookstore` each time. After figuring out what the real full class name is, it uses the mock builder from PHPUnit to create one and then returns it.

More helpers! This time, they are for controllers. Every single controller will always need the same dependencies: logger, database connection, template engine, and configuration reader. Knowing this, let's create a `ControllerTestCase` class from where all the tests covering controllers will extend. This class will contain a `setUp` method that creates all the common mocks and sets them in the dependency injector. Add it as your `tests/ControllerTestCase.php` file, as follows:

```php
<?php

namespace Bookstore\Tests;

use Bookstore\Utils\DependencyInjector;
use Bookstore\Core\Config;
use Monolog\Logger;
use Twig_Environment;
use PDO;

abstract class ControllerTestCase extends AbstractTestCase {
    protected $di;

    public function setUp() {
        $this->di = new DependencyInjector();
        $this->di->set('PDO', $this->mock(PDO::class));
        $this->di->set('Utils\Config', $this->mock(Config::class));
        $this->di->set(
            'Twig_Environment',
            $this->mock(Twig_Environment::class)
        );
        $this->di->set('Logger', $this->mock(Logger::class));
    }
}
```

Using mocks

Well, we've had enough of the helpers; let's start with the tests. The difficult part here is how to play with mocks. When you create one, you can add some expectations and return values. The methods are:

- `expects`: This specifies the amount of times the mock's method is invoked. You can send `$this->never()`, `$this->once()`, or `$this->any()` as an argument to specify 0, 1, or any invocations.

- `method`: This is used to specify the method we are talking about. The argument that it expects is just the name of the method.

- `with`: This is a method used to set the expectations of the arguments that the mock will receive when it is invoked. For example, if the mocked method is expected to get `basic` as the first argument and `123` as the second, the `with` method will be invoked as `with("basic", 123)`. This method is optional, but if we set it, PHPUnit will throw an error in case the mocked method does not get the expected arguments, so it works as an assertion.

- `will`: This is used to define what the mock will return. The two most common usages are `$this->returnValue($value)` or `$this->>throwException($exception)`. This method is also optional, and if not invoked, the mock will always return null.

Let's add the first test to see how it would work. Add the following code to the `tests/Controllers/BookControllerTest.php` file:

```php
<?php

namespace Bookstore\Tests\Controllers;

use Bookstore\Controllers\BookController;
use Bookstore\Core\Request;
use Bookstore\Exceptions\NotFoundException;
use Bookstore\Models\BookModel;
use Bookstore\Tests\ControllerTestCase;
use Twig_Template;

class BookControllerTest extends ControllerTestCase {
    private function getController(
        Request $request = null
    ): BookController {
        if ($request === null) {
            $request = $this->mock('Core\Request');
        }
        return new BookController($this->di, $request);
    }

    public function testBookNotFound() {
        $bookModel = $this->mock(BookModel::class);
        $bookModel
            ->expects($this->once())
            ->method('get')
            ->with(123)
            ->will(
                $this->throwException(
                    new NotFoundException()
```

```
                )
            );
        $this->di->set('BookModel', $bookModel);

        $response = "Rendered template";
        $template = $this->mock(Twig_Template::class);
        $template
            ->expects($this->once())
            ->method('render')
            ->with(['errorMessage' => 'Book not found.'])
            ->will($this->returnValue($response));
        $this->di->get('Twig_Environment')
            ->expects($this->once())
            ->method('loadTemplate')
            ->with('error.twig')
            ->will($this->returnValue($template));

        $result = $this->getController()->borrow(123);

        $this->assertSame(
            $result,
            $response,
            'Response object is not the expected one.'
        );
    }
}
```

The first thing the test does is to create a mock of the BookModel class. Then, it adds an expectation that goes like this: the get method will be called once with one argument, 123, and it will throw NotFoundException. This makes sense as the test tries to emulate a scenario in which we cannot find the book in the database.

The second part of the test consists of adding the expectations of the template engine. This is a bit more complex as there are two mocks involved. The loadTemplate method of Twig_Environment is expected to be called once with the error.twig argument as the template name. This mock should return Twig_Template, which is another mock. The render method of this second mock is expected to be called once with the correct error message, returning the response, which is a hardcoded string. After all the dependencies are defined, we just need to invoke the borrow method of the controller and expect a response.

Remember that this test does not have only one assertion, but four: the assertSame method and the three mock expectations. If any of them are not accomplished, the test will fail, so we can say that this method is quite robust.

With our first test, we verified that the scenario in which the book is not found works. There are two more scenarios that fail as well: when there are not enough copies of the book to borrow and when there is a database error when trying to save the borrowed book. However, you can see now that all of them share a piece of code that mocks the template. Let's extract this code to a `protected` method that generates the mocks when it is given the template name, the parameters are sent to the template, and the expected response is received. Run the following:

```
protected function mockTemplate(
    string $templateName,
    array $params,
    $response
) {
    $template = $this->mock(Twig_Template::class);
    $template
        ->expects($this->once())
        ->method('render')
        ->with($params)
        ->will($this->returnValue($response));
    $this->di->get('Twig_Environment')
        ->expects($this->once())
        ->method('loadTemplate')
        ->with($templateName)
        ->will($this->returnValue($template));
}

public function testNotEnoughCopies() {
    $bookModel = $this->mock(BookModel::class);
    $bookModel
        ->expects($this->once())
        ->method('get')
        ->with(123)
        ->will($this->returnValue(new Book()));
    $bookModel
        ->expects($this->never())
        ->method('borrow');
    $this->di->set('BookModel', $bookModel);

    $response = "Rendered template";
    $this->mockTemplate(
        'error.twig',
        ['errorMessage' => 'There are no copies left.'],
        $response
    );
```

```
        $result = $this->getController()->borrow(123);

        $this->assertSame(
            $result,
            $response,
            'Response object is not the expected one.'
        );
    }

    public function testErrorSaving() {
        $controller = $this->getController();
        $controller->setCustomerId(9);

        $book = new Book();
        $book->addCopy();
        $bookModel = $this->mock(BookModel::class);
        $bookModel
            ->expects($this->once())
            ->method('get')
            ->with(123)
            ->will($this->returnValue($book));
        $bookModel
            ->expects($this->once())
            ->method('borrow')
            ->with(new Book(), 9)
            ->will($this->throwException(new DbException()));
        $this->di->set('BookModel', $bookModel);

        $response = "Rendered template";
        $this->mockTemplate(
            'error.twig',
            ['errorMessage' => 'Error borrowing book.'],
            $response
        );

        $result = $controller->borrow(123);

        $this->assertSame(
            $result,
            $response,
            'Response object is not the expected one.'
        );
    }
```

The only novelty here is when we expect that the borrow method is never invoked. As we do not expect it to be invoked, there is no reason to use the with nor will method. If the code actually invokes this method, PHPUnit will mark the test as failed.

We already tested and found that all the scenarios that can fail have failed. Let's add a test now where a user can successfully borrow a book, which means that we will return valid books and customers from the database, the save method will be invoked correctly, and the template will get all the correct parameters. The test looks as follows:

```
public function testBorrowingBook() {
    $controller = $this->getController();
    $controller->setCustomerId(9);

    $book = new Book();
    $book->addCopy();
    $bookModel = $this->mock(BookModel::class);
    $bookModel
        ->expects($this->once())
        ->method('get')
        ->with(123)
        ->will($this->returnValue($book));
    $bookModel
        ->expects($this->once())
        ->method('borrow')
        ->with(new Book(), 9);
    $bookModel
        ->expects($this->once())
        ->method('getByUser')
        ->with(9)
        ->will($this->returnValue(['book1', 'book2']));
    $this->di->set('BookModel', $bookModel);

    $response = "Rendered template";
    $this->mockTemplate(
        'books.twig',
        [
            'books' => ['book1', 'book2'],
            'currentPage' => 1,
            'lastPage' => true
        ],
        $response
    );

    $result = $controller->borrow(123);

    $this->assertSame(
        $result,
```

```
            $response,
            'Response object is not the expected one.'
        );
    }
```

So this is it. You have written one of the most complex tests you will need to write during this book. What do you think of it? Well, as you do not have much experience with tests, you might be quite satisfied with the result, but let's try to analyze it a bit further.

Database testing

This will be the most controversial of the sections of this chapter by far. When it comes to database testing, there are different schools of thought. Should we use the database or not? Should we use our development database or one in memory? It is quite out of the scope of the book to explain how to mock the database or prepare a fresh one for each test, but we will try to summarize some of the techniques here:

- We will mock the database connection and write expectations to all the interactions between the model and the database. In our case, this would mean that we would inject a mock of the PDO object. As we will write the queries manually, chances are that we might introduce a wrong query. Mocking the connection would not help us detect this error. This solution would be good if we used ORM instead of writing the queries manually, but we will leave this topic out of the book.

- For each test, we will create a brand new database in which we add the data we would like to have for the specific test. This approach might take a lot of time, but it assures you that you will be testing against a real database and that there is no unexpected data that might make our tests fail; that is, the tests are fully isolated. In most of the cases, this would be the preferable approach, even though it might not be the one that performs faster. To solve this inconvenience, we will create in-memory databases.

- Tests run against an already existing database. Usually, at the beginning of the test we start a transaction that we roll back at the end of the test, leaving the database without any change. This approach emulates a real scenario, in which we can find all sorts of data and our code should always behave as expected. However, using a shared database always has some side effects; for example, if we want to introduce changes to the database schema, we will have to apply them to the database before running the tests, but the rest of the applications or developers that use the database are not yet ready for these changes.

In order to keep things small, we will try to implement a mixture of the second and third options. We will use our existing database, but after starting the transaction of each test, we will clean all the tables involved with the test. This looks as though we need a `ModelTestCase` to handle this. Add the following into `tests/ModelTestCase.php`:

```php
<?php

namespace Bookstore\Tests;

use Bookstore\Core\Config;
use PDO;

abstract class ModelTestCase extends AbstractTestCase {
    protected $db;
    protected $tables = [];

    public function setUp() {
        $config = new Config();

        $dbConfig = $config->get('db');
        $this->db = new PDO(
            'mysql:host=127.0.0.1;dbname=bookstore',
            $dbConfig['user'],
            $dbConfig['password']
        );
        $this->db->beginTransaction();
        $this->cleanAllTables();
    }

    public function tearDown() {
        $this->db->rollBack();
    }

    protected function cleanAllTables() {
        foreach ($this->tables as $table) {
            $this->db->exec("delete from $table");
        }
    }
}
```

The `setUp` method creates a database connection with the same credentials found in the `config/app.yml` file. Then, we will start a transaction and invoke the `cleanAllTables` method, which iterates the tables in the `$tables` property and deletes all the content from them. The `tearDown` method rolls back the transaction.

> **Extending from ModelTestCase**
>
> If you write a test extending from this class that needs to implement either the `setUp` or `tearDown` method, always remember to invoke the ones from the parent.

Let's write tests for the `borrow` method of the `BookModel` class. This method uses books and customers, so we would like to clean the tables that contain them. Create the `test` class and save it in `tests/Models/BookModelTest.php`:

```php
<?php

namespace Bookstore\Tests\Models;

use Bookstore\Models\BookModel;
use Bookstore\Tests\ModelTestCase;

class BookModelTest extends ModelTestCase {
    protected $tables = [
        'borrowed_books',
        'customer',
        'book'
    ];
    protected $model;

    public function setUp() {
        parent::setUp();

        $this->model = new BookModel($this->db);
    }
}
```

Note how we also overrode the `setUp` method, invoking the one in the parent and creating the model instance that all tests will use, which is safe to do as we will not keep any context on this object. Before adding the tests though, let's add some more helpers to `ModelTestCase`: one to create book objects given an array of parameters and two to save books and customers in the database. Run the following code:

```php
protected function buildBook(array $properties): Book {
    $book = new Book();
    $reflectionClass = new ReflectionClass(Book::class);

    foreach ($properties as $key => $value) {
```

```php
        $property = $reflectionClass->getProperty($key);
        $property->setAccessible(true);
        $property->setValue($book, $value);
    }

    return $book;
}

protected function addBook(array $params) {
    $default = [
        'id' => null,
        'isbn' => 'isbn',
        'title' => 'title',
        'author' => 'author',
        'stock' => 1,
        'price' => 10.0,
    ];
    $params = array_merge($default, $params);

    $query = <<<SQL
insert into book (id, isbn, title, author, stock, price)
values(:id, :isbn, :title, :author, :stock, :price)
SQL;
    $this->db->prepare($query)->execute($params);
}

protected function addCustomer(array $params) {
    $default = [
        'id' => null,
        'firstname' => 'firstname',
        'surname' => 'surname',
        'email' => 'email',
        'type' => 'basic'
    ];
    $params = array_merge($default, $params);

    $query = <<<SQL
insert into customer (id, firstname, surname, email, type)
values(:id, :firstname, :surname, :email, :type)
SQL;
    $this->db->prepare($query)->execute($params);
}
```

As you can note, we added default values for all the fields, so we are not forced to define the whole book/customer each time we want to save one. Instead, we just sent the relevant fields and merged them to the default ones.

Also, note that the `buildBook` method used a new concept, **reflection**, to access the private properties of an instance. This is way beyond the scope of the book, but if you are interested, you can read more at `http://php.net/manual/en/book.reflection.php`.

We are now ready to start writing tests. With all these helpers, adding tests will be very easy and clean. The `borrow` method has different use cases: trying to borrow a book that is not in the database, trying to use a customer not registered, and borrowing a book successfully. Let's add them as follows:

```
/**
 * @expectedException \Bookstore\Exceptions\DbException
 */
public function testBorrowBookNotFound() {
    $book = $this->buildBook(['id' => 123]);
    $this->model->borrow($book, 123);
}


/**
 * @expectedException \Bookstore\Exceptions\DbException
 */
public function testBorrowCustomerNotFound() {
    $book = $this->buildBook(['id' => 123]);
    $this->addBook(['id' => 123]);

    $this->model->borrow($book, 123);
}

public function testBorrow() {
    $book = $this->buildBook(['id' => 123, 'stock' => 12]);
    $this->addBook(['id' => 123, 'stock' => 12]);
    $this->addCustomer(['id' => 123]);

    $this->model->borrow($book, 123);
}
```

Impressed? Compared to the controller tests, these tests are way simpler, mainly because their code performs only one action, but also thanks to all the methods added to `ModelTestCase`. Once you need to work with other objects, such as `sales`, you can add `addSale` or `buildSale` to this same class to make things cleaner.

Test-driven development

You might realize already that there is no unique way to do things when talking about developing an application. It is out of the scope of this book to show you all of them—and by the time you are done reading these lines, more techniques will have been incorporated already—but there is one approach that is very useful when it comes to writing good, testable code: **test-driven development** (TDD).

This methodology consists of writing the unit tests before writing the code itself. The idea, though, is not to write all the tests at once and then write the class or method but rather to do it in a progressive way. Let's consider an example to make it easier. Imagine that your `Sale` class is yet to be implemented and the only thing we know is that we have to be able to add books. Rename your `src/Domain/Sale.php` file to `src/Domain/Sale2.php` or just delete it so that the application does not know about it.

Is all this verbosity necessary?
You will note in this example that we will perform an excessive amount of steps to come up with a very simple piece of code. Indeed, they are too many for this example, but there will be times when this amount is just fine. Finding these moments comes with experience, so we recommend you to practice first with simple examples. Eventually, it will come naturally to you.

The mechanics of TDD consist of four steps, as follows:

1. Write a test for some functionality that is not yet implemented.
2. Run the unit tests, and they should fail. If they do not, either your test is wrong, or your code already implements this functionality.
3. Write the minimum amount of code to make the tests pass.
4. Run the unit tests again. This time, they should pass.

We do not have the `sale` domain object, so the first thing, as we should start from small things and then move on to bigger things, is to assure that we can instantiate the `sale` object. Write the following unit test in `tests/Domain/SaleTest.php` as we will write all the existing tests, but using TDD; you can remove the existing tests in this file.

```php
<?php

namespace Bookstore\Tests\Domain;

use Bookstore\Domain\Sale;
use PHPUnit_Framework_TestCase;
```

```
class SaleTest extends PHPUnit_Framework_TestCase {
    public function testCanCreate() {
        $sale = new Sale();
    }
}
```

Run the tests to make sure that they are failing. In order to run one specific test, you can mention the file of the test when running PHPUnit, as shown in the following script:

```
1. vagrant@vagrant-ubuntu-trusty-64: /vagrant (bash)
vagrant@vagrant-ubuntu-trusty-64:/vagrant$ ./vendor/bin/phpunit tests/Domain/SaleTest.php

PHPUnit 5.1.3 by Sebastian Bergmann and contributors.

E                                                             1 / 1 (100%)

Time: 270 ms, Memory: 4.00Mb

There was 1 error:

1) Bookstore\Tests\Domain\SaleTest::testCanCreate
Error: Class 'Bookstore\Domain\Sale' not found

/vagrant/tests/Domain/SaleTest.php:10

FAILURES!
Tests: 1, Assertions: 0, Errors: 1.
vagrant@vagrant-ubuntu-trusty-64:/vagrant$
```

Good, they are failing. That means that PHP cannot find the object to instantiate it. Let's now write the minimum amount of code required to make this test pass. In this case, creating the class would be enough, and you can do this through the following lines of code:

```
<?php

namespace Bookstore\Domain;

class Sale {
}
```

Now, run the tests to make sure that there are no errors.

```
● ● ●                    1. vagrant@vagrant-ubuntu-trusty-64: /vagrant (bash)
vagrant@vagrant-ubuntu-trusty-64:/vagrant$ ./vendor/bin/phpunit tests/Domain/SaleTest.php

PHPUnit 5.1.3 by Sebastian Bergmann and contributors.

.                                                                    1 / 1 (100%)

Time: 110 ms, Memory: 4.00Mb

OK (1 test, 0 assertions)
vagrant@vagrant-ubuntu-trusty-64:/vagrant$
```

This is easy, right? So, what we need to do is repeat this process, adding more functionality each time. Let's focus on the books that a sale holds; when created, the book's list should be empty, as follows:

```
public function testWhenCreatedBookListIsEmpty() {
    $sale = new Sale();

    $this->assertEmpty($sale->getBooks());
}
```

Run the tests to make sure that they fail—they do. Now, write the following method in the class:

```
public function getBooks(): array {
return [];
}
```

Now, if you run... wait, what? We are forcing the getBooks method to return an empty array always? This is not the implementation that we need—nor the one we deserve—so why do we do it? The reason is the wording of step 3: "Write the minimum amount of code to make the tests pass.". Our test suite should be extensive enough to detect this kind of problem, and this is our way to make sure it does. This time, we will write bad code on purpose, but next time, we might introduce a bug unintentionally, and our unit tests should be able to detect it as soon as possible. Run the tests; they will pass.

Now, let's discuss the next functionality. When adding a book to the list, we should see this book with amount 1. The test should be as follows:

```
public function testWhenAddingABookIGetOneBook() {
    $sale = new Sale();
    $sale->addBook(123);
```

```
        $this->assertSame(
            $sale->getBooks(),
            [123 => 1]
        );
    }
```

This test is very useful. Not only does it force us to implement the addBook method, but also it helps us fix the getBooks method—as it is hardcoded right now—to always return an empty array. As the getBooks method now expects two different results, we cannot trick the tests any more. The new code for the class should be as follows:

```
class Sale {
    private $books = [];

    public function getBooks(): array {
        return $this->books;
    }

    public function addBook(int $bookId) {
        $this->books[123] = 1;
    }
}
```

A new test we can write is the one that allows you to add more than one book at a time, sending the amount as the second argument. The test would look similar to the following:

```
public function testSpecifyAmountBooks() {
    $sale = new Sale();
    $sale->addBook(123, 5);

    $this->assertSame(
        $sale->getBooks(),
        [123 => 5]
    );
}
```

Now, the tests do not pass, so we need to fix them. Let's refactor addBook so that it can accept a second argument as the amount :

```
public function addBook(int $bookId, int $amount = 1) {
    $this->books[123] = $amount;
}
```

The next functionality we would like to add is the same book invoking the method several times, keeping track of the total amount of books added. The test could be as follows:

```
public function testAddMultipleTimesSameBook() {
    $sale = new Sale();
    $sale->addBook(123, 5);
    $sale->addBook(123);
    $sale->addBook(123, 5);

    $this->assertSame(
        $sale->getBooks(),
        [123 => 11]
    );
}
```

This test will fail as the current execution will not add all the amounts but will instead keep the last one. Let's fix it by executing the following code:

```
public function addBook(int $bookId, int $amount = 1) {
    if (!isset($this->books[123])) {
        $this->books[123] = 0;
    }
    $this->books[123] += $amount;
}
```

Well, we are almost there. There is one last test we should add, which is the ability to add more than one different book. The test is as follows:

```
public function testAddDifferentBooks() {
    $sale = new Sale();
    $sale->addBook(123, 5);
    $sale->addBook(456, 2);
    $sale->addBook(789, 5);

    $this->assertSame(
        $sale->getBooks(),
        [123 => 5, 456 => 2, 789 => 5]
    );
}
```

This test fails due to the hardcoded book ID in our implementation. If we did not do this, the test would have already passed. Let's fix it then; run the following:

```
public function addBook(int $bookId, int $amount = 1) {
    if (!isset($this->books[$bookId])) {
        $this->books[$bookId] = 0;
    }
    $this->books[$bookId] += $amount;
}
```

We are done! Does it look familiar? It is the same code we wrote on our first implementation except for the rest of the properties. You can now replace the `sale` domain object with the previous one, so you have all the functionalities needed.

Theory versus practice

As mentioned before, this is a quite long and verbose process that very few experienced developers follow from start to end but one that most of them encourage people to follow. Why is this so? When you write all your code first and leave the unit tests for the end, there are two problems:

- Firstly, in too many cases developers are lazy enough to skip tests, telling themselves that the code already works, so there is no need to write the tests. You already know that one of the goals of tests is to make sure that future changes do not break the current features, so this is not a valid reason.

- Secondly, the tests written after the code usually test the code rather than the functionality. Imagine that you have a method that was initially meant to perform an action. After writing the method, we will not perform the action perfectly due to a bug or bad design; instead, we will either do too much or leave some edge cases untreated. When we write the test after writing the code, we will test what we see in the method, not what the original functionality was!

If you instead force yourself to write the tests first and then the code, you make sure that you always have tests and that they test what the code is meant to do, leading to a code that performs as expected and is fully covered. Also, by doing it in small intervals, you get quick feedback and don't have to wait for hours to know whether all the tests and code you wrote make sense at all. Even though this idea is quite simple and makes a lot of sense, many novice developers find it hard to implement.

Experienced developers have written code for several years, so they have already internalized all of this. This is the reason why some of them prefer to either write several tests before starting with the code or the other way around, that is, writing code and then testing it as they are more productive this way. However, if there is something that all of them have in common it is that their applications will always be full of tests.

Summary

In this chapter, you learned the importance of testing your code using unit tests. You now know how to configure PHPUnit on your application so that you can not only run your tests but also get good feedback. You got a good introduction on how to write unit tests properly, and now, it is safer for you to introduce changes in your application.

In the next chapter, we will study some existing frameworks, which you can use instead of writing your own every time you start an application. In this way, not only will you save time and effort, but also other developers will be able to join you and understand your code easily.

8
Using Existing PHP Frameworks

In the same way that you wrote your framework with PHP, other people did it too. It did not take long for people to realize that entire frameworks were reusable too. Of course, one man's meat is another man's poison, and as with many other examples in the IT world, loads of frameworks started to appear. You will never hear about most of them, but a handful of these frameworks got quite a lot of users.

As we write, there are four or five main frameworks that most PHP developers know of: **Symfony** and **Zend Framework** were the main characters of this last PHP generation, but Laravel is also there, providing a lightweight and fast framework for those who need fewer features. Due to the nature of this book, we will focus on the latest ones, **Silex** and **Laravel**, as they are quick enough to learn in a chapter — or at least their basics are.

In this chapter, you will learn about:

- The importance of frameworks
- Other features of frameworks
- Working with Laravel
- Writing applications with Silex

Reviewing frameworks

In *Chapter 6, Adapting to MVC*, we barely introduced the idea of frameworks using the MVC design pattern. In fact, we did not explain what a framework is; we just developed a very simple one. If you are looking for a definition, here it is: a framework is the structure that you choose to build your program on. Let's discuss this in more detail.

The purpose of frameworks

When you write an application, you need to add your models, views, and controllers if you use the MVC design pattern, which we really encourage you to do. These three elements, together with the JavaScript and CSS files that complete your views, are the ones that differentiate your application from others. There is no way you can skip on writing them.

On the other hand, there is a set of classes that, even though you need them for the correct functioning of your application, they are common to all other applications, or at least, they are very similar. Examples of these classes are the ones we have in the src/Core directory, such as the router, the configuration reader, and so on.

The purpose of frameworks is clear and necessary: they add some structure to your application and connect the different elements of it. In our example, it helped us route the HTTP requests to the correct controller, connect to the database, and generate dynamic HTML as the response. However, the idea that has to strive is the reusability of frameworks. If you had to write the framework each time you start an application, would that be okay?

So, in order for a framework to be useful, it must be easy to reuse in different environments. This means that the framework has to be downloaded from a source, and it has to be easy to install. Download and install a dependency? It seems Composer is going to be useful again! Even though this was quite different some years ago, nowadays, all the main frameworks can be installed using Composer. We will show you how to in a bit.

The main parts of a framework

If we open source our framework so that other developers can make use of it, we need to structure our code in a way that is intuitive. We need to reduce the learning curve as much as we can; nobody wants to spend weeks on learning how to work with a framework.

As MVC is the de facto web design pattern used in web applications, most frameworks will separate the three layers, model, view, and controller, in three different directories. Depending on the framework, they will be under a src/ directory, even though it is quite common to find the views outside of this directory, as we did with our own. Nevertheless, most frameworks will give you enough flexibility to decide where to place each of the layers.

The rest of the classes that complete the frameworks used to be all grouped in a separate directory—for example, `src/Core`. It is important to separate these elements from yours so that you do not mix the code and modify a core class unintentionally, thus messing up the whole framework. Even better, this last generation of PHP frameworks used to incorporate the core components as independent modules, which will be required via Composer. In doing so, the framework's `composer.json` file will require all the different components, such as routers, configuration, database connections, loggers, template engine, and so on, and Composer will download them in the `vendor/` directory, making them available with the autogenerated autoloader.

Separating the different components in different codebases has many benefits. First of all, it allows different teams of developers to work in an isolated way with the different components. Maintaining them is also easier as the code is separated enough not to affect each other. Finally, it allows the end user to choose which components to get for his application in an attempt to customize the framework, leaving out those heavy components that are not used.

Either the framework is organized in independent modules or everything is together; however, there are always the same common components, which are:

- **The router**: This is the class that, given an HTTP request, finds the correct controller, instantiates it, and executes it, returning the HTTP response.

- **The request**: This contains a handful of methods that allows you to access parameters, cookies, headers, and so on. This is mostly used by the router and sent to the controller.

- **The configuration handler**: This allows you to get the correct configuration file, read it, and use its contents to configure the rest of the components.

- **The template engine**: This merges HTML with content from the controller in order to render the template with the response.

- **The logger**: This adds entries to a log file with the errors or other messages that we consider important.

- **The dependency injector**: This manages all the dependencies that your classes need. Maybe the framework does not have a dependency injector, but it has something similar—that is, a service locator—which tries to help you in a similar way.

- **The way you can write and run your unit tests**: Most of the time, the frameworks include PHPUnit, but there are more options in the community.

Other features of frameworks

Most frameworks have more than just the features that we described in the previous section, even though these are enough to build simple applications as you already did by yourself. Still, most web applications have a lot more common features, so the frameworks tried to implement generic solutions to each of them. Thanks to this, we do not have to reinvent the wheel with features that virtually all medium and big web applications need to implement. We will try to describe some of the most useful ones so that you have a better idea when choosing a framework.

Authentication and roles

Most websites enforce users to authenticate in order to perform some action. The reason for this is to let the system know whether the user trying to perform certain action has the right to do so. Therefore, managing users and their roles is something that you will probably end up implementing in all your web applications. The problem comes when way too many people try to attack your system in order to get the information of other users or performing actions authenticated as someone else, which is called **impersonification**. It is for this reason that your authentication and authorization systems should be as secure as possible—a task that is never easy.

Several frameworks include a pretty secure way of managing users, permissions, and sessions. Most of the time, you can manage this through a configuration file probably by pointing the credentials to a database where the framework can add the user data, your customized roles, and some other customizations. The downside is that each framework has its own way of configuring it, so you will have to dig into the documentation of the framework you are using at this time. Still, it will save you more time than if you had to implement it by yourself.

ORM

Object-relational mapping (ORM) is a technique that converts data from a database or any other data storage into objects. The main goal is to separate the business logic as much as possible from the structure of the database and to reduce the complexity of your code. When using ORM, you will probably never write a query in MySQL; instead, you will use a chain of methods. Behind the scenes, ORM will write the query with each method invocation.

There are good and bad things when using ORM. On one hand, you do not have to remember all the SQL syntax all the time and only the correct methods to invoke, which can be easier if you work with an IDE that can autocomplete methods. It is also good to abstract your code from the type of storage system, because even though it is not very common, you might want to change it later. If you use ORM, you probably have to change only the type of connection, but if you were writing raw queries, you would have a lot of work to do in order to migrate your code.

The arguable downside of using ORM could be that it may be quite difficult to write complicated queries using method chains, and you will end up writing them manually. You are also at the mercy of ORM in order to speed up the performance of your queries, whereas when writing them manually, it is you who can choose better what and how to use when querying. Finally, something that OOP purists complain about quite a lot is that using ORM fills your code with a large amount of dummy objects, similar to the domain objects that you already know.

As you can see, using ORM is not always an easy decision, but just in case you choose to use it, most of the big frameworks include one. Take your time in deciding whether or not to use one in your applications; in case you do, choose wisely which one. You might end up requiring an ORM different from the one that the framework provides.

Cache

The bookstore is a pretty good example that may help in describing the cache feature. It has a database of books that is queried every time that someone either lists all the books or asks for the details of a specific one. Most of the time the information related to books will be the same; the only change would be the stock of the books from time to time. We could say that our system has way more reads than writes, where reads means querying for data and writes means updating it. In this kind of system, it seems like a waste of time and resources to access the database each time, knowing that most of the time, we will get the same results. This feeling increases if we do some expensive transformation to the data that we retrieve.

A **cache layer** allows the application to store temporary data in a storage system faster than our database, usually in memory rather than disk. Even though cache systems are getting more complex, they usually allow you to store data by key-value pairs, as in an array.

The idea is not to access the database for data that we know is the same as the last time we accessed it in order to save time and resources. Implementations can vary quite a lot, but the main flow is as follows:

1. You try to access a certain piece of data for the first time. We ask the cache whether a certain key is there, which it is not.

2. You query the database, getting back the result. After processing it—and maybe transforming it to your domain objects—you store the result in the cache. The key would be the same you used in step 1, and the value would be the object/array/JSON that you generated.

3. You try to access the same piece of data again. You ask the cache whether the key is there; here, it is, so you do not need to access the database at all.

It seems easy, right? The main problem with caches comes when we need to invalidate a certain key. How and when should we do it? There are a couple of approaches that are worth mentioning:

• You will set an expiration time to the key-value pair in the cache. After this time passes, the cache will remove the key-value pair automatically, so you will have to query the database again. Even though this system might work for some applications, it does not for ours. If the stock changes to 0 before the cache expires, the user will see books that they cannot borrow or buy.

• The data never expires, but each time we make a change in the database, we will identify which keys in the cache are affected by this change and then purge them. This is ideal since the data will be in the cache until it is no longer valid, whether this is 2 seconds or 3 weeks. The downside is that identifying these keys could be a hard task depending on your data structure. If you miss deleting some of them, you will have corrupted data in your cache, which is quite difficult to debug and detect.

You can see that cache is a double-edged sword, so we would recommend you to only use it when necessary and not just because your framework comes with it. As with ORM, if you are not convinced by the cache system that your framework provides, using a different one should not be difficult. In fact, your code should not be aware of which cache system you are using except when creating the connection object.

Internationalization

English is not the only language out there, and you would like to make your website as accessible as possible. Depending on your target, it would be a good idea to have your website translated to other languages too, but how do you do this? We hope that by now you did not answer: "Copy-pasting all the templates and translating them". This is way too inefficient; when making a little change in a template, you need to replicate the change everywhere.

There are tools that can be integrated with either controllers and/or template engines in order to translate strings. You usually keep a file for each language that you have, in which you will add all the strings that need to be translated plus their translation. One of the most common formats for this is PO files, in which you have a map of key-value pairs with originally translated pairs. Later on, you will invoke a `translate` method sending the original string, which will return the translated string depending on the language you selected.

When writing templates, it might be tiring to invoke the translation each time you want to display a string, but you will end up with only one template, which is much easier to maintain than any other option.

Usually, internationalization is very much tied to the framework that you use; however, if you have the opportunity to use the system of your choice, pay special attention to its performance, the translation files it uses, and how it manages strings with parameters—that is, how we can ask the system to translate messages such as "Hello %s, who are you?" in which "%s" needs to be injected each time.

Types of frameworks

Now that you know quite a lot about what a framework can offer you, you are in a position to decide what kind of framework you would like to use. In order to make this decision, it might be useful to know what kinds of frameworks are available. This categorization is nothing official, just some guidelines that we offer you to make your choice easier.

Complete and robust frameworks

This type of framework comes with the whole package. It contains all the features that we discussed earlier, so it will allow you to develop very complete applications. Usually, these frameworks allow you to create applications very easily with just a few configuration files that define things such as how to connect to a database, what kind of roles you need, or whether you want to use a cache. Other than this, you will just have to add your controllers, views, and models, which saves you a lot of time.

The problem with these frameworks is the learning curve. Given all the features they contain, you need to spend quite a lot of time on learning how to use each one, which is usually not very pleasant. In fact, most companies looking for web developers require that you have experience with the framework they use; otherwise, it will be a bad investment for them.

Another thing you should consider when choosing these frameworks is whether they are structured in modules or come as a huge monolith. In the first case, you will be able to choose which modules to use that add a lot of flexibility. On the other hand, if you have to stick with all of them, it might make your application slow even if you do not use all of the features.

Lightweight and flexible frameworks

Even when working on a small application, you would like to use a framework to save you a lot of time and pain, but you should avoid using one of the larger frameworks as they will be too much to handle for what you really need. In this case, you should choose a lightweight framework, one that contains very few features, similar to what we implemented in previous chapters.

The benefit of these frameworks is that even though you get the basic features such as routing, you are completely free to implement the login system, cache layer, or internationalization system that suits your specific application better. In fact, you could build a more complete framework using this one as the base and then adding all the complements you need, making it completely customized.

As you can note, both types have their pros and cons. It will be up to you to choose the correct one each time, depending on your needs, the time that you can spend, and the experience that you have with each one.

An overview of famous frameworks

You already have a good idea about what a framework can offer and what types there are. Now, it is time to review some of the most important ones out there so that you get an idea of where to start looking for your next PHP web application. Note that with the release of PHP 7, there will be quite a lot of new or improved PHP frameworks. Try to always be in the loop!

Symfony 2

Symfony has been one of the most favorite frameworks of developers during the last 10 years. After reinventing itself for its version 2, Symfony entered the generation of frameworks by modules. In fact, it is quite common to find other projects using Symfony 2 components mixed up with some other framework as you just need to add the name of the module in your Composer file to use it.

You can start applications with Symfony 2 by just executing a command. Symfony 2 creates all the directories, empty configuration files, and so on ready for you. You can also add empty controllers from the command line. They use Doctrine 2 as ORM, which is probably one of the most reliable ORMs that PHP can offer nowadays. For the template engine, you will find Twig, which is the same as what we used in our framework.

In general, this is a very attractive framework with a huge community behind it giving support; plus, a lot of companies also use it. It is always worth at least checking the list of modules in case you do not want to use the whole framework but want to take advantage of some bits of it.

Zend Framework 2

The second big PHP framework, at least since last year, is Zend Framework 2. As with Symfony, it has been out there for quite a long time too. Also, as with any other modern framework, it is built in an OOP way, trying to implement all the good design patterns used for web applications. It is composed of multiple components that you can reuse in other projects, such as their well-known authentication system. It lacks some elements, such as a template engine—usually they mix PHP and HTML—and ORM, but you can easily integrate the ones that you prefer.

There is a lot of work going on in order to release Zend Framework 3, which will come with support for PHP 7, performance improvements, and some other new components. We recommend you to keep an eye on it; it could be a good candidate.

Other frameworks

Even though Symfony and Zend Framework are the two big players, more and more PHP frameworks have appeared in these last years, evolving quite fast and bringing to the game more interesting features. Names such as CodeIgniter, Yii, PHPCake, and others will start to sound familiar as soon as you start browsing PHP projects. As some of them came into play later than Symfony and Zend Framework, they implement some new features that the others do not have, such as components related to JavaScript and jQuery, integration with Selenium for UI testing, and others.

Even though it is always a good thing to have diversification simply because you will probably get exactly what you need from one or the other, be smart when choosing your framework. The community plays an important role here because if you have any problem, it will help you to fix it or you can just help evolve the framework with each new PHP release.

The Laravel framework

Even though Symfony and Zend Framework have been the big players for quite a long time, during this last couple of years, a third framework came into play that has grown in popularity so much that nowadays it is the favorite framework among developers. Simplicity, elegant code, and high speed of development are the trump cards of this "framework for artisans". In this section, you will have a glance at what Laravel can do, taking the first steps to create a very simple application.

Installation

Laravel comes with a set of command-line tools that will make your life easier. Because of this, it is recommended to install it globally instead of per project—that is, to have Laravel as another program in your environment. You can still do this with Composer by running the following command:

```
$ composer global require "laravel/installer"
```

This command should download the Laravel installer to `~/.composer/vendor`. In order to be able to use the executable from the command line, you will need to run something similar to this:

```
$ sudo ln -s ~/.composer/vendor/bin/laravel /usr/bin/laravel
```

Now, you are able to use the `laravel` command. To ensure that everything went all right, just run the following:

```
$ laravel -version
```

If everything went OK, this should output the version installed.

Project setup

Yes, we know. Every single tutorial starts by creating a blog. However, we are building web applications, and this is the easiest approach we can take that adds some value to you. Let's start then; execute the following command wherever you want to add your application:

```
$ laravel new php-blog
```

This command will output something similar to what Composer does, simply because it fetches dependencies using Composer. After a few seconds, the application will hopefully tell you that everything was installed successfully and that you are ready to go.

Laravel created a new `php-blog` directory with quite a lot of content. You should have something similar to the directory structure shown in the following screenshot:

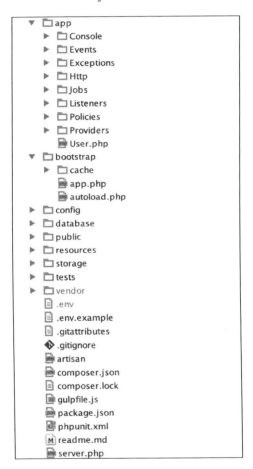

Let's set up the database. The first thing you should do is update the `.env` file with the correct database credentials. Update the `DB_DATABASE` values with your own; here's an example:

```
DB_HOST=localhost
DB_DATABASE=php_blog
DB_USERNAME=root
DB_PASSWORD=
```

You will also need to create the php_blog database. Do it with just one command, as follows:

```
$ mysql -u root -e "CREATE SCHEMA php_blog"
```

With Laravel, you have a migrations system; that is, you keep all the database schema changes under database/migrations so that anyone else using your code can quickly set up their database. The first step is to run the following command, which will create a migrations file for the blogs table:

```
$ php artisan make:migration create_posts_table --create=posts
```

Open the generated file, which should be something similar to database/ migrations/<date>_create_posts_table.php. The up method defines the table blogs with an autoincremental ID and timestamp field. We would like to add a title, the content of the post, and the user ID that created it. Replace the up method with the following:

```
public function up()
{
    Schema::create('posts', function (Blueprint $table) {
        $table->increments('id');
        $table->timestamps();
        $table->string('title');
        $table->text('content');
        $table->integer('user_id')->unsigned();
        $table->foreign('user_id')
            ->references('id')->on('users');
    });
}
```

Here, the title will be a string, whereas the content is a text. The difference is in the length of these fields, string being a simple VARCHAR and text a TEXT data type. For the user ID we defined INT UNSIGNED, which references the id field of the users table. Laravel already defined the users table when creating the project, so you do not have to worry about it. If you are interested in how it looks, check the database/ migrations/2014_10_12_000000_create_users_table.php file. You will note that a user is composed by an ID, a name, the unique e-mail, and the password.

So far, we have just written the migration files. In order to apply them, you need to run the following command:

```
$ php artisan migrate
```

If everything went as expected, you should have a `blogs` table now similar to the following:

```
● ● ●                 1. vagrant@vagrant-ubuntu-trusty-64: /vagrant (bash)
mysql> desc posts;
+------------+------------------+------+-----+---------------------+-----------------------------+
| Field      | Type             | Null | Key | Default             | Extra                       |
+------------+------------------+------+-----+---------------------+-----------------------------+
| id         | int(10) unsigned | NO   | PRI | NULL                | auto_increment              |
| created_at | timestamp        | NO   |     | CURRENT_TIMESTAMP   | on update CURRENT_TIMESTAMP |
| updated_at | timestamp        | NO   |     | 0000-00-00 00:00:00 |                             |
| title      | varchar(255)     | NO   |     | NULL                |                             |
| content    | text             | NO   |     | NULL                |                             |
| user_id    | int(10) unsigned | NO   | MUL | NULL                |                             |
+------------+------------------+------+-----+---------------------+-----------------------------+
6 rows in set (0.00 sec)

mysql>
```

To finish with all the preparations, we need to create a model for our `blogs` table. This model will extend from **Illuminate\Database\Eloquent\Model**, which is the ORM that Laravel uses. To generate this model automatically, run the following command:

```
$ php artisan make:model Post
```

The name of the model should be the same as that of the database table but in singular. After running this command, you can find the empty model in `app/Post.php`.

Adding the first endpoint

Let's add a quick endpoint just to understand how routes work and how to link controllers with templates. In order to avoid database access, let's build the add new post view, which will display a form that allows the user to add a new post with a title and text. Let's start by adding the route and controller. Open the `app/Http/routes.php` file and add the following:

```
Route::group(['middleware' => ['web']], function () {
    Route::get('/new', function () {
        return view('new');
    });
});
```

These three very simple lines say that for the `/new` endpoint, we want to reply with the `new` view. Later on, we will complicate things here in the controller, but for now, let's focus on the views.

Laravel uses Blade as the template engine instead of Twig, but the way they work is quite similar. They can also define layouts from where other templates can extend. The place for your layouts is in `resources/views/layouts`. Create an `app.blade.php` file with the following content inside this directory, as follows:

```
<!DOCTYPE html>
<html lang="en">
<head>
    <title>PHP Blog</title>
    <link rel="stylesheet" href="{{ URL::asset('css/layout.css') }}"
type="text/css">
    @yield('css')
</head>
<body>
<div class="navbar">
    <ul>
        <li><a href="/new">New article</a></li>
        <li><a href="/">Articles</a></li>
    </ul>
</div>
<div class="content">
@yield('content')
</div>
</body>
</html>
```

This is just a normal layout with a title, some CSS, and an `ul` list of sections in the body, which will be used as the navigation bar. There are two important elements to note here other than the HTML code that should already sound familiar:

- To define a block, Blade uses the `@yield` annotation followed by the name of the block. In our layout, we defined two blocks: `css` and `content`.

- There is a feature that allows you to build URLs in templates. We want to include the CSS file in `public/css/layout.css`, so we will use `URL::asset` to build this URL. It is also helpful to include JS files.

As you saw, we included a `layout.css` file. CSS and JS files are stored under the `public` directory. Create yours in `public/css/layout.css` with the following code:

```
.content {
    position: fixed;
    top: 50px;
    width: 100%
}
.navbar ul {
```

```
        position: fixed;
        top: 0;
        width: 100%;
        list-style-type: none;
        margin: 0;
        padding: 0;
        overflow: hidden;
        background-color: #333;
}
.navbar li {
        float: left;
        border-right: 1px solid #bbb;
}
.navbar li:last-child {
        border-right: none;
}
.navbar li a {
        display: block;
        color: white;
        text-align: center;
        padding: 14px 16px;
        text-decoration: none;
}
.navbar li a:hover {
        background-color: #111;
}
```

Now, we can focus on our view. Templates are stored in `resources/views`, and, as with layouts, they need the `.blade.php` file extension. Create your view in `resources/views/new.blade.php` with the following content:

```
@extends('layouts.app')

@section('css')
    <link rel="stylesheet" href="{{ URL::asset('css/new.css') }}"
type="text/css">
@endsection

@section('content')
    <h2>Add new post</h2>
    <form method="post" action="/new">
        <div class="component">
            <label for="title">Title</label>
            <input type="text" name="title"/>
        </div>
```

```
        <div class="component">
            <label>Text</label>
            <textarea rows="20" name="content"></textarea>
        </div>
        <div class="component">
            <button type="submit">Save</button>
        </div>
    </form>
@endsection
```

The syntax is quite intuitive. This template extends from the layouts' one and defines two sections or blocks: css and content. The CSS file included follows the same format as the previous one. You can create it in public/css/new.css with content similar to the following:

```
label {
    display: block;
}
input {
    width: 80%;
}
button {
    font-size: 30px;
    float: right;
    margin-right: 20%;
}
textarea {
    width: 80%;
}
.component {
    padding: 10px;
}
```

The rest of the template just defines the POST form pointing to the same URL with title and text fields. Everything is ready to test it in your browser! Try accessing http://localhost:8080/new or the port number of your choice. You should see something similar to the following screenshot:

Managing users

As explained before, user authentication and authorization is one of the features that most frameworks contain. Laravel makes our lives very easy by providing the user model and the registration and authentication controllers. It is quite easy to make use of them: you just need to add the routes pointing to the already existing controllers and add the views. Let's begin.

There are five routes that you need to consider here. There are two that belong to the registration step, one to get the form and another one for the form to submit the information provided by the user. The other three are related to the authentication part: one to get the form, one to post the form, and one for the logout. All five of them are included in the `Auth\AuthController` class. Add to your `routes.php` file the following routes:

```
// Registration routes...
Route::get('auth/register', 'Auth\AuthController@getRegister');
Route::post('auth/register', 'Auth\AuthController@postRegister');

// Authentication routes...
Route::get('/login', 'Auth\AuthController@getLogin');
Route::post('login', 'Auth\AuthController@postLogin');
Route::get('logout', 'Auth\AuthController@getLogout');
```

Note how we defined these routes. As opposed to the one that we created previously, the second argument of these is a string with the concatenation of the controller's class name and method. This is a better way to create routes because it separates the logic to a different class that can later be reused and/or unit tested.

If you are interested, you can browse the code for this controller. You will find a complex design, where the functions the routes will invoke are actually part of two traits that the `AuthController` class uses: `RegistersUsers` and `AuthenticatesUsers`. Checking these methods will enable you to understand what goes on behind the scenes.

Each `get` route expects a view to render. For the user's registration, we need to create a template in `resources/views/auth/register.blade.php`, and for the login view, we need a template in `resources/views/auth/login.blade.php`. As soon as we send the correct POST parameters to the correct URL, we can add any content that we think necessary.

User registration

Let's start with the registration form; this form needs four POST parameters: name, e-mail, password, and password confirmation, and as the route says, we need to submit it to `/auth/register`. The template could look similar to the following:

```
@extends('layouts.app')

@section('css')
    <link rel="stylesheet" href="{{ URL::asset('css/register.css') }}"
type="text/css">
@endsection

@section('content')
    <h2>Account registration</h2>

    <form method="post" action="/auth/register">
        {{ csrf_field() }}
        <div class="component">
            <label for="name">Name</label>
            <input type="text" name="name"
                    value="{{ old('name') }}" />
        </div>
        <div class="component">
            <label>Email</label>
            <input type="email" name="email"
                    value="{{ old('email') }}"/>
        </div>
```

```
        <div class="component">
            <label>Password</label>
            <input type="password" name="password" />
        </div>
        <div class="component">
            <label>Password confirmation</label>
            <input type="password" name="password_confirmation" />
        </div>
        <div class="component">
            <button type="submit">Create</button>
        </div>
    </form>
@endsection
```

This template is quite similar to the form for new posts: it extends the layout, adds a CSS file, and populates the content section with a form. The new addition here is the use of the `old` function that retrieves the value submitted on the previous request in case that the form was not valid and we showed it back to the user.

Before we try it, we need to add a `register.css` file with the styles for this form. A simple one could be as follows:

```
div.content {
    text-align: center;
}
label {
    display: block;
}
input {
    width: 250px;
}
button {
    font-size: 20px;
}
.component {
    padding: 10px;
}
```

Finally, we should edit the layout in order to add a link on the menu pointing to the registration and login pages. This is as simple as adding the following `li` elements at the end of the `ul` tag:

```
<li class="right"><a href="/auth/register">Sign up</a></li>
<li class="right"><a href="/login">Sign in</a></li>
```

Add also the style for the `right` class at the end of `layout.css`:

```css
div.alert {
    color: red;
}
```

To make things even more useful, we could add the information for what went wrong when submitting the form. Laravel flashes the errors into the session, and they can be accessed via the `errors` template variable. As this is common to all forms and not only to the registration one, we could add it to the `app.blade.php` layout, as follows:

```
<div class="content">
    @if (count($errors) > 0)
        <div class="alert">
            <strong>Whoops! Something went wrong!</strong>
            @foreach ($errors->all() as $error)
                <p>{{ $error }}</p>
            @endforeach
        </div>
    @endif
@yield('content')
```

In this piece of code, we will use Blade's `@if` conditional and `@foreach` loop. The syntax is the same as PHP; the only difference is the @ prefix.

Now, we are ready to go. Launch your application and click on the registration link on the right-hand side of the menu. Attempt to submit the form, but leave some fields blank so that we can note how the errors are displayed. The result should be something similar to this:

One thing that we should customize is where the user will be redirected once the registration is successful. In this case, we can redirect them to the login page. In order to achieve this, you need to change the value of the $redirectTo property of AuthController. So far, we only have the new post page, but later, you could add any path that you want via the following:

```
protected $redirectPath= '/new;
```

User login

The user's login has a few more changes other than the registration. We not only need to add the login view, we should also modify the menu in the layout in order to acknowledge the authenticated user, remove the register link, and add a logout one. The template, as mentioned earlier, has to be saved in resources/views/ auth/login.blade.php. The form needs an e-mail and password and optionally a checkbox for the *remember me* functionality. An example could be the following:

```
@extends('layouts.app')

@section('css')
    <link rel="stylesheet" href="{{ URL::asset('css/register.css') }}"
type="text/css">
@endsection

@section('content')
```

```
    <h2>Login</h2>

    <form method="POST" action="/login">
        {!! csrf_field() !!}
        <div class="component">
            <label>Email</label>
            <input type="email" name="email"
                    value="{{ old('email') }}">
        </div>
        <div class="component">
            <label>Password</label>
            <input type="password" name="password">
        </div>
        <div class="component">
            <input class="checkbox" type="checkbox" name="remember">
            Remember Me
        </div>
        <div class="component">
            <button type="submit">Login</button>
        </div>
    </form>
@endsection
```

The layout has to be changed slightly. Where we displayed the links to register and log in users, now we need to check whether there is a user already authenticated; if so, we should rather show a logout link. You can get the authenticated user through the Auth::user() method even from the view. If the result is not empty, it means that the user was authenticated successfully. Change the two links using the following code:

```
<ul>
    <li><a href="/new">New article</a></li>
    <li><a href="/">Articles</a></li>
    @if (Auth::user() !== null)
        <li class="right">
            <a href="/logout">Logout</a>
        </li>
    @else
        <li class="right">
            <a href="/auth/register">Sign up</a>
        </li>
        <li class="right">
            <a href="/login">Sign in</a>
        </li>
    @endif
</ul>
```

Protected routes

This last part of the user management session is probably the most important one. One of the main goals when authenticating users is to authorize them to certain content—that is, to allow them to visit certain pages that unauthenticated users cannot. In Laravel, you can define which routes are protected in this way by just adding the `auth` middleware. Update the new post route with the following code:

```
Route::get('/new', ['middleware' => 'auth', function () {
    return view('new');
}]);
```

Everything is ready! Try to access the new post page after logging out; you will be redirected automatically to the login page. Can you feel how powerful a framework can be?

Setting up relationships in models

As we mentioned before, Laravel comes with an ORM, Eloquent ORM, which makes dealing with models a very easy task. In our simple database, we defined one table for posts, and we already had another one for users. Posts contain the ID of the user that owns it—that is, `user_id`. It is good practice to use the singular of the name of the table followed by `_id` so that Eloquent will know where to look. This was all we did regarding the foreign key.

We should also mention this relationship on the model side. Depending on the type of the relationship (one to one, one to many, or many to many), the code will be slightly different. In our case, we have a one-to-many relationship because one user can have many posts. To say so in Laravel, we need to update both the `Post` and the `User` models. The `User` model needs to specify that it has many posts, so you need to add a `posts` method with the following content:

```
public function posts() {
    return $this->hasMany('App\Post');
}
```

This method says that the model for users has many posts. The other change that needs to be made in `Post` is similar: we need to add a `user` method that defines the relationship. The method should be similar to this one:

```
public function user() {
    return $this->belongsTo('App\User');
}
```

It looks like very little, but this is the whole configuration that we need. In the next section, you will see how easy it is to save and query using these two models.

Creating complex controllers

Even though the title of this section mentions complex controllers, you will note that we can create complete and powerful controllers with very little code. Let's start by adding the code that will manage the creation of posts. This controller needs to be linked to the following route:

```
Route::post('/new', 'Post\PostController@createPost');
```

As you can imagine, now, we need to create the Post\PostController class with the createPost method in it. Controllers should be stored in app/Http/Controllers, and if they can be organized in folders, it would be even better. Save the following class in app/Http/Controllers/Post/PostController.php:

```php
<?php

namespace App\Http\Controllers\Post;

use App\Http\Controllers\Controller;
use Illuminate\Http\Request;
use Illuminate\Support\Facades\Auth;
use Illuminate\Support\Facades\Validator;
use App\Post;

class PostController extends Controller {

    public function createPost(Request $request) {

    }
}
```

So far, the only two things we can note from this class are:

- Controllers extend from the App\Http\Controllers\Controller class, which contains some general helpers for all the controllers.
- Methods of controllers can get the Illuminate\Http\Request argument as the user's request. This object will contain elements such as the posted parameters, cookies, and so on. This is very similar to the one we created in our own application.

The first thing we need to do in this kind of controller is check whether the parameters posted are correct. For this, we will use the following code:

```
public function createPost(Request $request) {
    $validator = Validator::make($request->all(), [
        'title' => 'required|max:255',
        'content' => 'required|min:20',
    ]);

    if ($validator->fails()) {
        return redirect()->back()
            ->withInput()
            ->withErrors($validator);
    }
}
```

The first thing we did is create a validator. For this, we used the `Validator::make` function and sent two arguments: the first one contains all the parameters from the request, and the second one is an array with the expected fields and their constraints. Note that we expect two required fields: `title` and `content`. Here, the first one can be up to 255 characters long, and the second one needs to be at least 20 characters long.

Once the `validator` object is created, we can check whether the data posted by the user matches the requirements with the `fails` method. If it returns `true`—that is, the validation fails—we will redirect the user back to the previous page with `redirect()->back()`. To perform this invocation, we will add two more method calls: `withInput` will send the submitted values so that we can display them again, and `withErrors` will send the errors the same way `AuthController` did.

At this point, it would be helpful to the user if we show the previously submitted title and text in case the post is not valid. For this, use the already known `old` method in the view:

```
{{--...--}}
    <input type="text" name="title"
            value="{{ old('title') }}"/>
</div>
<div class="component">
    <label>Text</label>
    <textarea rows="20" name="content">
        {{ old('content') }}
    </textarea>
{{--...--}}
```

At this point, we can already test how the controller behaves when the post does not match the required validations. If you miss any of the parameters or they do not have correct lengths, you will get an error page similar to the following one:

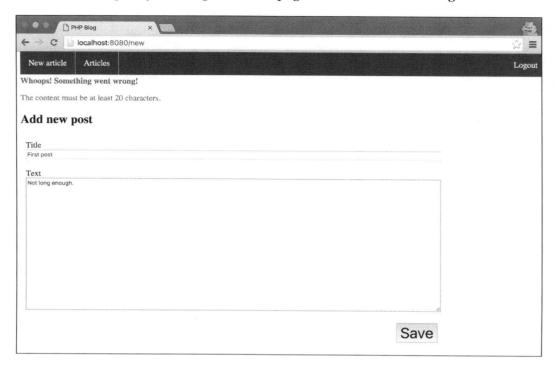

Let's now add the logic to save the post in case it is valid. If you remember the interaction with the models from our previous application, you will be gladly surprised at how easy it is to work with them here. Take a look at the following:

```php
public function createPost(Request $request) {
    $validator = Validator::make($request->all(), [
        'title' => 'required|max:255',
        'content' => 'required|min:20',
    ]);

    if ($validator->fails()) {
        return redirect()->back()
            ->withInput()
            ->withErrors($validator);
    }

    $post = new Post();
```

```
$post->title = $request->title;
$post->content = $request->content;

Auth::user()->posts()->save($post);

return redirect('/new');
}
```

The first thing we will do is create a `post` object setting the title and content from the request values. Then, given the result of `Auth::user()`, which gives us the instance of the currently authenticated user model, we will save the post that we just created through `posts()->save($post)`. If we wanted to save the post without the information of the user, we could use `$post->save()`. Really, that is all.

Let's quickly add another endpoint to retrieve the list of posts for a given user so that we can take a look at how Eloquent ORM allows us to fetch data easily. Add the following route:

```
Route::get('/', ['middleware' => 'auth', function () {
    $posts = Auth::user()
        ->posts()
        ->orderBy('created_at')
        ->get();
    return view('posts', ['posts' => $posts]);
}]);
```

The way we retrieve data is very similar to how we save it. We need the instance of a model—in this case, the authenticated user—and we will add a concatenation of method invocations that will internally generate the query to execute. In this case, we will ask for the posts ordered by the creation date. In order to send information to the view, we need to pass a second argument, which will be an array of parameter names and values.

Add the following template as `resources/views/posts.blade.php`, which will display the list of posts for the authenticated user as a table. Note how we will use the `$post` object, which is an instance of the model, in the following code:

```
@extends('layouts.app')

@section('css')
    <link rel="stylesheet" href="{{ URL::asset('css/posts.css') }}"
type="text/css">
@endsection

@section('content')
```

```
<h2>Your posts</h2>

<table>
@foreach ($posts as $post)
    <tr>
        <td>{{ $post->title }}</td>
        <td>{{ $post->created_at }}</td>
        <td>{{ str_limit($post->content, 100) }}</td>
    </tr>
@endforeach
</table>
@endsection
```

The lists of posts are finally displayed. The result should be something similar to the following screenshot:

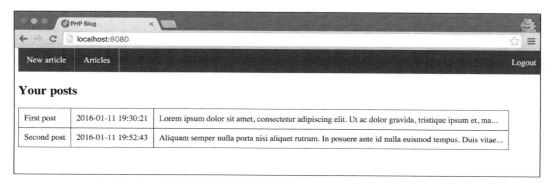

Adding tests

In a very short time, we created an application that allows you to register, log in, and create and list posts from scratch. We will end this section by talking about how to test your Laravel application with PHPUnit.

It is extremely easy to write tests in Laravel as it has a very nice integration with PHPUnit. There is already a phpunit.xml file, a customized TestCase class, customized assertions, and plenty of helpers in order to test with the database. It also allows you to test routes, emulating the HTTP request instead of testing the controllers. We will visit all these features while testing the creation of new posts.

First of all, we need to remove tests/ExampleTest.php because it tested the home page, and as we modified it, it will fail. Do not worry; this is an example test that helps developers to start testing, and making it fail is not a problem at all.

Now, we need to create our new test. To do this, we can either add the file manually or use the command line and run the following command:

```
$ php artisan make:test NewPostTest
```

This command creates the `tests/NewPostTest.php` file, which extends from `TestCase`. If you open it, you will note that there is already a dummy test, which you can also remove. Either way, you can run PHPUnit to make sure everything passes. You can do it in the same way we did previously, as follows:

```
$ ./vendor/bin/phpunit
```

The first test we can add is one where we try to add a new post but the data passed by the POST parameters is not valid. In this case, we should expect that the response contains errors and old data, so the user can edit it instead of rewriting everything again. Add the following test to the `NewPostTest` class:

```php
<?php

class NewPostTest extends TestCase
{
    public function testWrongParams() {
        $user = factory(App\User::class)
            ->make(['email' => 'test@user.laravel']);

        $this->be($user);

        $this->call(
            'POST',
            '/new',
            ['title' => 'the title', 'content' => 'ojhkjhg']
        );

        $this->assertSessionHasErrors('content');
        $this->assertHasOldInput();
    }
}
```

The first thing we can note in the test is the creation of a `user` instance using a factory. You can pass an array with any parameter that you want to set to the `make` invocation; otherwise, defaults will be used. After we get the `user` instance, we will send it to the `be` method to let Laravel know that we want that user to be the authorized one for this test.

Once we set the grounds for the test, we will use the `call` helper that will emulate a real HTTP request. To this method, we have to send the HTTP method (in this case, POST), the route to request, and optionally the parameters. Note that the `call` method returns the response object in case you need it.

We will send a title and the content, but this second one is not long enough, so we will expect some errors. Laravel comes with several customized assertions, especially when testing these kinds of responses. In this case, we could use two of them: `assertSessionHasErrors`, which checks whether there are any flash errors in the session (in particular, the ones for the content parameter), and `assertHasOldInput`, which checks whether the response contains old data in order to show it back to the user.

The second test that we would like to add is the case where the user posts valid data so that we can save the post in the database. This test is trickier as we need to interact with the database, which is usually a not a very pleasant experience. However, Laravel gives us enough tools to help us in this task. The first and most important is to let PHPUnit know that we want to use database transactions for each test. Then, we need to persist the authenticated user in the database as the post has a foreign key pointing to it. Finally, we should assert that the post is saved in the database correctly. Add the following code to the `NewPostTest` class:

```
use DatabaseTransactions;

//...

public function testNewPost() {
    $postParams = [
        'title' => 'the title',
        'content' => 'In a place far far away.'
    ];

    $user = factory(App\User::class)
        ->make(['email' => 'test@user.laravel']);
    $user->save();

    $this->be($user);

    $this->call('POST', '/new', $postParams);

    $this->assertRedirectedTo('http://localhost/new');
    $this->seeInDatabase('posts', $postParams);
}
```

The `DatabaseTransactions` trait will make the test to start a transaction at the beginning and then roll it back once the test is done, so we will not leave the database with data from tests. Saving the authenticated user in the database is also an easy task as the result of the factory is an instance of the user's model, and we can just invoke the `save` method on it.

The `assertRedirectedTo` assertion will make sure that the response contains the valid headers that redirect the user to the specified URL. More interestingly, `seeInDatabase` will verify that there is an entity in the `posts` table, which is the first argument, with the data provided in the array, which is the second argument.

There are quite a lot of assertions, but as you can note, they are extremely useful, reducing what could be a long test to a very few lines. We recommend you to visit the official documentation for the full list.

The Silex microframework

After a taste of what Laravel can offer you, you most likely do not want to hear about minimalist microframeworks. Still, we think it is good to know more than one framework. You can get to know different approaches, be more versatile, and everyone will want you in their team.

We chose Silex because it is a microframework, which is very different from Laravel, and also because it is part of the Symfony family. With this introduction to Silex, you will learn how to use your second framework, which is of a totally different type, and you will be one step closer to knowing Symfony as well, which is one of the big players.

What is the benefit of microframeworks? Well, they provide the very basics—that is, a router, a simple dependency injector, request helpers, and so on, but this is the end of it. You have plenty of room to choose and build what you really need, including external libraries or even your own ones. This means that you can have a framework specially customized for each different project. In fact, Silex provides a handful of built-in service providers that you can integrate very easily, from template engines to logging or security.

Installation

There's no news here. Composer does everything for you, as it does with Laravel. Execute the following command on your command line at the root of your new project in order to include Silex in your `composer.json` file:

```
$ composer require silex/silex
```

You may require more dependencies, but let's add them when we need them.

Project setup

Silex's most important class is `Silex\Application`. This class, which extends from **Pimple** (a lightweight dependency injector), manages almost anything. You can use it as an array as it implements the `ArrayAccess` interface, or you could invoke its methods to add dependencies, register services, and so on. The first thing to do is to instantiate it in your `public/index.php` file, as follows:

```php
<?php

use Silex\Application;

require_once __DIR__ . '/../vendor/autoload.php';

$app = new Application();
```

Managing configuration

One of the first things we like to do is load the configuration. We could do something very simple, such as including a file with PHP or JSON content, but let's make use of one of the service providers, `ConfigServiceProvider`. Let's add it with Composer via the following line:

```
$ composer require igorw/config-service-provider
```

This service allows us to have multiple configuration files, one for each environment we need. Imagining that we want to have two environments, `prod` and `dev`, this means we need two files: one in `config/prod.json` and one in `config/dev.json`. The `config/dev.json` file would look similar to this:

```json
{
  "debug": true,
  "cache": false,
  "database": {
    "user": "dev",
    "password": ""
  }
}
```

The `config/prod.json` file would look similar to this:

```json
{
  "debug": false,
  "cache": true,
  "database ": {
```

```
        "user": "root",
        "password": "fsd98na9nc"
    }
}
```

In order to work in a development environment, you will need to set the correct value to the environment variable by running the following command:

export APP_ENV=dev

The APP_ENV environment variable will be the one telling us which environment we are in. Now, it is time to use this service provider. In order to register it by reading from the configuration file of the current environment, add the following lines to your index.php file:

```
$env = getenv('APP_ENV') ?: 'prod';
$app->register(
    new Igorw\Silex\ConfigServiceProvider(
        __DIR__ . "/../config/$env.json"
    )
);
```

The first thing we did here is to get the environment from the environment variable. By default, we set it to prod. Then, we invoked register from the $app object to add an instance of ConfigServiceProvider by passing the correct configuration file path. From now on, the $app "array" will contain three entries: debug, cache, and db with the content of the configuration files. We will be able to access them whenever we have access to $app, which will be mostly everywhere.

Setting the template engine

Another of the handy service providers is Twig. As you might remember, Twig is the template engine that we used in our own framework, and it is, in fact, from the same people that developed Symfony and Silex. You also already know how to add the dependency with Composer; simply run the following:

$ composer require twig/twig

To register the service, we will need to add the following lines in our public/index. php file:

```
$app->register(
    new Silex\Provider\TwigServiceProvider(),
    ['twig.path' => __DIR__ . '/../views']
);
```

Also, create the views/ directory where we will later store our templates. Now, you have the Twig_Environment instance available by just accessing $app['twig'].

Adding a logger

The last one of the service providers that we will register for now is the logger. This time, the library to use is **Monolog**, and you can include this via the following:

```
$ composer require monolog/monolog
```

The quickest way to register a service is by just providing the path of the log file, which can be done as follows:

```
$app->register(
    new Silex\Provider\MonologServiceProvider(),
    ['monolog.logfile' => __DIR__ . '/../app.log']
);
```

If you would like to add more information to this service provider, such as what level of logs you want to save, the name of the log, and so on, you can add them to the array together with the log file. Take a look at the documentation at http://silex.sensiolabs.org/doc/providers/monolog.html for the full list of parameters available.

As with the template engine, from now on, you can access the Monolog\Logger instance from the Application object by accessing $app['monolog'].

Adding the first endpoint

It is time to see how the router works in Silex. We would like to add a simple endpoint for the home page. As we already mentioned, the $app instance can manage almost anything, including routes. Add the following code at the end of the public/index. php file:

```
$app->get('/', function(Application $app) {
    return $app['twig']->render('home.twig');
});
```

This is a similar way of adding routes to the one that Laravel follows. We invoked the get method as it is a GET endpoint, and we passed the route string and the Application instance. As we mentioned here, $app also acts as a dependency injector—in fact, it extends from one: Pimple—so you will notice the Application instance almost everywhere. The result of the anonymous function will be the response that we will send to the user—in this case, a rendered Twig template.

Right now, this will not do the trick. In order to let Silex know that you are done setting up your application, you need to invoke the run method at the very end of the public/index.php file. Remember that if you need to add anything else to this file, it has to be before this line:

```
$app->run();
```

You have already worked with Twig, so we will not spend too much time on this. The first thing to add is the `views/home.twig` template:

```
{% extends "layout.twig" %}

{% block content %}
    <h1>Hi visitor!</h1>
{% endblock %}
```

Now, as you might have already guessed, we will add the `views/layout.twig` template, as follows:

```
<html>
<head>
    <title>Silex Example</title>
</head>
<body>
{% block content %}
{% endblock %}
</body>
</html>
```

Try accessing the home page of your application; you should get the following result:

Accessing the database

For this section, we will write an endpoint that will create recipes for our cookbook. Run the following MySQL queries in order to set up the `cookbook` database and create the empty `recipes` table:

```
mysql> CREATE SCHEMA cookbook;
Query OK, 1 row affected (0.00 sec)
mysql> USE cookbook;
```

```
Database changed
mysql> CREATE TABLE recipes(
    -> id INT UNSIGNED NOT NULL AUTO_INCREMENT PRIMARY KEY,
    -> name VARCHAR(255) NOT NULL,
    -> ingredients TEXT NOT NULL,
    -> instructions TEXT NOT NULL,
    -> time INT UNSIGNED NOT NULL);
Query OK, 0 rows affected (0.01 sec)
```

Silex does not come with any ORM integration, so you will need to write your SQL queries by hand. However, there is a Doctrine service provider that gives you a simpler interface than the one PDO offers, so let's try to integrate it. To install this, run the following command:

```
$ composer require "doctrine/dbal:~2.2"
```

Now, we are ready to register the service provider. As with the rest of services, add the following code to your `public/index.php` before the route definitions:

```
$app->register(new Silex\Provider\DoctrineServiceProvider(), [
    'dbs.options' => [
        [
            'driver'    => 'pdo_mysql',
            'host'      => '127.0.0.1',
            'dbname'    => 'cookbook',
            'user'      => $app['database']['user'],
            'password'  => $app['database']['password']
        ]
    ]
]);
```

When registering, you need to provide the options for the database connection. Some of them will be the same regardless of the environment, such as the driver or even the host, but some will come from the configuration file, such as `$app['database']['user']`. From now on, you can access the database connection via `$app['db']`.

With the database set up, let's add the routes that will allow us to add and fetch recipes. As with Laravel, you can specify either the anonymous function, as we already did, or a controller and method to execute. Replace the current route with the following three routes:

```
$app->get(
    '/',
    'CookBook\\Controllers\\RecipesController::getAll'
);
$app->post(
```

```
    '/recipes',
    'CookBook\\Controllers\\RecipesController::create'
);
$app->get(
    '/recipes',
    'CookBook\\Controllers\\RecipesController::getNewForm'
);
```

As you can observe, there will be a new controller, CookBook\Controllers\
RecipesController, which will be placed in src/Controllers/
RecipesController.php. This means that you need to change the autoloader in
Composer. Edit your composer.json file with the following:

```
"autoload": {
    "psr-4": {"CookBook\\": "src/"}
}
```

Now, let's add the controller class, as follows:

```
<?php

namespace CookBook\Controllers;

class Recipes {

}
```

The first method we will add is the getNewForm method, which will just render the
add a new recipe page. The method looks similar to this:

```
public function getNewForm(Application $app): string {
    return $app['twig']->render('new_recipe.twig');
}
```

The method will just render new_recipe.twig. An example of this template could
be as follows:

```
{% extends "layout.twig" %}

{% block content %}
    <h1>Add recipe</h1>
    <form method="post">
        <div>
            <label for="name">Name</label>
            <input type="text" name="name"
                    value="{{ name is defined ? name : "" }}" />
        </div>
        <div>
```

```
            <label for="ingredients">Ingredients</label>
            <textarea name="ingredients">
                {{ ingredients is defined ? ingredients : "" }}
            </textarea>
        </div>
        <div>
            <label for="instructions">Instructions</label>
            <textarea name="instructions">
                {{ instructions is defined ? instructions : "" }}
            </textarea>
        </div>
        <div>
            <label for="time">Time (minutes)</label>
            <input type="number" name="time"
                value="{{ time is defined ? time : "" }}" />
        </div>
        <div>
            <button type="submit">Save</button>
        </div>
    </form>
{% endblock %}
```

This template sends the name, ingredients, instructions, and the time that it takes to prepare the dish. The endpoint that will get this form needs to get the response object in order to extract this information. In the same way that we could get the `Application` instance as an argument, we can get the `Request` one too if we specify it in the method definition. Accessing the POST parameters is as easy as invoking the `get` method by sending the name of the parameter or calling `$request->request->all()` to get all of them as an array. Add the following method that checks whether all the data is valid and renders the form again if it is not, sending the submitted data and errors:

```
public function create(Application $app, Request $request): string {
    $params = $request->request->all();
    $errors = [];

    if (empty($params['name'])) {
        $errors[] = 'Name cannot be empty.';
    }
    if (empty($params['ingredients'])) {
        $errors[] = 'Ingredients cannot be empty.';
    }
    if (empty($params['instructions'])) {
        $errors[] = 'Instructions cannot be empty.';
    }
    if ($params['time'] <= 0) {
        $errors[] = 'Time has to be a positive number.';
    }
```

```
    if (!empty($errors)) {
        $params = array_merge($params, ['errors' => $errors]);
        return $app['twig']->render('new_recipe.twig', $params);
    }
}
```

The `layout.twig` template needs to be edited too in order to show the errors returned. We can do this by executing the following:

```
{# ... #}
{% if errors is defined %}
    <p>Something went wrong!</p>
    <ul>
    {% for error in errors %}
        <li>{{ error }}</li>
    {% endfor %}
    </ul>
{% endif %}
{% block content %}
{# ... #}
```

At this point, you can already try to access `http://localhost/recipes`, fill the form leaving something empty, submitting, and getting the form back with the errors. It should look something similar to this (with some extra CSS styles):

The continuation of the controller should allow us to store the correct data as a new recipe in the database. To do so, it would be a good idea to create a separate class, such as `CookBook\Models\RecipeModel`; however, to speed things up, let's add the following few lines that would go into the model to the controller. Remember that we have the Doctrine service provider, so there is no need to use PDO directly:

```php
$sql = 'INSERT INTO recipes (name, ingredients, instructions, time) '
    . 'VALUES(:name, :ingredients, :instructions, :time)';
$result = $app['db']->executeUpdate($sql, $params);

if (!$result) {
    $params = array_merge($params, ['errors' => $errors]);
    return $app['twig']->render('new_recipe.twig', $params);
}


return $app['twig']->render('home.twig');
```

Doctrine also helps when fetching data. To see it working, check the third and final method, in which we will fetch all the recipes in order to show the user:

```php
public function getAll(Application $app): string {
    $recipes = $app['db']->fetchAll('SELECT * FROM recipes');
    return $app['twig']->render(
        'home.twig',
        ['recipes' => $recipes]
    );
}
```

With only one line, we performed a query. It is not as clean as the Eloquent ORM of Laravel, but at least it is much less verbose than using raw PDO. Finally, you can update your `home.twig` template with the following content in order to display the recipes that we just fetched from the database:

```twig
{% extends "layout.twig" %}

{% block content %}
    <h1>Hi visitor!</h1>
    <p>Check our recipes!</p>
    <table>
        <th>Name</th>
        <th>Time</th>
        <th>Ingredients</th>
        <th>Instructions</th>
    {% for recipe in recipes %}
        <tr>
```

```
          <td>{{ recipe.name }}</td>
          <td>{{ recipe.time }}</td>
          <td>{{ recipe.ingredients }}</td>
          <td>{{ recipe.instructions }}</td>
        </tr>
    {% endfor %}
    </table>
{% endblock %}
```

Silex versus Laravel

Even though we did some similar comparison before starting the chapter, it is time to recapitulate what we said and compare it with what you noted by yourself. Laravel belongs to the type of framework that allows you to create great things with very little work. It contains all the components that you, as a web developer, will ever need. There has to be some good reason for how fast it became the most popular framework of the year!

On the other hand, Silex is a microframework, which by itself does very little. It is just the skeleton on which you can build the framework that you exactly need. It already provides quite a lot of service providers, and we did not discuss even half of them; we recommend you to visit http://silex.sensiolabs.org/doc/ providers.html for the full list. However, if you prefer, you can always add other dependencies with Composer and use them. If, for some reason, you stop liking the ORM or the template engine that you use, or it just happens that a new and better one appears in the community, switching them should be easy. On the other hand, when working with Laravel, you will probably stick to what it comes with it.

There is always an occasion for each framework, and we would like to encourage you to be open to all the possibilities that there are out there, keep up to date, and explore new frameworks or technologies from time to time.

Summary

In this chapter, you learned how important it is to know some of the most important frameworks. You also learned the basics of two famous ones: Laravel and Silex. Now, you are ready to either use your framework or to use these two for your next application. With this, you also have the capacity to take any other similar framework and understand it easily.

In the next chapter, we will study what REST APIs are and how to write one with Laravel. This will expand your set of skills and give you more flexibility for when you need to decide which approach to take when designing and writing applications.

9
Building REST APIs

Most non-developers probably think that creating applications means building either software for your PC or Mac, games, or web pages, because that is what they can see and use. But once you join the developers' community, either by your own or professionally, you will eventually realize how much work is done for applications and tools that do not have a user interface.

Have you ever wondered how someone's website can access your Facebook profile, and later on, post an automatic message on your wall? Or how websites manage to send/receive information in order to update the content of the page, without refreshing or submitting any form? All of these features, and many more interesting ones, are possible thanks to the integration of applications working "behind the scenes". Knowing how to use them will open the doors for creating more interesting and useful web applications.

In this chapter, you will learn the following:

- Introduction to APIs and REST APIs, and their use
- The foundation of REST APIs
- Using third-party APIs
- Tools for REST API developers
- Designing and writing REST APIs with Laravel
- Different ways of testing your REST APIs

Introducing APIs

API stands for **Application Program Interface**. Its goal is to provide an interface so that other programs can send commands that will trigger some process inside the application, possibly returning some output. The concept might seem a bit abstract, but in fact, there are APIs virtually in everything which is somehow related to computers. Let's see some real life examples:

- Operating systems or OS, like Windows or Linux, are the programs that allow you to use computers. When you use any application from your computer, it most probably needs to talk to the OS in one way or another, for example by requesting a certain file, sending some audio to the speakers, and so on. All these interactions between the application and the OS are possible thanks to the APIs that the OS provides. In this way, the application need not interact with the hardware straight away, which is a very tiring task.

- To interact with the user, a mobile application provides a GUI. The interface captures all the events that the user triggers, like clicking or typing, in order to send them to the server. The GUI communicates with the server using an API in the same way the program communicates with the OS as explained earlier.

- When you create a website that needs to display tweets from the user's Twitter account, you need to communicate with Twitter. They provide an API that can be accessed via HTTP. Once authenticated, by sending the correct HTTP requests, you can update and/or retrieve data from their application.

As you can see, there are different places where APIs are useful. In general, when you have a system that should be accessed externally, you need to provide potential users an API. When we say externally, we mean from another application or library, but it can very well be inside the same machine.

Introducing REST APIs

REST APIs are a specific type of APIs. They use HTTP as the protocol to communicate with them, so you can imagine that they will be the most used ones by web applications. In fact, they are not very different from the websites that you've already built, since the client sends an HTTP request, and the server replies with an HTTP response. The difference here is that REST APIs make heavy use of HTTP status codes to understand what the response is, and instead of returning HTML resources with CSS and JS, the response uses JSON, XML, or any other document format with just information, and not a graphic user interface.

Let's take an example. The Twitter API, once authenticated, allows developers to get the tweets of a given user by sending an HTTP GET request to `https://api.twitter.com/1.1/statuses/user_timeline.json`. The response to this request is an HTTP message with a JSON map of tweets as the body and the status code 200. We've already mentioned status code in *Chapter 2, Web Applications with PHP*, but we will review them shortly.

The REST API also allows developers to post tweets on behalf of the user. If you were already authenticated, as in the previous example, you just need to send a POST request to `https://api.twitter.com/1.1/statuses/update.json` with the appropriate POST parameters in the body, like the text that you want to tweet. Even though this request is not a GET, and thus, you are not requesting data but rather sending it, the response of this request is quite important too. The server will use the status codes of the response to let the requester know if the tweet was posted successfully, or if they could not understand the request, there was an internal server error, the authentication was not valid, and so on. Each of these scenarios has a different status code, which is the same across all applications. This makes it very easy to communicate with different APIs, since you will not need to learn a new list of status code each time. The server can also add some extra information to the body in order to throw some light on why the error happened, but that will depend on the application.

You can imagine that these REST APIs are provided to developers so they can integrate them with their applications. They are not user-friendly, but HTTP-friendly.

The foundations of REST APIs

Even though REST APIs do not have an official standard, most developers agree on the same foundation. It helps that HTTP, which is the protocol that this technology uses to communicate, does have a standard. In this section, we will try to describe how REST APIs should work.

HTTP request methods

We've already introduced the idea of HTTP methods in *Chapter 2, Web Applications with PHP*. We explained that an HTTP method is just the verb of the request, which defines what kind of action it is trying to perform. We've already defined this method when working with HTML forms: the `form` tag can get an optional attribute, `method`, which will make the form submit with that specific HTTP method.

You will not use forms when working with REST APIs, but you can still specify the method of the request. In fact, two requests can go to the same endpoint with the same parameters, headers, and so on, and yet have completely different behaviors due to their methods, which makes them a very important part of the request.

As we are giving so much importance to HTTP methods in order to identify what a request is trying to do, it is natural that we will need a handful of them. So far, we have introduced GET and POST, but there are actually eight different methods: GET, POST, PUT, DELETE, OPTIONS, HEAD, TRACE, and CONNECT. You will usually work with just four of them. Let's look at them in detail.

GET

When a request uses the GET method, it means that it is requesting for information about a given entity. The endpoint should contain information of what that entity is, like the ID of a book. GET can also be used to query for a list of objects, either all of them, filtered, or paginated.

GET requests can add extra information to the request when needed. For example, if we are try to retrieve all the books that contain the string "rings", or if we want the page number 2 of the full list of books. As you already know, this extra information is added to the query string as GET parameters, which is a list of key-value pairs concatenated by an ampersand (&). So, that means that the request for http:// bookstore.com/books?year=2001&page3 is probably used for getting the second page of the list of books published during 2001.

REST APIs have extensive documentation on the available endpoints and parameters, so it should be easy for you to learn to query properly. Still, even though it will be documented, you should expect parameters with intuitive names, like the ones in the example.

POST and PUT

POST is the second type of HTTP method that you already know about. You used it in forms with the intention of "posting" data, that is, trying to update a resource on the server side. When you wanted to add or update a new book, you sent a POST request with the data of the book as the POST parameters.

POST parameters are sent in a format similar to the GET parameters, but instead of being part of the query string, they are included as part of the request's body. Forms in HTML are already doing that for you, but when you need to talk to a REST API, you should know how to do this by yourself. In the next section, we will show you how to perform POST using tools other than forms. Also note that you can add any data to the body of the request; it is quite common to send JSON in the body instead of POST parameters.

The PUT method is quite similar to the POST method. This too tries to add or update data on the server side, and for this purpose, it also adds extra information on the body of the request. Why should we have two different methods that do the same thing? There are actually two main differences between these methods:

- PUT requests either create a resource or update it, but the affected resource is the one defined by the endpoint and nothing else. That means that if we want to update a book, the endpoint should state that the resource is a book, and specify it, for example, `http://bookstore.com/books/8734`. On the other hand, if you do not identify the resource to be created or updated in the endpoint, or you affect other resources at the same time, you should use POST requests.

- Idempotent is a complicated word for a simple concept. An idempotent HTTP method is one that can be called many times, and the result will always be the same. For example, if you are trying to update the title of a book to "Don Quixote", it does not matter how many times you call it, the result will always be the same: the resource will have the title "Don Quixote". On the other hand, non-idempotent methods might return different results when executing the same request. An example could be an endpoint that increases the stock of some book. Each time you call it, you will increase the stock more and more, and thus, the result is not the same. PUT requests are idempotent, whereas POST requests are not.

Even with this explanation in mind, misusing POST and PUT is quite a common mistake among developers, especially when they lack enough experience in developing REST APIs. Since forms in HTML only send data with POST and not PUT, the first one is more popular. You might find REST APIs where all the endpoints that update data are POST, even though some of them should be PUT.

DELETE

The DELETE HTTP method is quite self-explanatory. It is used when you want to delete a resource on the server. As with PUT requests, DELETE endpoints should identify the specific resource to be deleted. An example would be when we want to remove one book from our database. We could send a DELETE request to an endpoint similar to `http://bookstore.com/books/23942`.

DELETE requests just delete resources, and they are already determined by the URL. Still, if you need to send extra information to the server, you could use the body of the request as you do with POST or PUT. In fact, you can always send information within the body of the request, including GET requests, but that does not mean it is a good practice to do so.

Status codes in responses

If HTTP methods are very important for requests, status codes are almost indispensable for responses. With just one number, the client will know what happened with the request. This is especially useful when you know that status codes are a standard, and they are extensively documented on the Internet.

We've already described the most important ones in *Chapter 2, Web Applications with PHP*, but let's list them again, adding a few more that are important for REST APIs. For the full list of status codes, you can visit `https://www.w3.org/Protocols/rfc2616/rfc2616-sec10.html`.

2xx – success

All the status codes that start with 2 are used for responses where the request was processed successfully, regardless of whether it was a GET or POST. Some of the most commonly used ones in this category are as follows:

- **200 OK**: It is the generic "everything was OK" response. If you were asking for a resource, you will get it in the body of the response, and if you were updating a resource, this will mean that the new data has been successfully saved.

- **201 created**: It is the response used when resources are created successfully with POST or PUT.

- **202 accepted**: This response means that the request has been accepted, but it has not been processed yet. This might be useful when the client needs a straightforward response for a very heavy operation: the server sends the accepted response, and then starts processing it.

3xx – redirection

Even though you might think there is only one type of redirection, there are a few refinements:

- **301 moved permanently**: This means that the resource has been moved to a different URL, so from then on, you should try to access it through the URL provided in the body of the response.

- **303 see other**: This means that the request has been processed but, in order to see the response, you need to access the URL provided in the body of the response.

4xx – client error

This category has status codes describing what went wrong due to the client's request:

- **400 bad request**: This is a generic response to a malformed request, that is, there is a syntax error in the endpoint, or some of the expected parameters were not provided.

- **401 unauthorized**: This means the client has not been authenticated successfully yet, and the resource that it is trying to access needs this authentication.

- **403 forbidden**: This error message means that even though the client has been authenticated, it does not have enough permissions to access that resource.

- **404 not found**: The specific resource has not been found.

- **405 method not allowed**: This means that the endpoint exists, but it does not accept the HTTP method used on the request, for example, we were trying to use PUT, but the endpoint only accepts POST requests.

5xx – server error

There are up to 11 different errors on the server side, but we are only interested in one: the **500 internal server** error. You could use this status code when something unexpected, like a database error, happens while processing the request.

REST API security

REST APIs are a powerful tool since they allow developers to retrieve and/or update data from the server. But with great power comes great responsibility, and when designing a REST API, you should think about making your data as secure as possible. Imagine— anyone could post tweets on your behalf with a simple HTTP request!

Similar to using web applications, there are two concepts here: **authentication** and **authorization**. Authenticating someone is identifying who he or she is, that is, linking his or her request to a user in the database. On the other hand, authorizing someone is to allow that specific user to perform certain actions. You could think of authentication as the login of the user, and authorization as giving permissions.

REST APIs need to manage these two concepts very carefully. Just because a developer has been authenticated does not mean he can access all the data on the server. Sometimes, users can access only their own data, whereas sometimes you would like to implement a roles system where each role has different access levels. It always depends on the type of application you are building.

Although authorization happens on the server side, that is, it's the server's database that will decide whether a given user can access a certain resource or not, authentications have to be triggered by the client. This means that the client has to know what authentication system the REST API is using in order to proceed with the authentication. Each REST API will implement its own authentication system, but there are some well known implementations.

Basic access authentication

Basic access authentication—BA for short—is, as its name suggests, basic. The client adds the information about the user in the headers of each request, that is, username and password. The problem is that this information is only encoded using BASE64 but not encrypted, making it extremely easy for an intruder to decode the header and obtain the password in plain text. If you ever have to use it, since, to be honest, it is a very easy way of implementing some sort of authentication, we would recommend you to use it with HTTPS.

In order to use this method, you need to concatenate the username and password like `username:password`, encode the resultant string using Base64, and add the authorization header as:

```
Authorization: Basic <encoded-string>
```

OAuth 2.0

If basic authentication was very simple, and insecure, OAuth 2.0 is the most secure system that REST APIs use in order to authenticate, and so was the previous OAuth 1.0. There are actually different versions of this standard, but all of them work on the same foundation:

1. There are no usernames and passwords. Instead, the provider of the REST API assigns a pair of credentials—a token and the secret—to the developer.

2. In order to authenticate, the developer needs to send a POST request to the "token" endpoint, which is different in each REST API but has the same concept. This request has to include the encoded developer credentials.

3. The server replies to the previous request with a session token. This (and not the credentials mentioned in the first step) is to be included in each request that you make to the REST API. The session token expires for security reasons, so you will have to repeat the second step again when that happens.

Even though this standard is kind of recent (2012 onwards), several big companies like Google or Facebook have already implemented it for their REST APIs. It might look a bit overcomplicated, but you will soon get to use it, and even implement it.

Using third-party APIs

That was enough theory about REST APIs; it is time to dive into a real world example. In this section, we will write a small PHP application that interacts with Twitter's REST API; that includes requesting developer credentials, authenticating, and sending requests. The goal is to give you your first experience in working with REST APIs, and showing you that it is easier than you could expect. It will also help you to understand better how they work, so it will be easier to build your own later.

Getting the application's credentials

REST APIs usually have the concept of application. An application is like an account on their development site that identifies who uses the API. The credentials that you will use to access the API will be linked to this application, which means that you can have multiple applications linked to the same account.

Assuming that you have a Twitter account, go to `https://apps.twitter.com` in order to create a new application. Click on the **Create New App** button in order to access the form for application details. The fields are very self-explanatory—just a name for the application, the description, and the website URL. The callback URL is not necessary here, since that will be used only for applications that require access to someone else's account. Agree with the terms and conditions in order to proceed.

Once you have been redirected to your application's page, you will see all sort of information that you can edit. Since this is just an example, let's go straight to what matters: the credentials. Click on the **Keys and Access Tokens** tab to see the values of **Consumer key (API key)** and **Consumer Secret (API secret)**. There is nothing else that we need from here. You can save them on your filesystem, as `~/.twitter_php7.json`, for example:

```
{
    "key": "iTh4Mzl0EAPn9HAm98hEhAmVEXS",
    "secret": "PfoWM9yq4Bh6rGbzzJhr893j4r4sMIAeVRaPMYbkDer5N6F"
}
```

Securing your credentials

Securing your REST API credentials should be taken seriously. In fact, you should take care of all kinds of credentials, like the database ones. But the difference is that you will usually host your database in your server, which makes things slightly more difficult to whoever wants to attack. On the other hand, the third-party REST API is not part of your system, and someone with your credentials can use your account freely on your behalf.

Never include your credentials in your code base, especially if you have your code in GitHub or some other repository. One solution would be to have a file in your server, outside your code, with the credentials; if that file is encrypted, that is even better. And try to refresh your credentials regularly, which you can probably do on the provider's website.

Setting up the application

Our application will be extremely simple. It will consist of one class that will allow us to fetch tweets. This will be managed by our app.php script.

As we have to make HTTP requests, we can either write our own functions that use **cURL** (a set of PHP native functions), or make use of the famous PHP library, **Guzzle**. This library can be found in **Packagist**, so we will use Composer to include it:

```
$ composer require guzzlehttp/guzzle
```

We will have a Twitter class, which will get the credentials from the constructor, and one public method: fetchTwits. For now, just create the skeleton so that we can work with it; we will implement such methods in later sections. Add the following code to src/Twitter.php:

```php
<?php

namespace TwitterApp;

class Twitter {

    private $key;
    private $secret;

    public function __construct(String $key, String $secret) {
        $this->key = $key;
        $this->secret = $secret;
    }

    public function fetchTwits(string name, int $count): array {
        return [];
    }

}
```

Since we set the namespace `TwitterApp`, we need to update our `composer.json` file with the following addition. Remember to run `composer update` to update the autoloader.

```
"autoload": {
    "psr-4": {"TwitterApp\\": "src"}
}
```

Finally, we will create a basic `app.php` file, which includes the Composer autoloader, reads the credentials file, and creates a Twitter instance:

```php
<?php

use TwitterApp\Twitter;

require __DIR__ . '/vendor/autoload.php';

$path = $_SERVER['HOME'] . '/.twitter_php7.json';
$jsonCredentials = file_get_contents($path);
$credentials = json_decode($jsonCredentials, true);

$twitter = new Twitter($credentials['key'], $credentials['secret']);
```

Requesting an access token

In a real world application, you would probably want to separate the code related to authentication from the one that deals with operations like fetching or posting data. To keep things simple here, we will let the `Twitter` class know how to authenticate by itself.

Let's start by adding a `$client` property to the class which will contain an instance of Guzzle's `Client` class. This instance will contain the base URI of the Twitter API, which we can have as the constant `TWITTER_API_BASE_URI`. Instantiate this property in the constructor so that the rest of the methods can make use of it. You can also add an `$accessToken` property which will contain the access token returned by the Twitter API when authenticating. All these changes are highlighted here:

```php
<?php

namespace TwitterApp;

use Exception;
use GuzzleHttp\Client;
```

```
class Twitter {

    const TWITTER_API_BASE_URI = 'https://api.twitter.com';

    private $key;
    private $secret;
    private $accessToken;
    private $client;

    public function __construct(String $key, String $secret) {
        $this->key = $key;
        $this->secret = $secret;

        $this->client = new Client(
            ['base_uri' => self::TWITTER_API_BASE_URI]
        );
    }

    //...
}
```

The next step would be to write a method that, given the key and secret are provided, requests an access token to the provider. More specifically:

- Concatenate the key and the secret with a `:`. Encode the result using Base64.
- Send a POST request to `/oauth2/token` with the encoded credentials as the `Authorization` header. Also include a `Content-Type` header and a body (check the code for more information).

We now invoke the `post` method of Guzzle's `client` instance sending two arguments: the endpoint string (`/oauth2/token`) and an array with options. These options include the headers and the body of the request, as you will see shortly. The response of this invocation is an object that identifies the HTTP response. You can extract the content (body) of the response with `getBody`. Twitter's API response is a JSON with some arguments. The one that you care about the most is the `access_token`, the token that you will need to include in each subsequent request to the API. Extract it and save it. The full method looks as follows:

```
private function requestAccessToken() {
    $encodedString = base64_encode(
        $this->key . ':' . $this->secret
    );
    $headers = [
        'Authorization' => 'Basic ' . $encodedString,
```

```
            'Content-Type' => 'application/x-www-form-
    urlencoded;charset=UTF-8'
        ];
        $options = [
            'headers' => $headers,
            'body' => 'grant_type=client_credentials'
        ];

        $response = $this->client->post(self:: OAUTH_ENDPOINT, $options);
        $body = json_decode($response->getBody(), true);

        $this->accessToken = $body['access_token'];
    }
```

You can already try this code by adding these two lines at the end of the constructor:

```
$this->requestAccessToken();
var_dump($this->accessToken);
```

Run the application in order to see the access token given by the provider using the following command. Remember to remove the preceding two lines in order to proceed with the section.

$ php app.php

Keep in mind that, even though having a key and secret and getting an access token is the same across all OAuth authentications, the specific way of encoding, the endpoint used, and the response received from the provider are exclusive from Twitter's API. It could be that several others are exactly the same, but always check the documentation for each one.

Fetching tweets

We finally arrive to the section where we actually make use of the API. We will implement the fetchTwits method in order to get a list of the last *N* number of tweets for a given user. In order to perform requests, we need to add the Authorization header to each one, this time with the access token. Since we want to make this class as reusable as possible, let's extract this to a private method:

```
private function getAccessTokenHeaders(): array {
    if (empty($this->accessToken)) {
        $this->requestAccessToken();
    }

    return ['Authorization' => 'Bearer ' . $this->accessToken];
}
```

As you can see, the preceding method also allows us to fetch the access token from the provider. This is useful, since if we make more than one request, we will just request the access token once, and we have one unique place to do so. Add now the following method implementation:

```
const GET_TWITS = '/1.1/statuses/user_timeline.json';
//...
public function fetchTwits(string $name, int $count): array {
    $options = [
        'headers' => $this->getAccessTokenHeaders(),
        'query' => [
            'count' => $count,
            'screen_name' => $name
        ]
    ];

    $response = $this->client->get(self::GET_TWITS, $options);
    $responseTwits = json_decode($response->getBody(), true);

    $twits = [];
    foreach ($responseTwits as $twit) {
        $twits[] = [
            'created_at' => $twit['created_at'],
            'text' => $twit['text'],
            'user' => $twit['user']['name']
        ];
    }

    return $twits;
}
```

The first part of the preceding method builds the `options` array with the access token headers and the query string arguments—in this case, with the number of tweets to retrieve and the user. We perform the GET request and decode the JSON response into an array. This array contains a lot of information that we might not need, so we iterate it in order to extract those fields that we really want—in this example, the date, the text, and the user.

In order to test the application, just invoke the `fetchTwits` method at the end of the `app.php` file, specifying the Twitter ID of one of the people you are following, or yourself.

```
$twits = $twitter->fetchTwits('neiltyson', 10);
var_dump($twits);
```

You should get a response similar to ours, shown in the following screenshot:

```
[7]=>
array(3) {
  ["created_at"]=>
  string(30) "Sat Jan 23 14:40:47 +0000 2016"
  ["text"]=>
  string(123) "@bobgourley Thanks for the poke. My arguments on exploration are more fully developed in th
is book: https://t.co/wPCOJkOeJ8"
  ["user"]=>
  string(19) "Neil deGrasse Tyson"
}
[8]=>
array(3) {
  ["created_at"]=>
  string(30) "Tue Jan 19 23:37:16 +0000 2016"
  ["text"]=>
  string(130) "Technically, the zillion Pomegranate "seeds" would each need to be seedless. But this shoul
d be easy - we invented lap dogs."
  ["user"]=>
  string(19) "Neil deGrasse Tyson"
}
[9]=>
array(3) {
  ["created_at"]=>
  string(30) "Tue Jan 19 23:30:13 +0000 2016"
  ["text"]=>
  string(125) "Seedless grapes. Seedless oranges. Seedless watermelons. All good. My vote for the next fru
it to invent: Seedless pomegranate"
  ["user"]=>
  string(19) "Neil deGrasse Tyson"
}
```

One thing to keep in mind is that access tokens expire after some time, returning an HTTP response with a 4xx status code (usually, 401 unauthorized). Guzzle throws an exception when the status code is either 4xx or 5xx, so it is easy manage these scenarios. You could add this code when performing the GET request:

```
try {
    $response = $this->client->get(self::GET_TWITS, $options);
} catch (ClientException $e) {
    if ($e->getCode() == 401) {
        $this->requestAccessToken();
        $response = $this->client->get(self::GET_TWITS, $options);
    } else {
        throw $e;
    }
}
```

The toolkit of the REST API developer

While you are developing your own REST API, or writing an integration for a third-party one, you might want to test it before you start writing your code. There are a handful of tools that will help you with this task, whether you want to use your browser, or you are a fan of the command line.

Testing APIs with browsers

There are actually several add-ons that allow you to perform HTTP requests from browsers, depending on which one you use. Some famous names are *Advanced Rest Client* for Chrome and *RESTClient* for Firefox. At the end of the day, all those clients allow you to perform the same HTTP requests, where you can specify the URL, the method, the headers, the body, and so on. These clients will also show you all the details you can imagine from the response, including the status code, the time spent, and the body. The following screenshot displays an example of a request using Chrome's *Advanced Rest Client*:

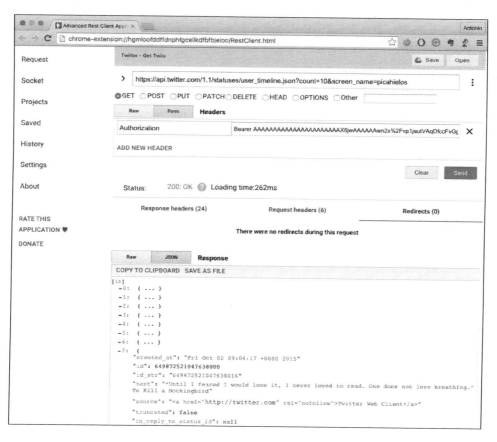

If you want to test GET requests with your own API, and all that you need is the URL, that is, you do not need to send any headers, you can just use your browser as if you were trying to access any other website. If you do so, and if you are working with JSON responses, you can install another add-on to your browser that will help you in viewing your JSON in a more "beautiful" way. Look for *JSONView* on any browser for a really handy one.

Testing APIs using the command line

Some people feel more comfortable using the command line; so luckily, for them there are tools that allow them to perform any HTTP request from their consoles. We will give a brief introduction to one of the most famous ones: cURL. This tool has quite a lot of features, but we will focus only on the ones that you will be using more often: the HTTP method, post parameters, and headers:

- `-X <method>`: This specifies the HTTP method to use
- `--data`: This adds the parameters specified, which can be added as key-value pairs, JSON, plain text, and so on
- `--header`: This adds a header to the request

The following is an example of the way to send a POST request with cURL:

```
curl -X POST --data "text=This is sparta!" \
> --header "Authorization: Bearer 8s8d7bf8asdbf8sbdf8bsa" \
>  https://api.twitter.com/1.1/statuses/update.json
{"errors":[{"code":89,"message":"Invalid or expired token."}]}
```

If you are using a Unix system, you will probably be able to format the resulting JSON by appending | `python -m json.tool` so that it gets easier to read:

```
$ curl -X POST --data "text=This is sparta!" \
> --header "Authorization: Bearer 8s8d7bf8asdbf8sbdf8bsa" \
>  https://api.twitter.com/1.1/statuses/update.json \
> | python -m json.tool
{
    "errors": [
        {
            "code": 89,
            "message": "Invalid or expired token."
        }
    ]
}
```

cURL is quite a powerful tool that lets you do quite a few tricks. If you are interested, go ahead and check the documentation or some tutorial on how to use all its features.

Best practices with REST APIs

We've already gone through some of the best practices when writing REST APIs, like using HTTP methods properly, or choosing the correct status code for your responses. We also described two of the most used authentication systems. But there is still a lot to learn about creating proper REST APIs. Remember that they are meant to be used by developers like yourself, so they will always be grateful if you do things properly, and make their lives easier. Ready?

Consistency in your endpoints

When deciding how to name your endpoints, try keeping them consistent. Even though you are free to choose, there is a set of spoken rules that will make your endpoints more intuitive and easy to understand. Let's list some of them:

- For starters, an endpoint should point to a specific resource (for example, books or tweets), and you should make that clear in your endpoint. If you have an endpoint that returns the list of all books, do not name it /library, as it is not obvious what it will be returning. Instead, name it /books or / books/all.

- The name of the resource can be either plural or singular, but make it consistent. If sometimes you use /books and sometimes /user, it might be confusing, and people will probably make mistakes. We personally prefer to use the plural form, but that is totally up to you.

- When you want to retrieve a specific resource, do it by specifying the ID whenever possible. IDs must be unique in your system, and any other parameter might point to two different entities. Specify the ID next to the name of the resource, such as /books/249234-234-23-42.

- If you can understand what an endpoint does by just the HTTP method, there is no need to add this information as part of the endpoint. For example, if you want to get a book, or you want to delete it, /books/249234-234-23-42 along with the HTTP methods GET and DELETE are more than enough. If it is not obvious, state it as a verb at the end of the endpoint, like / employee/9218379182/promote.

Document as much as you can

The title says everything. You are probably not going to be the one using the REST API, others will. Obviously, even if you design a very intuitive set of endpoints, developers will still need to know the whole set of available endpoints, what each of them does, what optional parameters are available, and so on.

Write as much documentation as possible, and keep it up to date. Take a look at other documented APIs to gather ideas on how to display the information. There are plenty of templates and tools that will help you deliver a well-presented documentation, but you are the one that has to be consistent and methodical. Developers have a special hate towards documenting anything, but we also like to find clear and beautifully presented documentation when we need to use someone else's APIs.

Filters and pagination

One of the common usages of an API is to list resources and filter them by some criteria. We already saw an example when we were building our own bookstore; we wanted to get the list of books that contained a certain string in their titles or authors.

Some developers try to have beautiful endpoints, which a priori is a good thing to do. Imagine that you want to filter just by title, you might end up having an endpoint like `/books/title/<string>`. We add also the ability to filter by author, and we now get two more endpoints: `/books/title/<string>/author/<string>` and `/books/author/<string>`. Now let's add the description too — do you see where we are going?

Even though some developers do not like to use query strings as arguments, there is nothing wrong with it. In fact, if you use them properly, you will end up with cleaner endpoints. You want to get books? Fine, just use `/books`, and add whichever filter you need using the query string.

Pagination occurs when you have way too many resources of the same type to retrieve all at once. You should think of pagination as another optional filter to be specified as a GET parameter. You should have pages with a default size, let's say 10 books, but it is a good idea to give the developers the ability to define their own size. In this case, developers can specify the length and the number of pages to retrieve.

API versioning

Your API is a reflection of what your application can do. Chances are that your code will evolve, improving the already existing features or adding new ones. Your API should be updated too, exposing those new features, updating existing endpoints, or even removing some of them.

Imagine now that someone else is using your REST API, and their whole website relies on it. If you change your existing endpoints, their website will stop working! They will not be happy at all, and will try to find someone else that can do what you were doing. Not a good scenario, but then, how do you improve your API?

The solution is to use versioning. When you release a new version of the API, do not nuke down the existing one; you should give some time to the users to upgrade their integrations. And how can two different versions of the API coexist? You already saw one of the options—the one that we recommend you: by specifying the version of the API to use as part of the endpoint. Do you remember the endpoint of the Twitter API /1.1/statuses/user_timeline.json? The 1.1 refers to the version that we want to use.

Using HTTP cache

If the main feature of REST APIs is that they make heavy use of HTTP, why not take advantage of HTTP cache? Well, there are actual reasons for not using it, but most of them are due to a lack of knowledge about using it properly. It is out of the scope of this book to explain every single detail of its implementation, but let's try to give a short introduction to the topic. Plenty of resources on the Internet can help you to understand the parts that you are more interested in.

HTTP responses can be divided as public and private. Public responses are shared between all users of the API, whereas the private ones are meant to be unique for each user. You can specify which type of response is yours using the Cache-Control header, allowing the response to be cached if the method of the request was a GET. This header can also expose the expiration of the cache, that is, you can specify the duration for which your response will remain the same, and thus, can be cached.

Other systems rely on generating a hash of the representation of a resource, and add it as the ETag (Entity tag) header in order to know if the resource has changed or not. In a similar way, you can set the Last-Modified header to let the client know when was the last time that the given resource changed. The idea behind those systems is to identify when the client already contains valid data. If so, the provider does not process the request, but returns an empty response with the status code 304 (not modified) instead. When the client gets that response, it uses its cached content.

Creating a REST API with Laravel

In this section, we will build a REST API with Laravel from scratch. This REST API will allow you to manage different clients at your bookstore, not only via the browser, but via the UI as well. You will be able to perform pretty much the same actions as before, that is, listing books, buying them, borrowing for free, and so on.

Once the REST API is done, you should remove all the business logic from the bookstore that you built during the previous chapters. The reason is that you should have one unique place where you can actually manipulate your databases and the REST API, and the rest of the applications, like the web one, should able to communicate with the REST API for managing data. In doing so, you will be able to create other applications for different platforms, like mobile apps, that will use the REST API too, and both the website and the mobile app will always be synchronized, since they will be using the same sources.

As with our previous Laravel example, in order to create a new project, you just need to run the following command:

```
$ laravel new bookstore_api
```

Setting OAuth2 authentication

The first thing that we are going to implement is the authentication layer. We will use OAuth2 in order to make our application more secure than basic authentication. Laravel does not provide support for OAuth2 out of the box, but there is a service provider which does that for us.

Installing OAuth2Server

To install OAuth2, add it as a dependency to your project using Composer:

```
$ composer require "lucadegasperi/oauth2-server-laravel:5.1.*"
```

This service provider needs quite a few changes. We will go through them without going into too much detail on how things work exactly. If you are more interested in the topic, or if you want to create your own service providers for Laravel, we recommend you to go though the extensive official documentation.

To start with, we need to add the new OAuth2Server service provider to the array of providers in the config/app.php file. Add the following lines at the end of the providers array:

```
/*
 * OAuth2 Server Service Providers...
 */
        LucaDegasperi\OAuth2Server\Storage\FluentStorageServiceProvid
er::class,        LucaDegasperi\OAuth2Server\OAuth2ServerServiceProvid
er::class,
```

In the same way, you need to add a new alias to the `aliases` array in the same file:

```
'Authorizer' => LucaDegasperi\OAuth2Server\Facades\Authorizer::class,
```

Let's move to the `app/Http/Kernel.php` file, where we need to make some changes too. Add the following entry to the `$middleware` array property of the `Kernel` class:

```
\LucaDegasperi\OAuth2Server\Middleware\OAuthExceptionHandlerMiddlewar
e::class,
```

Add the following key-value pairs to the `$routeMiddleware` array property of the same class:

```
'oauth' => \LucaDegasperi\OAuth2Server\Middleware\
OAuthMiddleware::class,
'oauth-user' => \LucaDegasperi\OAuth2Server\Middleware\OAuthUserOwnerM
iddleware::class,
'oauth-client' => \LucaDegasperi\OAuth2Server\Middleware\OAuthClientOw
nerMiddleware::class,
'check-authorization-params' => \LucaDegasperi\OAuth2Server\
Middleware\CheckAuthCodeRequestMiddleware::class,
'csrf' => \App\Http\Middleware\VerifyCsrfToken::class,
```

We added a CSRF token verifier to the `$routeMiddleware`, so we need to remove the one already defined in `$middlewareGroups`, since they are incompatible. Use the following line to do so:

```
\App\Http\Middleware\VerifyCsrfToken::class,
```

Setting up the database

Let's set up the database now. In this section, we will assume that you already have the bookstore database in your environment. If you do not have it, go back to *Chapter 5, Using Databases*, to create it in order to proceed with this setup.

The first thing to do is to update the database credentials in the `.env` file. They should look something similar to the following lines, but with your username and password:

```
DB_HOST=localhost
DB_DATABASE=bookstore
DB_USERNAME=root
DB_PASSWORD=
```

In order to prepare the configuration and database migration files from the OAuth2Server service provider, we need to publish it. In Laravel, you do it by executing the following command:

```
$ php artisan vendor:publish
```

Now the `database/migrations` directory contains all the necessary migration files that will create the necessary tables related to OAuth2 in our database. To execute them, we run the following command:

```
$ php artisan migrate
```

We need to add at least one client to the `oauth_clients` table, which is the table that stores the key and secrets for all clients that want to connect to our REST API. This new client will be the one that you will use during the development process in order to test what you have done. We can set a random ID—the key—and the secret as follows:

```
mysql> INSERT INTO oauth_clients(id, secret, name)
    -> VALUES('iTh4Mz10EAPn90sK4EhAmVEXS',
    -> 'PfoWM9yq4Bh6rGbzzJhr8oDDsNZwGlsMIAeVRaPM',
    -> 'Toni');
Query OK, 1 row affected, 1 warning (0.00 sec)
```

Enabling client-credentials authentication

Since we published the plugins in `vendor` in the previous step, now we have the configuration files for the OAuth2Server. This plugin allows us different authentication systems (all of them with OAuth2), depending on our necessities. The one that we are interested in for our project is the `client_credentials` type. To let Laravel know, add the following lines at the end of the array in the `config/oauth2.php` file:

```
'grant_types' => [
    'client_credentials' => [
        'class' =>
            '\League\OAuth2\Server\Grant\ClientCredentialsGrant',
        'access_token_ttl' => 3600
    ]
]
```

These preceding lines grant access to the `client_credentials` type, which are managed by the `ClientCredentialsGrant` class. The `access_token_ttl` value refers to the time period of the access token, that is, for how long someone can use it. In this case, it is set to 1 hour, that is, 3,600 seconds.

Finally, we need to enable a route so we can post our credentials in exchange for an access token. Add the following route to the routes file in `app/Http/routes.php`:

```
Route::post('oauth/access_token', function() {
    return Response::json(Authorizer::issueAccessToken());
});
```

Requesting an access token

It is time to test what we have done so far. To do so, we need to send a POST request to the /oauth/access_token endpoint that we enabled just now. This request needs the following POST parameters:

- client_id with the key from the database
- client_secret with the secret from the database
- grant_type to specify the type of authentication that we are trying to perform, in this case client_credentials

The request issued using the *Advanced REST Client* add-on from Chrome looks as follows:

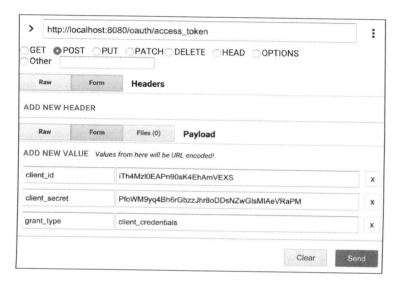

The response that you should get should have the same format as this one:

```
{
    "access_token": "MPCovQda354d10zzUXpZVOFzqe491E7ZHQAhSAax"
    "token_type": "Bearer"
    "expires_in": 3600
}
```

Note that this is a different way of requesting for an access token than what the Twitter API does, but the idea is still the same: given a key and a secret, the provider gives us an access token that will allow us to use the API for some time.

Preparing the database

Even though we've already done the same in the previous chapter, you might think: "Why do we start by preparing the database?". We could argue that you first need to know the kind of endpoints you want to expose in your REST API, and only then you can start thinking about what your database should look like. But you could also think that, since we are working with an API, each endpoint should manage one resource, so first you need to define the resources you are dealing with. This *code first versus database/model first* is an ongoing war on the Internet. But whichever way you think is better, the fact is that we already know what the users will need to do with our REST API, since we already built the UI previously; so it does not really matter.

We need to create four tables: books, sales, sales_books, and borrowed_books. Remember that Laravel already provides a users table, which we can use as our customers. Run the following four commands to create the migrations files:

```
$ php artisan make:migration create_books_table --create=books
$ php artisan make:migration create_sales_table --create=sales
$ php artisan make:migration create_borrowed_books_table \
--create=borrowed_books
$ php artisan make:migration create_sales_books_table \
--create=sales_books
```

Now we have to go file by file to define what each table should look like. We will try to replicate the data structure from *Chapter 5, Using Databases*, as much as possible. Remember that the migration files can be found inside the database/migrations directory. The first file that we can edit is the create_books_table.php. Replace the existing empty up method by the following one:

```
public function up()
{
    Schema::create('books', function (Blueprint $table) {
        $table->increments('id');
        $table->string('isbn')->unique();
        $table->string('title');
        $table->string('author');
        $table->smallInteger('stock')->unsigned();
        $table->float('price')->unsigned();
    });
}
```

The next one in the list is `create_sales_table.php`. Remember that this one has a foreign key pointing to the `users` table. You can use `references (field)->on(tablename)` to define this constraint.

```
public function up()
{
    Schema::create('sales', function (Blueprint $table) {
        $table->increments('id');
        $table->string('user_id')->references('id')->on('users');
        $table->timestamps();
    });
}
```

The `create_sales_books_table.php` file contains two foreign keys: one pointing to the ID of the sale, and one to the ID of the book. Replace the existing `up` method by the following one:

```
public function up()
{
    Schema::create('sales_books', function (Blueprint $table) {
        $table->increments('id');
        $table->integer('sale_id')->references('id')->on('sales');
        $table->integer('book_id')->references('id')->on('books');
        $table->smallInteger('amount')->unsigned();
    });
}
```

Finally, edit the `create_borrowed_books_table.php` file, which has the `book_id` foreign key and the `start` and `end` timestamps:

```
public function up()
{
    Schema::create('borrowed_books', function (Blueprint $table) {
        $table->increments('id');
        $table->integer('book_id')->references('id')->on('books');
        $table->string('user_id')->references('id')->on('users');
        $table->timestamp('start');
        $table->timestamp('end');
    });
}
```

The migration files are ready so we just need to migrate them in order to create the database tables. Run the following command:

```
$ php artisan migrate
```

Also, add some books to the database manually so that you can test later. For example:

```
mysql> INSERT INTO books (isbn,title,author,stock,price) VALUES
    -> ("9780882339726","1984","George Orwell",12,7.50),
    -> ("9789724621081","1Q84","Haruki Murakami",9,9.75),
    -> ("9780736692427","Animal Farm","George Orwell",8,3.50),
    -> ("9780307350169","Dracula","Bram Stoker",30,10.15),
    -> ("9780753179246","19 minutes","Jodi Picoult",0,10);
Query OK, 5 rows affected (0.01 sec)
Records: 5  Duplicates: 0  Warnings: 0
```

Setting up the models

The next thing to do on the list is to add the relationships that our data has, that is, to translate the foreign keys from the database to the models. First of all, we need to create those models, and for that we just run the following commands:

```
$ php artisan make:model Book
$ php artisan make:model Sale
$ php artisan make:model BorrowedBook
$ php artisan make:model SalesBook
```

Now we have to go model by model, and add the one to one and one to many relationships as we did in the previous chapter. For BookModel, we will only specify that the model does not have timestamps, since they come by default. To do so, add the following highlighted line to your app/Book.php file:

```php
<?php

namespace App;

use Illuminate\Database\Eloquent\Model;

class Book extends Model
{
    public $timestamps = false;
}
```

For the `BorrowedBook` model, we need to specify that it has one book, and it belongs to a user. We also need to specify the fields we will fill once we need to create the object—in this case, `book_id` and `start`. Add the following two methods in `app/BorrowedBook.php`:

```php
<?php

namespace App;

use Illuminate\Database\Eloquent\Model;

class BorrowedBook extends Model
{
    protected $fillable = ['user_id', 'book_id', 'start'];
    public $timestamps = false;

    public function user() {
        return $this->belongsTo('App\User');
    }

    public function book() {
        return $this->hasOne('App\Book');
    }
}
```

Sales can have many "sale books" (we know it might sound a little awkward), and they also belong to just one user. Add the following to your `app/Sale.php`:

```php
<?php

namespace App;

use Illuminate\Database\Eloquent\Model;

class Sale extends Model
{
    protected $fillable = ['user_id'];

    public function books() {
        return $this->hasMany('App\SalesBook');
    }

    public function user() {
        return $this->belongsTo('App\User');
    }
}
```

Like borrowed books, sale books can have one book and belong to one sale instead of to one user. The following lines should be added to app/SalesBook.php:

```php
<?php

namespace App;

use Illuminate\Database\Eloquent\Model;

class SaleBook extends Model
{
    public $timestamps = false;
    protected $fillable = ['book_id', 'sale_id', 'amount'];

    public function sale() {
        return $this->belongsTo('App\Sale');
    }

    public function books() {
        return $this->hasOne('App\Book');
    }
}
```

Finally, the last model that we need to update is the User model. We need to add the opposite relationship to the belongs we used earlier in Sale and BorrowedBook. Add these two functions, and leave the rest of the class intact:

```php
<?php

namespace App;

use Illuminate\Foundation\Auth\User as Authenticatable;

class User extends Authenticatable
{
    //...

    public function sales() {
        return $this->hasMany('App\Sale');
    }

    public function borrowedBooks() {
        return $this->hasMany('App\BorrowedBook');
    }
}
```

Designing endpoints

In this section, we need to come up with the list of endpoints that we want to expose to the REST API clients. Keep in mind the "rules" explained in the *Best practices with REST APIs* section. In short, keep the following rules in mind:

- One endpoint interacts with one resource
- A possible schema could be `<API version>/<resource name>/<optional id>/<optional action>`
- Use GET parameters for filtering and pagination

So what will the user need to do? We already have a good idea about that, since we created the UI. A brief summary would be as follows:

- List all the available books with some filtering (by title and author), and paginated when necessary. Also retrieve the information on a specific book, given the ID.
- Allow the user to borrow a specific book if available. In the same way, the user should be able to return books, and list the history of borrowed books too (filtered by date and paginated).
- Allow the user to buy a list of books. This could be improved, but for now let's force the user to buy books with just one request, including the full list of books in the body. Also, list the sales of the user following the same rules as that with borrowed books.

We will start straightaway with our list of endpoints, specifying the path, the HTTP method, and the optional parameters. It will also give you an idea on how to document your REST APIs.

- GET `/books`
    - `title`: Optional and filters by title
    - `author`: Optional and filters by author
    - `page`: Optional, default is 1, and specifies the page to return
    - `page-size`: Optional, default is 50, and specifies the page size to return
- GET `/books/<book id>`
- POST `/borrowed-books`
    - `book-id`: Mandatory and specifies the ID of the book to borrow

- GET `/borrowed-books`
  - ○ `from`: Optional and returns borrowed books from the specified date
  - ○ `page`: Optional, default is 1, and specifies the page to return
  - ○ `page-size`: Optional, default is 50, and specifies the number of borrowed books per page

- PUT `/borrowed-books/<borrowed book id>/return`

- POST `/sales`
  - ○ `books`: Mandatory and it is an array listing the book IDs to buy and their amounts, that is, *{"book-id-1": amount, "book-id-2": amount, ...}*

- GET `/sales`
  - ○ `from`: Optional and returns borrowed books from the specified date
  - ○ `page`: Optional, default is 1, and specifies the page to return
  - ○ `page-size`: Optional, default is 50, and specifies the number of sales per page

- GET `/sales/<sales id>`

We use POST requests when creating sales and borrowed books, since we do not know the ID of the resource that we want to create a priori, and posting the same request will create multiple resources. On the other hand, when returning a book, we do know the ID of the borrowed book, and sending the same request multiple times will leave the database in the same state. Let's translate these endpoints to routes in `app/Http/routes.php`:

```
/*
 * Books endpoints.
 */
Route::get('books', ['middleware' => 'oauth',
    'uses' => 'BookController@getAll']);
Route::get('books/{id}', ['middleware' => 'oauth',
    'uses' => 'BookController@get']);
/*
 * Borrowed books endpoints.
 */
Route::post('borrowed-books', ['middleware' => 'oauth',
    'uses' => 'BorrowedBookController@borrow']);
Route::get('borrowed-books', ['middleware' => 'oauth',
    'uses' => 'BorrowedBookController@get']);
Route::put('borrowed-books/{id}/return', ['middleware' => 'oauth',
    'uses' => 'BorrowedBookController@returnBook']);
```

```
/*
 * Sales endpoints.
 */
Route::post('sales', ['middleware' => 'oauth',
    'uses' => 'SalesController@buy']);
Route::get('sales', ['middleware' => 'oauth',
    'uses' => 'SalesController@getAll']);
Route::get('sales/{id}', ['middleware' => 'oauth',
    'uses' => 'SalesController@get']);
```

In the preceding code, note how we added the middleware oauth to all the endpoints. This will require the user to provide a valid access token in order to access them.

Adding the controllers

From the previous section, you can imagine that we need to create three controllers: BookController, BorrowedBookController, and SalesController. Let's start with the easiest one: returning the information of a book given the ID. Create the file app/Http/Controllers/BookController.php, and add the following code:

```php
<?php

namespace App\Http\Controllers;

use App\Book;
use Illuminate\Http\JsonResponse;
use Illuminate\Http\Response;

class BookController extends Controller {

    public function get(string $id): JsonResponse {
        $book = Book::find($id);

        if (empty($book)) {
            return new JsonResponse (
                null,
                JsonResponse::HTTP_NOT_FOUND
            );
        }

        return response()->json(['book' => $book]);
    }
}
```

Even though this preceding example is quite easy, it contains most of what we will need for the rest of the endpoints. We try to fetch a book given the ID from the URL, and when not found, we reply with a 404 (not found) empty response—the constant `Response::HTTP_NOT_FOUND` is 404. In case we have the book, we return it as JSON with `response->json()`. Note how we add the seemingly unnecessary key `book`; it is true that we do not return anything else and, since we ask for the book, the user will know what we are talking about, but as it does not really hurt, it is good to be as explicit as possible.

Let's test it! You already know how to get an access token—check the *Requesting an access token* section. So get one, and try to access the following URLs:

- `http://localhost/books/0?access_token=12345`
- `http://localhost/books/1?access_token=12345`

Assuming that `12345` is your access token, that you have a book in the database with ID `1`, and you do not have a book with ID `0`, the first URL should return a 404 response, and the second one, a response something similar to the following:

```
{
    "book": {
        "id": 1
        "isbn": "9780882339726"
        "title": "1984"
        "author": "George Orwell"
        "stock": 12
        "price": 7.5
    }
}
```

Let's now add the method to get all the books with filters and pagination. It looks quite verbose, but the logic that we use is quite simple:

```php
public function getAll(Request $request): JsonResponse {
    $title = $request->get('title', '');
    $author = $request->get('author', '');
    $page = $request->get('page', 1);
    $pageSize = $request->get('page-size', 50);

    $books = Book::where('title', 'like', "%$title%")
        ->where('author', 'like', "%$author%")
        ->take($pageSize)
        ->skip(($page - 1) * $pageSize)
        ->get();

    return response()->json(['books' => $books]);
}
```

We get all the parameters that can come from the request, and set the default values of each one in case the user does not include them (since they are optional). Then, we use the Eloquent ORM to filter by title and author using `where()`, and limiting the results with `take()->skip()`. We return the JSON in the same way we did with the previous method. In this one though, we do not need any extra check; if the query does not return any book, it is not really a problem.

You can now play with your REST API, sending different requests with different filters. The following are some examples:

- `http://localhost/books?access_token=12345`
- `http://localhost/books?access_token=12345&title=19&page-size=1`
- `http://localhost/books?access_token=12345&page=2`

The next controller in the list is `BorrowedBookController`. We need to add three methods: `borrow`, `get`, and `returnBook`. As you already know how to work with requests, responses, status codes, and the Eloquent ORM, we will write the entire class straightaway:

```php
<?php

namespace App\Http\Controllers;

use App\Book;
use App\BorrowedBook;
use Illuminate\Http\JsonResponse;
use Illuminate\Http\Request;
use LucaDegasperi\OAuth2Server\Facades\Authorizer;

class BorrowedBookController extends Controller {

    public function get(): JsonResponse {
        $borrowedBooks = BorrowedBook::where(
            'user_id', '=', Authorizer::getResourceOwnerId()
        )->get();

        return response()->json(
            ['borrowed-books' => $borrowedBooks]
        );
    }

    public function borrow(Request $request): JsonResponse {
        $id = $request->get('book-id');
```

```php
        if (empty($id)) {
            return new JsonResponse(
                ['error' => 'Expecting book-id parameter.'],
                JsonResponse::HTTP_BAD_REQUEST
            );
        }

        $book = Book::find($id);

        if (empty($book)) {
            return new JsonResponse(
                ['error' => 'Book not found.'],
                JsonResponse::HTTP_BAD_REQUEST
            );
        } else if ($book->stock < 1) {
            return new JsonResponse(
                ['error' => 'Not enough stock.'],
                JsonResponse::HTTP_BAD_REQUEST
            );
        }

        $book->stock--;
        $book->save();

        $borrowedBook = BorrowedBook::create(
            [
                'book_id' => $book->id,
                'start' => date('Y-m-d H:i:s'),
                'user_id' => Authorizer::getResourceOwnerId()
            ]
        );

        return response()->json(['borrowed-book' => $borrowedBook]);
}

public function returnBook(string $id): JsonResponse {
    $borrowedBook = BorrowedBook::find($id);

    if (empty($borrowedBook)) {
        return new JsonResponse(
            ['error' => 'Borrowed book not found.'],
            JsonResponse::HTTP_BAD_REQUEST
        );
```

```
            }

        $book = Book::find($borrowedBook->book_id);
        $book->stock++;
        $book->save();

        $borrowedBook->end = date('Y-m-d H:m:s');
        $borrowedBook->save();

        return response()->json(['borrowed-book' => $borrowedBook]);
    }
}
```

The only thing to note in the preceding code is how we also update the stock of the book by increasing or decreasing the stock, and invoke the save method to save the changes in the database. We also return the borrowed book object as the response when borrowing a book so that the user can know the borrowed book ID, and use it when querying or returning the book.

You can test how this set of endpoints works with the following use cases:

- Borrow a book. Check that you get a valid response.
- Get the list of borrowed books. The one that you just created should be there with a valid starting date and an empty end date.
- Get the information of the book you borrowed. The stock should be one less.
- Return the book. Fetch the list of borrowed books to check the end date and the returned book to check the stock.

Of course, you can always try to trick the API and ask for books without stock, non-existing borrowed books, and the like. All these edge cases should respond with the correct status codes and error messages.

We finish this section, and the REST API, by creating the SalesController. This controller is the one that contains more logic, since creating a sale implies adding entries to the sales books table, prior to checking for enough stock for each one. Add the following code to app/Html/SalesController.php:

```php
<?php

namespace App\Http\Controllers;

use App\Book;
use App\Sale;
use App\SalesBook;
```

```
use Illuminate\Http\JsonResponse;
use Illuminate\Http\Request;
use LucaDegasperi\OAuth2Server\Facades\Authorizer;

class SalesController extends Controller {

    public function get(string $id): JsonResponse {
        $sale = Sale::find($id);

        if (empty($sale)) {
            return new JsonResponse(
                null,
                JsonResponse::HTTP_NOT_FOUND
            );
        }

        $sale->books = $sale->books()->getResults();
        return response()->json(['sale' => $sale]);
    }

    public function buy(Request $request): JsonResponse {
        $books = json_decode($request->get('books'), true);

        if (empty($books) || !is_array($books)) {
            return new JsonResponse(
                ['error' => 'Books array is malformed.'],
                JsonResponse::HTTP_BAD_REQUEST
            );
        }

        $saleBooks = [];
        $bookObjects = [];
        foreach ($books as $bookId => $amount) {
            $book = Book::find($bookId);
            if (empty($book) || $book->stock < $amount) {
                return new JsonResponse(
                    ['error' => "Book $bookId not valid."],
                    JsonResponse::HTTP_BAD_REQUEST
                );
            }

            $bookObjects[] = $book;
            $saleBooks[] = [
                'book_id' => $bookId,
```

```
                              'amount' => $amount
                ];
        }

        $sale = Sale::create(
            ['user_id' => Authorizer::getResourceOwnerId()]
        );
        foreach ($bookObjects as $key => $book) {
            $book->stock -= $saleBooks[$key]['amount'];

            $saleBooks[$key]['sale_id'] = $sale->id;
            SalesBook::create($saleBooks[$key]);
        }

        $sale->books = $sale->books()->getResults();
        return response()->json(['sale' => $sale]);
    }

    public function getAll(Request $request): JsonResponse {
        $page = $request->get('page', 1);
        $pageSize = $request->get('page-size', 50);

        $sales = Sale::where(
                'user_id', '=', Authorizer::getResourceOwnerId()
            )
            ->take($pageSize)
            ->skip(($page - 1) * $pageSize)
            ->get();

        foreach ($sales as $sale) {
            $sale->books = $sale->books()->getResults();
        }

        return response()->json(['sales' => $sales]);
    }
}
```

In the preceding code, note how we first check the availability of all the books before creating the sales entry. This way, we make sure that we do not leave any unfinished sale in the database when returning an error to the user. You could change this, and use transactions instead, and if a book is not valid, just roll back the transaction.

In order to test this, we can follow similar steps as we did with borrowed books. Just remember that the books parameter, when posting a sale, is a JSON map; for example, {"1": 2, "4": 1} means that I am trying to buy two books with ID 1 and one book with ID 4.

Testing your REST APIs

You have already been testing your REST API after finishing each controller by making some request and expecting a response. As you might imagine, this can be handy sometimes, but it is for sure not the way to go. Testing should be automatic, and should cover as much as possible. We will have to think of a solution similar to unit testing.

In *Chapter 10, Behavioral Testing*, you will learn more methodologies and tools for testing an application end to end, and that will include REST APIs. However, due to the simplicity of our REST API, we can add some pretty good tests with what Laravel provides us as well. Actually, the idea is very similar to the tests that we wrote in *Chapter 8, Using Existing PHP Frameworks*, where we made a request to some endpoint, and expected a response. The only difference will be in the kind of assertions that we use (which can check if a JSON response is OK), and the way we perform requests.

Let's add some tests to the set of endpoints related to books. We need some books in the database in order to query them, so we will have to populate the database before each test, that is, use the `setUp` method. Remember that in order to leave the database clean of test data, we need to use the trait `DatabaseTransactions`. Add the following code to `tests/BooksTest.php`:

```php
<?php

use Illuminate\Foundation\Testing\DatabaseTransactions;
use App\Book;

class BooksTest extends TestCase {

    use DatabaseTransactions;

    private $books = [];

    public function setUp() {
        parent::setUp();

        $this->addBooks();
    }

    private function addBooks() {
        $this->books[0] = Book::create(
            [
                'isbn' => '293842983648273',
                'title' => 'Iliad',
                'author' => 'Homer',
                'stock' => 12,
```

```
                    'price' => 7.40
            ]
        );
        $this->books[0]->save();
        $this->books[0] = $this->books[0]->fresh();

        $this->books[1] = Book::create(
            [
                'isbn' => '9879287342342',
                'title' => 'Odyssey',
                'author' => 'Homer',
                'stock' => 8,
                'price' => 10.60
            ]
        );
        $this->books[1]->save();
        $this->books[1] = $this->books[1]->fresh();

        $this->books[2] = Book::create(
            [
                'isbn' => '312312314235324',
                'title' => 'The Illuminati',
                'author' => 'Larry Burkett',
                'stock' => 22,
                'price' => 5.10
            ]
        );
        $this->books[2]->save();
        $this->books[2] = $this->books[2]->fresh();
    }
}
```

As you can see in the preceding code, we add three books to the database, and to the class property $books too. We will need them when we want to assert that a response is valid. Also note the use of the fresh method; this method synchronizes the model that we have with the content in the database. We need to do this in order to get the ID inserted in the database, since we do not know it a priori.

There is another thing we need to do before we run each test: authenticating our client. We will need to make a POST request to the access token generation endpoint sending valid credentials, and storing the access token that we receive so that it can be used in the remaining requests. You are free to choose how to provide the credentials, since there are different ways to do it. In our case, we just provide the credentials of a client test that we know exists in the database, but you might prefer to insert that client into the database each time. Update the test with the following code:

```
<?php

use Illuminate\Foundation\Testing\DatabaseTransactions;
```

```
use App\Book;

class BooksTest extends TestCase {

    use DatabaseTransactions;

    private $books = [];
    private $accessToken;

    public function setUp() {
        parent::setUp();

        $this->addBooks();
        $this->authenticate();
    }

    //...

    private function authenticate() {
        $this->post(
            'oauth/access_token',
            [
                'client_id' => 'iTh4Mzl0EAPn90sK4EhAmVEXS',
                'client_secret' => 'PfoWM9yq4Bh6rhr8oDDsNZM',
                'grant_type' => 'client_credentials'
            ]
        );
        $response = json_decode(
            $this->response->getContent(), true
        );
        $this->accessToken = $response['access_token'];
    }
}
```

In the preceding code, we use the post method in order to send a POST request. This method accepts a string with the endpoint, and an array with the parameters to be included. After making a request, Laravel saves the response object into the $response property. We can JSON-decode it, and extract the access token that we need.

It is time to add some tests. Let's start with an easy one: requesting a book given an ID. The ID is used to make the GET requests with the ID of the book (do not forget the access token), and check if the response matches the expected one. Remember that we have the $books array already, so it will be pretty easy to perform these checks.

We will be using two assertions: seeJson, which compares the received JSON response with the one that we provide, and assertResponseOk, which you already know from previous tests—it just checks that the response has a 200 status code. Add this test to the class:

```php
public function testGetBook() {
    $expectedResponse = [
        'book' => json_decode($this->books[1], true)
    ];
    $url = 'books/' . $this->books[1]->id
        . '?' . $this->getCredentials();

    $this->get($url)
        ->seeJson($expectedResponse)
        ->assertResponseOk();
}

private function getCredentials(): string {
    return 'grant_access=client_credentials&access_token='
        . $this->accessToken;
}
```

We use the get method instead of post, since this is a GET request. Also note that we use the getCredentials helper, since we will have to use it in each test. To see another example, let's add a test that checks the response when requesting the books that contain the given title:

```php
public function testGetBooksByTitle() {
    $expectedResponse = [
        'books' => [
            json_decode($this->books[0], true),
            json_decode($this->books[2], true)
        ]
    ];

    $url = 'books/?title=Il&' . $this->getCredentials();
    $this->get($url)
        ->seeJson($expectedResponse)
        ->assertResponseOk();
}
```

The preceding test is pretty much the same as the previous one, isn't it? The only changes are the endpoint and the expected response. Well, the remaining tests will all follow the same pattern, since so far, we can only fetch books and filter them.

To see something different, let's check how to test an endpoint that creates resources. There are different options, one of them being to first make the request, and then going to the database to check that the resource has been created. Another option, the one that we prefer, is to first send the request that creates the resource, and then, with the information in the response, send a request to fetch the newly created resource. This is preferable, since we are testing only the REST API, and we do not need to know the specific schema that the database is using. Also, if the REST API changes its database, the tests will keep passing — and they should — since we test through the interface only.

One good example could be borrowing a book. The test should first send a POST in order to borrow the book, specifying the book ID, then extract the borrowed book ID from the response, and finally send a GET request asking for that borrowed book. To save time, you can add the following test to the already existing `tests/BooksTest.php`:

```php
public function testBorrowBook() {
    $params = ['book-id' => $this->books[1]->id];
    $params = array_merge($params, $this->postCredentials());

    $this->post('borrowed-books', $params)
        ->seeJsonContains(['book_id' => $this->books[1]->id])
        ->assertResponseOk();

    $response = json_decode($this->response->getContent(), true);

    $url = 'borrowed-books' . '?' . $this->getCredentials();
    $this->get($url)
        ->seeJsonContains(['id' => $response['borrowed-book']['id']])
        ->assertResponseOk();
}

private function postCredentials(): array {
    return [
        'grant_access' => 'client_credentials',
        'access_token' => $this->accessToken
    ];
}
```

Summary

In this chapter, you learned the importance of REST APIs in the web world. Now you are able not only to use them, but also write your own REST APIs, which has turned you into a more resourceful developer. You can also integrate your applications with third-party APIs to give more features to your users, and for making your websites more interesting and useful.

In the next and last chapter, we will end this book discovering a type of testing other than unit testing: behavioral testing, which improves the quality and reliability of your web applications.

10
Behavioral Testing

In *Chapter 7, Testing Web Applications*, you learned how to write unit tests in order to test small pieces of code in an isolated way. Even though this is a must, it is not enough alone to make sure your application works as it should. The scope of your test could be so small that even though the algorithm that you test makes sense, it would not be what the business asked you to create.

Acceptance tests were born in order to add this level of security to the business side, complementing the already existing unit tests. In the same way, BDD originated from TDD in order to write code based on these acceptance tests in an attempt to involve business and managers in the development process. As PHP is one of the favorite languages of web developers, it is just natural to find powerful tools to implement BDD in your projects. You will be positively surprised by what you can do with **Behat** and **Mink**, the two most popular BDD frameworks at the moment.

In this chapter, you will learn about:

- Acceptance tests and BDD
- Writing features with Gherkin
- Implementing and running tests with Behat
- Writing tests against browsers with Mink

Behavior-driven development

We already exposed in *Chapter 7, Testing Web Applications*, the different tools we can use in order to make our applications bug-free, such as automated tests. We described what unit tests are and how they can help us achieve our goals, but this is far from enough. In this section, we will describe the process of creating a real-world application, how unit tests are not enough, and what other techniques we can include in this life cycle in order to succeed in our task—in this case, behavioral tests.

Introducing continuous integration

There is a huge difference between developing a small web application by yourself and being part of a big team of developers, managers, marketing people, and so on, that works around the same big web application. Working on an application used by thousands or millions of users has a clear risk: if you mess it up, there will be a huge number of unhappy affected users, which may translate into sales going down, partnerships terminated, and so on.

From this scenario, you can imagine that people would be scared when they have to change anything in production. Before doing so, they will make sure that everything works perfectly fine. For this reason, there is always a heavy process around all the changes affecting a web application in production, including loads of tests of all kinds.

Some think that by reducing the number of times they deploy to production, they can reduce the risk of failure, which ends up with them having releases every several months with an uncountable number of changes.

Now, imagine releasing the result of two or three months of code changes at once and something mysteriously fails in production: do you know where to even start looking for the cause of the problem? What if your team is good enough to make perfect releases, but the end result is not what the market needs? You might end up wasting months of work!

Even though there are different approaches and not all companies use them, let's try to describe one of the most famous ones from the last few years: **continuous integration (CI)**. The idea is to integrate small pieces of work often rather than big ones every once in a while. Of course, releasing is still a constraint in your system, which means that it takes a lot of time and resources. CI tries to automatize this process as much as possible, reducing the amount of time and resources that you need to invest. There are huge benefits with this approach, which are as follows:

- Releases do not take forever to be done, and there isn't an entire team focused on releasing as this is done automatically.

- You can release changes one by one as they come. If something fails, you know exactly what the change was and where to start looking for the error. You can even revert the changes easily if you need to.

- As you release so often, you can get quick feedback from everyone. You will be able to change your plans in time if you need to instead of waiting for months to get any feedback and wasting all the effort you put on this release.

The idea seems perfect, but how do we implement it? First, let's focus on the manual part of the process: developing the features using a **version control system (VCS)**. The following diagram shows a very common approach:

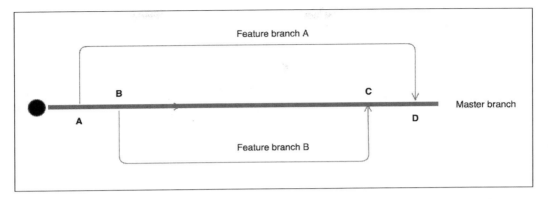

As we already mentioned, a VCS allows developers to work on the same codebase, tracking all the changes that everyone makes and helping on the resolution of conflicts. A VCS usually allows you to have different branches; that is, you can diverge from the main line of development and continue to do work without messing with it. The previous graph shows you how to use branches to write new features and can be explained as follows:

- **A**: A team needs to start working on feature A. They create a new branch from the master, in which they will add all the changes for this feature.

- **B**: A different team also needs to start working on a feature. They create a new branch from master, same as before. At this point, they are not aware of what the first team is doing as they do it on their own branch.

- **C**: The second team finishes their job. No one else changed master, so they can merge their changes straight away. At this point, the CI process will start the release process.

- **D**: The first team finishes the feature. In order to merge it to master, they need to first rebase their branch with the new changes of master and solve any conflicts that might take place. The older the branch is the more chances of getting conflicts you will have, so you can imagine that smaller and faster features are preferred.

Now, let's take a look at how the automated side of the process looks. The following graph shows you all the steps from the merging into master to production deployment:

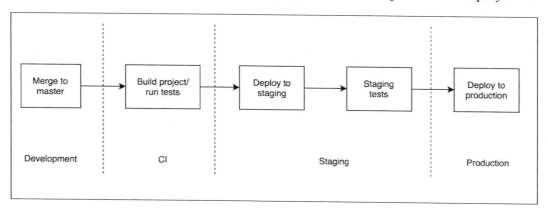

Until you merge your code into master, you are in the development environment. The CI tool will listen to all the changes on the master branch of your project, and for each of them, it will trigger a job. This job will take care of building the project if necessary and then run all the tests. If there is any error or test failure, it will let everyone now, and the team that triggered this job should take care of fixing it. The master branch is considered unstable at this point.

If all tests pass, the CI tool will deploy your code into staging. Staging is an environment that emulates production as much as possible; that is, it has the same server configuration, database structure, and so on. Once the application is here, you can run all the tests that you need until you are confident to continue the deployment to production. As you make small changes, you do not need to manually test absolutely everything. Instead, you can test your changes and the main use cases of your application.

Unit tests versus acceptance tests

We said that the goal of CI is to have a process as automatized as possible. However, we still need to manually test the application in staging, right? Acceptance tests to the rescue!

Writing unit tests is nice and a must, but they test only small pieces of code in an isolated way. Even if your entire unit tests suite passes, you cannot be sure that your application works at all as you might not integrate all the parts properly because you are missing functionalities or the functionalities that you built were not what the business needed. Acceptance tests test the entire flow of a specific use case.

If your application is a website, acceptance tests will probably launch a browser and emulate user actions, such as clicking and typing, in order to assert that the page returns what is expected. Yes, from a few lines of code, you can execute all the tests that were previously manual in an automated way.

Now, imagine that you wrote acceptance tests for all the features of your application. Once the code is in staging, the CI tool can automatically run all of these tests and make sure that the new code does not break any existing functionality. You can even run them using as many different browsers as you need to make sure that your application works fine in all of them. If a test fails, the CI tool will notify the team responsible, and they will have to fix it. If all the tests pass, the CI tool can automatically deploy your code into production.

Why do we need to write unit tests then, if acceptance tests test what the business really cares about? There are several reasons to keep both acceptance and unit tests; in fact, you should have way more unit tests than acceptance tests.

- Unit tests check small pieces of code, which make them orders-of-magnitude faster than acceptance tests, which test the whole flow against a browser. That means that you can run all your unit tests in a few seconds or minutes, but it will take much longer to run all your acceptance tests.
- Writing acceptance tests that cover absolutely all the possible combinations of use cases is virtually impossible. Writing unit tests that cover a high percentage of use cases for a given method or piece of code is rather easy. You should have loads of unit tests testing as many edge cases as possible but only some acceptance tests testing the main use cases.

When should you run each type of test then? As unit tests are faster, they should be executed during the first stages of deployment. Only once we know that they all have passed do we want to spend time deploying to staging and running acceptance tests.

TDD versus BDD

In *Chapter 7, Testing Web Applications*, you learned that TDD or test-driven development is the practice of writing first the unit tests and then the code in an attempt to write testable and cleaner code and to make sure that your test suite is always up to date. With the appearance of acceptance tests, TDD evolved to BDD or behavior-driven development.

BDD is quite similar to TDD, in that you should write the tests first and then the code that makes these tests pass. The only difference is that with BDD, we write tests that specify the desired behavior of the code, which can be translated to acceptance tests. Even though it will always depend on the situation, you should write acceptance tests that test a very specific part of the application rather than long use cases that contain several steps. With BDD, as with TDD, you want to get quick feedback, and if you write a broad test, you will have to write a lot of code in order to make it pass, which is not the goal that BDD wants to achieve.

Business writing tests

The whole point of acceptance tests and BDD is to make sure that your application works as expected, not only your code. Acceptance tests, then, should not be written by developers but by the business itself. Of course, you cannot expect that managers and executives will learn how to code in order to create acceptance tests, but there is a bunch of tools that allow you to translate plain English instructions or **behavioral specifications** into acceptance tests' code. Of course, these instructions have to follow some patterns. Behavioral specifications have the following parts:

- A title, which describes briefly, but in a very clear way, what use case the behavioral specification covers.

- A narrative, which specifies who performs the test, what the business value is, and what the expected outcome is. Usually the format of the narrative is the following:

  ```
  In order to <business value>
  As a <stakeholder>
  I want to <expected outcome>
  ```

- A set of scenarios, which is a description and a set of steps of each specific use case that we want to cover. Each scenario has a description and a list of instructions in the `Given-When-Then` format; we will discuss more on this in the next section. A common patterns is:

  ```
  Scenario: <short description>
  Given <set up scenario>
  When <steps to take>
  Then <expected outcome>
  ```

In the next two sections, we will discover two tools in PHP that you can use in order to understand behavioral scenarios and run them as acceptance tests.

BDD with Behat

The first of the tools we will introduce is Behat. Behat is a PHP framework that can transform behavioral scenarios into acceptance tests and then run them, providing feedback similar to PHPUnit. The idea is to match each of the steps in English with the scenarios in a PHP function that performs some action or asserts some results.

In this section, we will try to add some acceptance tests to our application. The application will be a simple database migration script that will allow us to keep track of the changes that we will add to our schema. The idea is that each time that you want to change your database, you will write the changes on a migration file and then execute the script. The application will check what was the last migration executed and will perform new ones. We will first write the acceptance tests and then introduce the code progressively as BDD suggests.

In order to install Behat on your development environment, you can use Composer. The command is as follows:

```
$ composer require behat/behat
```

Behat actually does not come with any set of assertion functions, so you will have to either implement your own by writing conditionals and throwing exceptions or you could integrate any library that provides them. Developers usually choose PHPUnit for this as they are already used to its assertions. Add it, then, to your project via the following:

```
$ composer require phpunit/phpunit
```

As with PHPUnit, Behat needs to know where your test suite is located. You can either have a configuration file stating this and other configuration options, which is similar to the phpunit.xml configuration file for PHPUnit, or you could follow the conventions that Behat sets and skip the configuration step. If you choose the second option, you can let Behat create the folder structure and PHP test class for you with the following command:

```
$ ./vendor/bin/behat --init
```

After running this command, you should have a features/bootstrap/ FeatureContext.php file, which is where you need to add the steps of the PHP functions' matching scenarios. More on this shortly, but first, let's find out how to write behavioral specifications so that Behat can understand them.

Introducing the Gherkin language

Gherkin is the language, or rather the format, that behavioral specifications have to follow. Using Gherkin naming, each behavioral specification is a **feature**. Each feature is added to the `features` directory and should have the `.feature` extension. Feature files should start with the `Feature` keyword followed by the title and the narrative in the same format that we already mentioned before—that is, the *In order to–As a–I need to* structure. In fact, Gherkin will only print these lines, but keeping it consistent will help your developers and business know what they are trying to achieve.

Our application will have two features: one for the setup of our database to allow the migrations tool to work, and the other one for the correct behavior when adding migrations to the database. Add the following content to the `features/setup.feature` file:

```
Feature: Setup
  In order to run database migrations
  As a developer
  I need to be able to create the empty schema and migrations table.
```

Then, add the following feature definition to the `features/migrations.feature` file:

```
Feature: Migrations
  In order to add changes to my database schema
  As a developer
  I need to be able to run the migrations script
```

Defining scenarios

The title and narrative of features does not really do anything more than give information to the person who runs the tests. The real work is done in scenarios, which are specific use cases with a set of steps to take and some assertions. You can add as many scenarios as you need to each feature file as long as they represent different use cases of the same feature. For example, for `setup.feature`, we can add a couple of scenarios: one where it is the first time that the user runs the script, so the application will have to set up the database, and one where the user already executed the script previously, so the application does not need to go through the setup process.

As Behat needs to be able to translate the scenarios written in plain English to PHP functions, you will have to follow some conventions. In fact, you will see that they are very similar to the ones that we already mentioned in the behavioral specifications section.

Writing Given-When-Then test cases

A scenario must start with the `Scenario` keyword followed by a short description of what use case the scenario covers. Then, you need to add the list of steps and assertions. Gherkin allows you to use four keywords for this: `Given`, `When`, `Then`, and `And`. In fact, they all have the same meaning when it comes to code, but they add a lot of semantic value to your scenarios. Let's consider an example; add the following scenario at the end of your `setup.feature` file:

```
Scenario: Schema does not exist and I do not have migrations
    Given I do not have the "bdd_db_test" schema
    And I do not have migration files
    When I run the migrations script
    Then I should have an empty migrations table
    And I should get:
        """
        Latest version applied is 0.
        """
```

This scenario tests what happens when we do not have any schema information and run the migrations script. First, it describes the state of the scenario: *Given I do not have the bdd_db_test schema And I do not have migration files*. These two lines will be translated to one method each, which will remove the schema and all migration files. Then, the scenario describes what the user will do: *When I run the migrations script*. Finally, we set the expectations for this scenario: *Then I should have an empty migrations table And I should get Latest version applied is 0..*

In general, the same step will always start by the same keyword—that is, *I run the migrations script* will always be preceded by `When`. The `And` keyword is a special one as it matches all the three keywords; its only purpose is to have steps as English-friendly as possible; although if you prefer, you could write *Given I do not have migration files*.

Another thing to note in this example is the use of arguments as part of the step. The line *And I should get* is followed by a string enclosed by `"""`. The PHP function will get this string as an argument, so you can have one unique step definition—that is, the function—for a wide variety of situations just using different strings.

Reusing parts of scenarios

It is quite common that for a given feature, you always start from the same scenario. For example, `setup.feature` has a scenario in which we can run the migrations for the first time without any migration file, but we will also add another scenario in which we want to run the migrations script for the first time with some migration files to make sure that it will apply all of them. Both scenarios have in common one thing: they do not have the database set up.

Gherkin allows you to define some steps that will be applied to all the scenarios of the feature. You can use the `Background` keyword and a list of steps, usually `Given`. Add these two lines between the `feature` narrative and `scenario` definition:

```
Background:
    Given I do not have the "bdd_db_test" schema
```

Now, you can remove the first step from the existing scenario as `Background` will take care of it.

Writing step definitions

So far, we have written features using the Gherkin language, but we still have not considered how any of the steps in each scenario is translated to actual code. The easiest way to note this is by asking Behat to run the acceptance tests; as the steps are not defined anywhere, Behat will print out all the functions that you need to add to your `FeatureContext` class. To run the tests, just execute the following command:

```
$ ./vendor/bin/behat
```

The following screenshot shows the output that you should get if you have no step definitions:

As you can note, Behat complained about some missing steps and then printed in yellow the methods that you could use in order to implement them. Copy and paste them into your autogenerated features/bootstrap/FeatureContext.php file. The following FeatureContext class has already implemented all of them:

```php
<?php

use Behat\Behat\Context\Context;
use Behat\Behat\Context\SnippetAcceptingContext;
use Behat\Gherkin\Node\PyStringNode;

require_once __DIR__ . '/../../vendor/phpunit/phpunit/src/Framework/Assert/Functions.php';

class FeatureContext implements Context, SnippetAcceptingContext
{
    private $db;
    private $config;
    private $output;

    public function __construct() {
        $configFileContent = file_get_contents(
            __DIR__ . '/../../config/app.json'
        );
        $this->config = json_decode($configFileContent, true);
    }

    private function getDb(): PDO {
        if ($this->db === null) {
            $this->db = new PDO(
                "mysql:host={$this->config['host']}; "
                    . "dbname=bdd_db_test",
                $this->config['user'],
                $this->config['password']
            );
        }

        return $this->db;
    }

    /**
     * @Given I do not have the "bdd_db_test" schema
     */
    public function iDoNotHaveTheSchema()
```

```
    {
        $this->executeQuery('DROP SCHEMA IF EXISTS bdd_db_test');
    }

    /**
     * @Given I do not have migration files
     */
    public function iDoNotHaveMigrationFiles()
    {
        exec('rm db/migrations/*.sql > /dev/null 2>&1');
    }

    /**
     * @When I run the migrations script
     */
    public function iRunTheMigrationsScript()
    {
        exec('php migrate.php', $this->output);
    }

    /**
     * @Then I should have an empty migrations table
     */
    public function iShouldHaveAnEmptyMigrationsTable()
    {
        $migrations = $this->getDb()
            ->query('SELECT * FROM migrations')
            ->fetch();
        assertEmpty($migrations);
    }

    private function executeQuery(string $query)
    {
        $removeSchemaCommand = sprintf(
            'mysql -u %s %s -h %s -e "%s"',
            $this->config['user'],
            empty($this->config['password'])
                ? '' : "-p{$this->config['password']}",
            $this->config['host'],
            $query
        );

        exec($removeSchemaCommand);
    }
}
```

As you can note, we read the configuration from the `config/app.json` file. This is the same configuration file that the application will use, and it contains the database's credentials. We also instantiated a `PDO` object to access the database so that we could add or remove tables or take a look at what the script did.

Step definitions are a set of methods with a comment on each of them. This comment is an annotation as it starts with @ and is basically a regular expression matching the plain English step defined in the feature. Each of them has its implementation: either removing a database or migration files, executing the migrations script, or checking what the migrations table contains.

The parameterization of steps

In the previous `FeatureContext` class, we intentionally missed the `iShouldGet` method. As you might recall, this step has a string argument identified by a string enclosed between `"""`. The implementation for this method looks as follows:

```
/**
 * @Then I should get:
 */
public function iShouldGet(PyStringNode $string)
{
    assertEquals(implode("\n", $this->output), $string);
}
```

Note how the regular expression does not contain the string. This happens when using long strings with `"""`. Also, the argument is an instance of `PyStringNode`, which is a bit more complex than a normal string. However, fear not; when you compare it with a string, PHP will look for the `__toString` method, which just prints the content of the string.

Running feature tests

In the previous sections, we wrote acceptance tests using Behat, but we have not written a single line of code yet. Before running them, though, add the `config/app.json` configuration file with the credentials of your database user so that the `FeatureContext` constructor can find it, as follows:

```
{
    "host": "127.0.0.1",
    "schema": "bdd_db_test",
    "user": "root",
    "password": ""
}
```

Now, let's run the acceptance tests, expecting them to fail; otherwise, our tests will not be valid at all. The output should be something similar to this:

```
● ● ●                        1. vagrant@vagrant-ubuntu-trusty-64: /vagrant (bash)
vagrant@vagrant-ubuntu-trusty-64:/vagrant$ ./vendor/bin/behat
Feature: Setup
  In order to run database migrations
  As a developer
  I need to be able to create the empty schema and migrations table.

  Background:
    Given I do not have the "bdd_db_test" schema

  Scenario: Schema does not exist and I do not have migrations
    Given I do not have migration files
    When I run the migrations script
    Then I should have an empty migrations table
      SQLSTATE[HY000] [1049] Unknown database 'bdd_db_test' (PDOException)
    And I should get:
      """
      Latest version applied is 0.
      """

--- Failed scenarios:

    features/setup.feature:9

1 scenario (1 failed)
5 steps (3 passed, 1 failed, 1 skipped)
0m0.33s (7.05Mb)
vagrant@vagrant-ubuntu-trusty-64:/vagrant$
```

As expected, the `Then` steps failed. Let's implement the minimum code necessary in order to make the tests pass. For starters, add the autoloader into your `composer.json` file and run `composer update`:

```
"autoload": {
    "psr-4": {
        "Migrations\\": "src/"
    }
}
```

We would like to implement a `Schema` class that contains the helpers necessary to set up a database, run migrations, and so on. Right now, the feature is only concerned about the setup of the database—that is, creating the database, adding the empty migrations table to keep track of all the migrations added, and the ability to get the latest migration registered as successful. Add the following code as `src/Schema.php`:

```php
<?php

namespace Migrations;

use Exception;
use PDO;
```

```
class Schema {

    const SETUP_FILE = __DIR__ . '/../db/setup.sql';
    const MIGRATIONS_DIR = __DIR__ . '/../db/migrations/';

    private $config;
    private $connection;

    public function __construct(array $config)
    {
        $this->config = $config;
    }



    private function getConnection(): PDO
    {
        if ($this->connection === null) {
            $this->connection = new PDO(
                "mysql:host={$this->config['host']};"
                    . "dbname={$this->config['schema']}",
                $this->config['user'],
                $this->config['password']
            );
        }

        return $this->connection;
    }
}
```

Even though the focus of this chapter is to write acceptance tests, let's go through the different implemented methods:

- The constructor and getConnection just read the configuration file in config/app.json and instantiated the PDO object.

- The createSchema executed CREATE SCHEMA IF NOT EXISTS, so if the schema already exists, it will do nothing. We executed the command with exec instead of PDO as PDO always needs to use an existing database.

- The getLatestMigration will first check whether the migrations table exists; if not, we will create it using setup.sql and then fetch the last successful migration.

We also need to add the `migrations/setup.sql` file with the query to create the migrations table, as follows:

```
CREATE TABLE IF NOT EXISTS migrations(
   version INT UNSIGNED NOT NULL,
   `time` TIMESTAMP NOT NULL DEFAULT CURRENT_TIMESTAMP,
   status ENUM('success', 'error'),
   PRIMARY KEY (version, status)
);
```

Finally, we need to add the `migrate.php` file, which is the one that the user will execute. This file will get the configuration, instantiate the `Schema` class, set up the database, and retrieve the last migration applied. Run the following code:

```php
<?php

require_once __DIR__ . '/vendor/autoload.php';

$configFileContent = file_get_contents(__DIR__ . '/config/app.json');
$config = json_decode($configFileContent, true);

$schema = new Migrations\Schema($config);

$schema->createSchema();

$version = $schema->getLatestMigration();
echo "Latest version applied is $version.\n";
```

You are now good to run the tests again. This time, the output should be similar to this screenshot, where all the steps are in green:

Now that our acceptance test is passing, we need to add the rest of the tests. To make things quicker, we will add all the scenarios, and then we will implement the necessary code to make them pass, but it would be better if you add one scenario at a time. The second scenario of `setup.feature` could look as follows (remember that the feature contains a `Background` section, in which we clean the database):

```
Scenario: Schema does not exists and I have migrations
  Given I have migration file 1:
    """
    CREATE TABLE test1(id INT);
    """
  And I have migration file 2:
    """
    CREATE TABLE test2(id INT);
    """
  When I run the migrations script
  Then I should only have the following tables:
    | migrations |
    | test1      |
    | test2      |
  And I should have the following migrations:
    | 1 | success |
    | 2 | success |
  And I should get:
    """
    Latest version applied is 0.
    Applied migration 1 successfully.
    Applied migration 2 successfully.
    """
```

This scenario is important as it used parameters inside the step definitions. For example, the *I have migration file* step is presented twice, each time with a different migration file number. The implementation of this step is as follows:

```
/**
 * @Given I have migration file :version:
 */
public function iHaveMigrationFile(
    string $version,
    PyStringNode $file
) {
    $filePath = __DIR__ . "/../../db/migrations/$version.sql";
    file_put_contents($filePath, $file->getRaw());
}
```

The annotation of this method, which is a regular expression, used :version as a wildcard. Any step that starts with *Given I have migration file* followed by something else will match this step definition, and the "something else" bit will be received as the $version argument as a string.

Here, we introduced yet another type of argument: tables. The *Then I should only have the following tables* step defined a table of two rows of one column each, and the *Then I should have the following migrations* bit sent a table of two rows of two columns each. The implementation for the new steps is as follows:

```php
/**
 * @Then I should only have the following tables:
 */
public function iShouldOnlyHaveTheFollowingTables(TableNode $tables) {
    $tablesInDb = $this->getDb()
        ->query('SHOW TABLES')
        ->fetchAll(PDO::FETCH_NUM);

    assertEquals($tablesInDb, array_values($tables->getRows()));
}

/**
 * @Then I should have the following migrations:
 */
public function iShouldHaveTheFollowingMigrations(
    TableNode $migrations
) {
    $query = 'SELECT version, status FROM migrations';
    $migrationsInDb = $this->getDb()
        ->query($query)
        ->fetchAll(PDO::FETCH_NUM);

    assertEquals($migrations->getRows(), $migrationsInDb);
}
```

The tables are received as TableNode arguments. This class contains a getRows method that returns an array with the rows defined in the feature file.

The other feature that we would like to add is features/migrations.feature. This feature will assume that the user already has the database set up, so we will add a Background section with this step. We will add one scenario in which the migration file numbers are not consecutive, in which case the application should stop at the last consecutive migration file. The other scenario will make sure that when there is an error, the application does not continue the migration process. The feature should look similar to the following:

```
Feature: Migrations
  In order to add changes to my database schema
  As a developer
  I need to be able to run the migrations script

  Background:
    Given I have the bdd_db_test

  Scenario: Migrations are not consecutive
    Given I have migration 3
    And I have migration file 4:
      """
      CREATE TABLE test4(id INT);
      """
    And I have migration file 6:
      """
      CREATE TABLE test6(id INT);
      """
    When I run the migrations script
    Then I should only have the following tables:
      | migrations |
      | test4      |
    And I should have the following migrations:
      | 3 | success |
      | 4 | success |
    And I should get:
      """
      Latest version applied is 3.
      Applied migration 4 successfully.
      """

  Scenario: A migration throws an error
    Given I have migration file 1:
      """
      CREATE TABLE test1(id INT);
      """
    And I have migration file 2:
      """
      CREATE TABLE test1(id INT);
      """
    And I have migration file 3:
      """
      CREATE TABLE test3(id INT);
      """
```

```
When I run the migrations script
Then I should only have the following tables:
  | migrations |
  | test1      |
And I should have the following migrations:
  | 1 | success |
  | 2 | error   |
And I should get:
  """

  Latest version applied is 0.
  Applied migration 1 successfully.
  Error applying migration 2: Table 'test1' already exists.
  """
```

There aren't any new Gherkin features. The two new step implementations look as follows:

```php
/**
 * @Given I have the bdd_db_test
 */
public function iHaveTheBddDbTest()
{
    $this->executeQuery('CREATE SCHEMA bdd_db_test');
}


/**
 * @Given I have migration :version
 */
public function iHaveMigration(string $version)
{
    $this->getDb()->exec(
        file_get_contents(__DIR__ . '/../../db/setup.sql')
    );

    $query = <<<SQL
INSERT INTO migrations (version, status)
VALUES(:version, 'success')
SQL;
    $this->getDb()
        ->prepare($query)
        ->execute(['version' => $version]);
}
```

Now, it is time to add the needed implementation to make the tests pass. There are only two changes needed. The first one is an `applyMigrationsFrom` method in the `Schema` class that, given a version number, will try to apply the migration file for this number. If the migration is successful, it will add a row in the migrations table, with the new version added successfully. If the migration failed, we would add the record in the migrations table as a failure and then throw an exception so that the script is aware of it. Finally, if the migration file does not exist, the returning value will be `false`. Add this code to the `Schema` class:

```php
public function applyMigrationsFrom(int $version): bool
{
    $filePath = self::MIGRATIONS_DIR . "$version.sql";

    if (!file_exists($filePath)) {
        return false;
    }

    $connection = $this->getConnection();
    if ($connection->exec(file_get_contents($filePath)) === false) {
        $error = $connection->errorInfo()[2];
        $this->registerMigration($version, 'error');
        throw new Exception($error);
    }

    $this->registerMigration($version, 'success');
    return true;
}

private function registerMigration(int $version, string $status)
{
    $query = <<<SQL
INSERT INTO migrations (version, status)
VALUES(:version, :status)
SQL;
    $params = ['version' => $version, 'status' => $status];

    $this->getConnection()->prepare($query)->execute($params);
}
```

The other bit missing is in the `migrate.php` script. We need to call the newly created `applyMigrationsFrom` method with consecutive versions starting from the latest one, until we get either a `false` value or an exception. We also want to print out information about what is going on so that the user is aware of what migrations were added. Add the following code at the end of the `migrate.php` script:

```
do {
    $version++;

    try {
        $result = $schema->applyMigrationsFrom($version);
        if ($result) {
            echo "Applied migration $version successfully.\n";
        }
    } catch (Exception $e) {
        $error = $e->getMessage();
        echo "Error applying migration $version: $error.\n";
        exit(1);
    }
} while ($result);
```

Now, run the tests and voilà! They all pass. You now have a library that manages database migrations, and you are 100% sure that it works thanks to your acceptance tests.

Testing with a browser using Mink

So far, we have been able to write acceptance tests for a script, but most of you are reading this book in order to write nice and shiny web applications. How can you take advantage of acceptance tests then? It is time to introduce the second PHP tool of this chapter: Mink.

Mink is actually an extension of Behat, which adds implementations of several steps related to web browser testing. For example, if you add Mink to your application, you will be able to add scenarios where Mink will launch a browser and click or type as requested, saving you a lot of time and effort in manual testing. However, first, let's take a look at how Mink can achieve this.

Types of web drivers

Mink makes use of web drivers—that is, libraries that have an API that allows you to interact with a browser. You can send commands, such as *go to this page*, *click on this link*, *fill this input field with this text*, and so on, and the web driver will translate this into the correct instruction for your browser. There are several web drivers, each of them implemented following a different approach. It is for this reason that depending on the web driver, you will have some features or others.

Web drivers can be divided into two groups depending on how they work:

- **Headless browsers**: These drivers do not really launch a browser; they only try to emulate one. They actually request for the web page and render the HTML and JavaScript code, so they are aware of how the page looks, but they do not display it. They have a huge benefit: they are easy to install and manage, and as they do not have to build the graphical representation, they are extremely fast. The disadvantage is that they have severe restrictions in terms of CSS and some JavaScript functionalities, especially AJAX.

- **Web drivers that launch real browsers like a user would do**: These web drivers can do almost anything and are way more powerful than headless browsers. The problem is that they can be a bit tricky to install and are very, very slow—as slow as a real user trying to go through the scenarios.

So, which one should you choose? As always, it will depend on what your application is. If you have an application that does not make heavy use of CSS and JavaScript and it is not critical for your business, you could use headless browsers. Instead, if the application is the cornerstone of your business and you need to be absolutely certain that all the UI features work as expected, you might want to go for web drivers that launch browsers.

Installing Mink with Goutte

In this chapter, we will use **Goutte**, a headless web driver written by the same guys that worked on **Symfony**, to add some acceptance tests to the repositories page of GitHub. The required components of your project will be Behat, Mink, and the Goutte driver. Add them with Composer via the following commands:

```
$ composer require behat/behat
$ composer require behat/mink-extension
$ composer require behat/mink-goutte-driver
```

Now, execute the following line to ask Behat to create the basic directory structure:

```
$ ./vendor/bin/behat -init
```

The only change we will add to the `FeatureContext` class is where it extends from. This time, we will use `MinkContext` in order to get all the step definitions related to web testing. The `FeatureContext` class should look similar to this:

```php
<?php

use Behat\MinkExtension\Context\MinkContext;

require __DIR__ . '/../../vendor/autoload.php';

class FeatureContext extends MinkContext {
}
```

Mink also needs some configuration in order to let Behat know which web driver we want to use or what the base URL for our tests is. Add the following information to `behat.yml`:

```yaml
default:
  extensions:
    Behat\MinkExtension:
      base_url: "https://github.com"
      sessions:
        default_session:
          goutte: ~
```

With this configuration, we let Behat know that we are using the Mink extension, that Mink will use Goutte in all the sessions (you could actually define different sessions with different web drivers if necessary), and that the base URL for these tests is the GitHub one. Behat is already instructed to look for the `behat.yml` file in the same directory that we executed it in, so there is nothing else that we need to do.

Interaction with the browser

Now, let's look at the magic. If you know the steps to use, writing acceptance tests with Mink will be like a game. First, add the following feature in `feature/search.feature`:

```
Feature: Search
  In order to find repositories
  As a website user
  I need to be able to search repositories by name

  Background:
    Given I am on "/picahielos"
```

```
    And I follow "Repositories"

Scenario: Searching existing repository
   When I fill in "zap" for "q"
   And I press "Search"
   Then I should see "picahielos/zap"

Scenario: Searching non-existing repository
   When I fill in "yolo" for "q"
   And I press "Search"
   Then I should not see "picahielos/yolo"
```

The first thing to note is that we have a `Background` section. This section assumes that the user visited the `https://github.com/picahielos` page and clicked on the **Repositories** link. Using *I follow* with some string is the equivalent of trying to find a link with this string and clicking on it.

The first scenario used the *When I fill <field> with <value>* step, which basically tries to find the input field on the page (you can either specify the ID or name), and types the value for you. In this case, the q field was the search bar, and we typed zap. Then, similar to when clicking on the links, the *I press <button>* line will try to find the button by name, ID, or value, and will click on it. Finally, *Then I should see* followed by a string will assert that the given string could be found on the page. In short, the test launched a browser, going to the specified URL, clicking on the **Repositories** link, searching for the zap repository, and asserting that it could find it. In a similar way, the second scenario tried to find a repository that does not exist.

If you run the tests, they should pass, but you will not see any browser. Remember that Goutte is a headless browser web driver. However, check how fast these tests are executed; in my laptop, it took less than 3 seconds! Can you imagine anyone performing these two tests manually in less than this time?

One last thing: having a cheat sheet of predefined Mink steps is one of the handiest things to have near your desk; you can find one at `http://blog.lepine.pro/images/2012-03-behat-cheat-sheet-en.pdf`. As you can see, we did not write a single line of code, and we still have two tests making sure that the website works as expected. Also, if you need to add a fancier step, do not worry; you can still implement your step definitions as we did in Behat previously while taking advantage of the web driver's interface that Mink provides. We recommend you to go through the official documentation in order to take a look at the complete list of things that you can do with Mink.

Summary

In this concluding chapter, you learned how important it is to coordinate the business with the application. For this, you saw what BDD is and how to implement it with your PHP web applications using Behat and Mink. This also gives you the ability to test the UI with web drivers, which you could not do it with unit tests and PHPUnit. Now, you can make sure that not only is your application bug-free and secure, but also that it does what the business needs it to do.

Congratulations on reaching the end of the book! You started as an inexperienced developer, but now you are able to write simple and complex websites and REST APIs with PHP and have an extensive knowledge of good test practices. You have even worked with a couple of famous PHP frameworks, so you are ready to either start a new project with them or join a team that uses one of them.

Now, you might be wondering: what do I do next? You already know the theory — well, some of it — so we would recommend that you practice a lot. There are several ways you can do this: by creating your own application, joining a team working on open source projects, or working for a company. Try to keep up to date with new releases of the language or the tools and frameworks, discover a new framework from time to time, and never stop reading. Expanding your set of skills is always a great idea!

If you run out of ideas on what to read next, here are some hints. We did not go through the frontend part too much, so you might be interested in reading about CSS and specially JavaScript. JavaScript has become the main character in these last few years, so do not miss it out. If you are rather interested in the backend side and how to manage applications properly, try discovering new technologies, such as continuous integration tools similar to Jenkins. Finally, if you prefer to focus on the theory and "science" side, you can read about how to write quality code with *Code Complete, Steve McConnell*, or how to make good use of design patterns with *Design Patterns: Elements of Reusable Object-Oriented Software, Erich Gamma, John Vlissides, Ralph Johnson, and Richard Helm*, a gang of four.

Always enjoy and have fun when developing. Always!

Index

Symbols

2xx - success status codes
200 OK 320
201 created 320
202 accepted 320
3xx - redirection status codes
301 moved permanently 320
303 see other 320
4xx - client error status codes
400 bad request 321
401 unauthorized 321
403 forbidden 321
404 not found 321
405 method not allowed 321
5xx - server error 321
500 internal server error 321
__autoload function
using 90, 91

A

abstract classes 97-100
acceptance tests
about 235
versus unit tests 362, 363
aliases
URL 178
anonymous functions 128-131
Apache
reference link 26
Application Program Interface (API)
about 316
testing, with browsers 330, 331
testing, with command line 331

arguments by value
versus arguments by reference 65
arithmetic operators 34
array functions 48, 49
arrays
about 40
accessing 43
elements, searching in 45
empty function 44
initializing 41, 42
isset function 44
ordering 45, 46
populating 42, 43
assertions
about 244-248
reference 244
assignment operators 34
authentication, OAuth2
access token, requesting 338
client-credentials authentication, enabling 337
database, setting up 336
authorization 321
autoloader 90

B

BDD
versus TDD 363
Behat, using 365
Behat 359, 365
behavioral specifications 364
behavior-driven development 359

best practices, REST APIs
about 332
API versioning 333
consistency, in endpoints 332
documenting 333
filters 333
HTTP cache, using 334
pagination 333
browsers
APIs, testing with 330, 331
business writing tests 364

C

cache layer 277
callable 129
casting
about 50
versus type juggling 50
class
about 76
autoloading 90
constructors 79, 80
conventions 83
methods 77, 78
properties 76, 77
code coverage 237
command line
APIs, testing with 331
comparison operators 35, 36
components, frameworks
configuration handler 275
dependency injector 275
logger 275
request 275
router 275
template engine 275
Composer
autoloader, with PSR-4 179
dependencies, managing 176-178
index.php file 181
metadata, adding 180
using 176
conditionals 54-57
constraints 143

continuous integration (CI) 360-362
controller
about 176
book controller 220-223
books, borrowing 223, 224
defining 215-218
error controller 218
login controller 219, 220
sales controller 225
control structures
about 54
conditionals 54-57
loops 59
cookies
data, persisting with 52, 53
CSS 22, 24
cURL 324

D

data
deleting 169, 170
inserting 149-152
persisting, with cookies 52, 53
querying 152-155
updating 165-168
databases
about 133, 134, 138
date and time data types 140
list of values 139
numeric data types 138
MySQL 134, 135
string data types 139
testing 260-264
versus files 72
data providers 250, 251
data providing 250
Data Source Name (DSN) 156
data types
about 32, 33
Booleans 32
floats 32
integers 32
strings 32

date and time data types
about 140
reference link 141
decrementing operators 36
DELETE method 319
dependency injection
about 226
defining 226
need for 226, 227
dependency injector
implementing 228-232
design patterns
about 121
factory 121, 123
singleton 124-128
DesignPatternsPHP
reference link 121
DI
models, injecting with 252
doubles
testing with 251
do...while loop 60

E

elements
searching, in array 45
Eloquent JavaScript
reference link 23
empty function 44
encapsulation 83-86
environment
setting up, with Vagrant 1
environment setup, on OS X
about 5
Composer, installing 9
MySQL, installing 7, 8
Nginx, installing 9
PHP, installing 5-7
environment setup, on Ubuntu
about 13
MySQL, installing 14
Nginx, installing 14
PHP, installing 14

environment setup, on Windows
about 9
Composer, installing 13
MySQL, installing 10-12
Nginx, installing 12, 13
PHP, installing 10
escape characters 40
exceptions
catching 117-120
handling 112
handling, finally block used 115-11
handling, try catch block 113, 114
exit condition 61
expecting exceptions 249
expression 34

F

factory design pattern 121, 123
feature 366
features, frameworks
about 276
authentication 276
cache 277, 278
internationalization 279
object-relational mapping (ORM) 276, 277
roles 276
feature tests
running 371-380
fetch mode
advantages 200
disadvantages 200
files
reading 68, 69
versus databases 72
writing 70, 71
filesystem
about 68
functions 73
finally block 115-117
foreach loop 61-63
foreign keys
about 145-148
behaviors 168, 169

for loop 60, 61
foundations, REST APIs
  HTTP request methods 317
  REST API security 321
  status codes, in responses 320
frameworks
  components 275
  features 276
  overview 280
  parts 274, 275
  purpose 274
  reviewing 273
  Symfony 2 281
  Zend Framework 2 281
framework, types
  about 279
  complete 279
  flexible 280
  lightweight 280
  robust 279
functions
  about 63
  arguments 64, 65
  declaring 63
functions, date and time data types
  CURRENT_DATE() 140
  CURRENT_TIME() 140
  DATE_ADD() 140
  DATE_FORMAT() 140
  DAY() 140
  HOUR() 140
  MINUTE() 140
  MONTH() 140
  NOW() 140
  SECOND() 140
  YEAR() 140
functions, PDO
  beginTransaction 171
  commit 171
  rollBack 171
functions, PHP files
  include 30
  include_once 30
  require 30
  require_once 30

functions, strings
  strlen 39
  strpos 39
  str_replace 39
  strtolower 39
  strtoupper 39
  substr 39
  trim 39

G

GET method 318
getter 84
Gherkin language 366
Given-When-Then test cases
  writing 367
Goutte
  Mink, installing with 381, 382
Graphical User Interface (GUI) 134
Guzzle 324

H

HTML 22, 24
HTML forms 51, 52
HTTP message, components
  about 18
  body 19
  headers 19, 20
  HTTP method 19
  status code 20
  URI 18, 19
HTTP protocol
  about 17
  complex example 20, 21
  interchange of messages, example 18
HTTP request methods
  about 317
  DELETE 319
  GET 318
  POST 318, 319
  PUT 318, 319
HyperText Transfer Protocol (HTTP)
    methods
  about 17-19
  DELETE 19

GET 19
OPTION 19
POST 19
PUT 19

I

impersonification 276
incrementing operators 36
indexes 149
infinite loops 59
information hiding 83
inheritance
    about 92-95
    abstract classes 97-100
    methods, overriding 96
installation
    Mink, with Goutte 381, 382
    Vagrant 2
integration tests 235
interface 100-104
internationalization 279
isset function 44

J

JavaScript 22-24
join queries 162

K

keys
    about 143
    foreign keys 145-148
    primary keys 143, 144
    unique keys 148

L

lambda functions 128
Laravel
    about 273
    versus Silex 313
Laravel framework
    about 282
    complex controllers, creating 296-300

    first endpoint, adding 285-288
    installation 282
    project setup 282-285
    relationships, setting up in models 295, 296
    tests, adding 300-303
    users, managing 289, 290
layout 210
lazy load 204
left joins 163
list of values 139
lists 40
logical operators 36
loops
    about 54, 59
    do...while loop 60
    foreach 61-63
    for loop 60, 61
    while loop 59

M

magic methods 80
maps 40
methods
    overriding 96, 97
    visibility 81
model
    about 176
    book model 198-202
    customer model 196, 197
    defining 194-196
    injecting, with DI 252
    sales model 203-207
Mink
    about 359
    browser interaction 382, 383
    installing, with Goutte 381, 382
    used, for testing with browser 380
mocks
    using 254-259
Monolog
    about 306
    reference link 306

MVC (model-view-controller) pattern
   about 175
   defining 175, 176
MySQL 134, 136
MySQL server installer
   reference link 7
MySQL Workbench
   reference link 8

N

namespaces 88, 90
Nginx
   reference link 26
numeric data types 138

O

OAuth 2.0 322
OAuth2Server
   installing 335, 336
object-relational mapping (ORM) 276, 277
objects 76
operator precedence 37, 38
operators
   about 33
   arithmetic operators 34
   assignment operators 34
   comparison operators 35, 36
   decrementing operators 36
   incrementing operators 36
   logical operators 36
optional arguments 64
overindexing 149
overloaded functions 64

P

Packagist
   about 180, 324
   reference links 181
PDO
   connecting, to database 156
   prepared statements 159-161
   queries, performing 157, 158
   using 156

PHP
   and HTML, mixing 57
   built-in server 25, 26
   reference link 179
PHP Data Objects. *See* **PDO**
PHP files
   about 29-31
   functions 30
PHP functions, filesystem
   file_exists 73
   is_writable 73
   reference link 73
PHP, in web applications
   about 49
   data, persisting with cookies 52
   HTML forms 51, 52
   information, obtaining from user 49, 50
PHPUnit
   about 237
   integrating 237, 238
phpunit.xml file 238, 239
Pimple 304
polymorphism 105, 106
POST method 318, 319
prepared statements 159-61
primary keys 143, 144
production web servers 26
project setup, Silex microframework
   about 304
   configuration, managing 304, 305
   logger, adding 306
   template engine, setting 305
property visibility 81
PUT method 319

Q

queries
   grouping 164, 165

R

receiver 18
reflection
   about 264
   reference link 264

requests
  parameters, filtering from 183-185
  request object 182, 183
  router 189, 190
  routes, mapping to controllers 186-188
  working with 181
REST API, creating with Laravel
  about 334
  controllers, adding 346-352
  database, preparing 339, 340
  endpoints, designing 344, 345
  models, setting up 341-343
  OAuth2 authentication, setting 335
REST API developer
  toolkit 330
REST APIs
  about 316, 317
  best practices 332
  foundations 317
  testing 353-357
REST API security
  about 321
  basic access authentication 322
  OAuth 2.0 322
return statement 66
return type 66-68
router
  about 189, 190
  arguments, extracting of URL 192
  controller, executing 192, 193
  URLs matching, with regular
      expressions 190, 191

S

scenarios
  defining 366
  Given-When-Then test cases, writing 367
  parts, reusing of 367
schemas 136, 137
sender 18
setter 84

Silex
  about 273
  reference link 313
  versus Laravel 313
Silex microframework
  about 303
  database, accessing 307-312
  first endpoint, adding 306, 307
  installation 303
  project setup 304
singleton design pattern 124-128
spl_autoload_register function
  using 92
standards, PHP
  PSR-0 179
  PSR-4 179
static methods 87
static properties 87
status codes
  about 20
  reference 320
status codes, in responses
  2xx - success 320
  3xx - redirection 320
  4xx - client error 321
  5xx - server error 321
  about 320
step
  definitions, writing 368-371
  parameterization 371
strings
  working with 38, 39
superglobals
  about 53
  reference 54
Symfony 273, 381
Symfony 2 281

T

tables
  about 136
  fields 141
  joining 161-163
  managing 141-143

TestCase
customizing 252, 253
test-driven development (TDD)
about 265-270
theory, versus practice 270, 271
versus BDD 363
tests
about 239-241
acceptance tests 235
integration tests 235
need for 233
running 241, 242
types 234-236
unit tests 235
third-party APIs
access token, requesting 325-327
application's credentials, obtaining 323, 324
application, setting up 324, 325
tweets, fetching 327-329
using 323
timestamps 52
tools installation, with Composer
reference link 238
traits 106-112
transactions
working with 171-173
try catch block 113, 114
Twig 208
Twitter
reference link 323
type hinting 66-68
type juggling
about 33
versus casting 50

U

unique keys 148
unit tests
about 235, 236
end 243
start 243
versus acceptance tests 362, 363
writing 242

user management, Laravel framework
about 289, 290
protected routes 295
user login 293, 294
user registration 290-293

V

Vagrant
about 2
download page link 2
environment, setting up with 1
installing 2
using 2-5
variables
about 31, 32
expanding 40
scope 64
version control systems (VCS) 361
view
about 176
blocks 210, 211
book view 208, 209
defining 207
error template 214
layouts 210, 211
login template 215
paginated book list 211, 212
sales view 212, 213
Twig, defining 207, 208
visibility
about 81
private 81
protected 81
public 81
working 82, 83

W

web applications 21
web drivers
types 381
web forms
submitting 21

web page 21
web servers
  about 24
  working 24, 25
website 21
while loop 59

Z

Zend Framework 273
Zend Framework 2 281
ZIP file, Nginx
  reference link 12